THE HANDBOOK OF DIRECT MARKETING FOR NON-PROFIT ORGANIZATIONS

By Billy Sharma

The Handbook of Direct Marketing for Nonprofit Organizations

Published by Civil Sector Press
Box 86, Station C
Toronto, Ontario, M6J 3M7
Telephone: 416- 345-9403

Printed in Canada by: Harmony Printing..
Design by: Billy Sharma

ISBN# 1-895589-61-4

To my wife Ellen, without whom
I would be lost for words.

PAGE	CONTENTS

CONTENTS | PAGE

PAGE | CONTENTS

CONTENTS	PAGE

PREFACE

Despite the often-predicted demise of Direct Mail fundraising, it continues to be the most practical way to raise funds.

However, direct mail works most effectively if you stick to the basic principles. This does not mean following rules blindly, but instead intelligently. This book is about the fundamentals of direct marketing.

Direct marketing is about relevance, responsibility, results and a return on investment.

Direct marketing has become more important than just finding new ways to generate leads and sales. In today's world we must create genuine value for the people we are targeting to buy into our cause.

Direct marketing is a strategic tool that can help nurture connections with different donors by recognizing their individuality and by communicating relevant information in a responsible way, thereby attaining results and real value for both parties.

Advances in computing and communications have broadened the process and the scope of direct marketing with new channels and sophisticated database capabilities. The Internet is propelling direct marketing into a whole new world of possibilities.

Direct mail fundraising works exceedingly well if you stick to the basics. By applying these key rules you can get predictable and stable results.

I thank experts in the field, Michael Johnston and Ptofessor Jim Higgonson, for their valuable input.

FOREWORD

A lot of people may be surprised to discover that direct marketing is the highly productive work horse of the charity and business world. If that includes you, or your staff, volunteers or board, you need to read this book.

No, strike that. Direct marketing is not a *horse* about to be put out to pasture. Make that the work *truck*, reliably delivering the goods. "Rolling down the highway, smiling," as the inimitable Canadian legend, Stompin' Tom Connors sang.

Oh sure, spiffy new on-line campaigns may seem flashier and faster and attract a lot of admiring glances, but when it comes time to pick up another truck-full of money, nothing beats direct marketing.

Now for a lot of those work trucks, it's time for a tune up. Your direct marketing could get probably better mileage. And with today's high costs, tough competition and growing needs, who wouldn't like to do better?

Too many organizations only take the mail truck out for a run once or twice a year. But just as the industrial sector has discovered that 'Just in Time Delivery' makes sense, direct marketers are discovering that more frequent contact produces better results. Billy tells you how.

Is direct marketing for everyone? Pretty nearly. It works best for well known organizations, or those with popular causes. It is a mass market technique, more than a narrow niche. Small organizations can use the technique – and perhaps even better than big groups – by crafting genuinely personal cards and letters and phone calls, not just personalized approaches.

Environmentalists in particular will complain that direct mail is not green. They hate the wasted paper. On one level, it is true, and I agree. The fact is that when you write fundraising appeals to people who have never supported you before, to acquire new donors, only one in a hundred typically respond. Ninety-nine per cent will trash your piece. Let's hope it goes into a recycling bin, but it is still a waste. Even when you write to your most loyal supporters, it is a rare letter that will produce responses from the majority of people on the mailing list. More typically 20% to 40% will respond to any single mailing (although over the courses of a year 80% of the people on the list will respond, if you write often enough).

On the other hand, few charities have seen significant responses to email campaigns. Perhaps this will change in future, but not so far.

So what can you do? Use recycled paper, of course. Test packages to find out whether you can eliminate the brochure, or write shorter letters. You can and must also create truly great campaigns (following Billy's advice in this book will help a lot) so that no tree need die in vain.

If you want sustainable funding, direct marketing is pretty much essential.

Telephone campaigns? Yuk! Perhaps the most hated, reviled, and humourized part of the direct marketing mix. From Jerry Seinfeld to Bob Newhart and on, it seems everyone has a favourite joke about how to hang up on a telemarketer. Millions of people signed up for the Do Not Call List in Canada, and they complain that it is not effective.

Yet telephone fundraising and phone-mail combinations are still powerful tools raising millions for those who use them effectively. (Hint: they work better with current and lapsed supporters than for acquiring new first-time givers.) While high-tech auto-dialers and recorded calls (or scripts that make humans sound like recordings) may drive you batty, there is a reason why call centres are one of the growth industries of the decade. Lots of people welcome calls made by real people who want to have real conversations about really important issues. And they give. Generously. If you call. In the right way. At the right time. With the right approach.

Did you mom complain "You never call! You never write!"? If so, this book will tell you how to get in touch with all the moms (and dads) (and young people) who want to hear from you.

Billy Sharma has drawn a road map that will help so many non-profit organizations (and for-profit businesses, too) get the results they need.

Twenty five years ago my book '***Everything You Need to Know to Get Started in Direct Mail Fundraising***' became must reading across Canada and in fundraisers' offices around the world. I still meet people who tell me that my books were their bibles and helped establish their campaigns.

This is a worthy successor.

This will be the new textbook in the direct marketing course I teach in the post-graduate Fundraising and Volunteer Management program at Humber College, in Toronto.

Even if you can't enroll, you'll get a lot from studying this book. Billy's years of experience as a direct marketing consultant, as a columnist for ***Direct Marketing News*** where he regularly profiles top practitioners, and as a teacher in Humber's School of Business are all distilled here. It is easy to read and full of wisdom.

Of course direct marketing is just one vehicle in the fleet. Direct mail is a great way to get new supporters to sign up. Letters are the low-cost way to get repeat donations year after year from long-term supporters. Phone calls effectively renew supporters who are slipping away, and can up-grade donations. DM is a superb way to build a broad base of loyal supporters. But direct marketing should not be the only fundraising method you use.

From that wonderful base of supporters you build through direct marketing, a few will rise up as major individual donors. Develop a plan to find them and ask them for more than they might give as a result of direct marketing.

I'll never forget the experience, as a young fundraiser, of opening the business reply envelopes (BREs) from an appeal I had crafted for Oxfam-Canada, the international development charity, and discovering a huge cheque. I think was for $7,000. Here was the proof that people cared. Here was the proof that controversial methods like direct marketing really worked. Here was the proof that *my very own* direct marketing packages could move people to action. Unfortunately, here too was the proof that an organization could be so fixated on one fundraising method that it could miss the very large red flag that a donor was waving. 'Come see me,' read the invisible message. 'I might have much more to give you,' was the sub-text we missed. Had we known enough to arrange to have a volunteer visit that family we might have received ten times the $7,000 gift.

Of course Oxfam and I and so many others have long since learned the importance of integrated fundraising.

Direct marketing provides the reliable base, and from there you can find the opportunities to approach people for much larger donations. Find the top 20% of your supporters – the people who give the most in total dollars; the people who have supported you the longest; the people who support you the most often – and arrange for volunteers to visit them to explore the potential for major life time donations and planned gifts through wills and bequests.

This is an important way to increase the return on your substantial investment in good direct marketing.

Similarly, there are many people who do not respond to direct marketing at all. They are the party people. Some call them the socialites. If you want their support you need to hold special events. It could be a gala or a marathon. It could include an auction or a balloon-pop. You can send them an invitation by snail mail or email, but they will respond best if a friend personally asks them to buy a ticket or a table. You can ask socialites to sponsor you in a race (or any kind of challenging activity) by getting them to sign up on your customized mini-website, but this unique breed will rarely respond unless there is an event. Don't leave them out of your mix of fundraising techniques.

Finally, don't mistake direct marketing for grant writing. Corporations may respond to a direct mail package with contributions into the hundreds of dollars. However you might have received tens of thousands if you had done the careful research to put together customized proposals for grants or sponsorships. Not just personalized letters with their name added on the laser printer, but careful research to produce a unique approach.

So direct marketing, useful though it is, is not a one-size fits-all garment. And in reality, one-size fits-all clothes rarely look good on most people.

Your best plan is to use direct marketing, and to use it as part of an integrated campaign.

Whether you are saving the whales, worrying about your school, caring for people who need better health, praying for a miracle, providing social services, creating art, sporting fitness, changing the world – or even selling widgets – following Billy's advice will help you.

Professor Ken Wyman CFRE
Coordinator, Graduate Program in Fundraising
and Volunteer Management
Humber College
Toronto
November. 2009

A recent survey conducted in the UK reported that regular donors appreciate the reasons charities must use direct mail:

- 74% of respondents said they were happy to be contacted via direct mail by charities they support;
- 53% think that direct mail is a good way for charities to raise money for their work;
- 50% do not mind charities contacting them on a regular basis, while 12% did;
- 80% of donors want their charities to be environmentally friendly and use recycled materials.

CHAPTER 1

DIRECT MARKETING: IT'S NOT AN EVENT IT'S A PROCESS

Direct marketing is not an event, it's a process. It's a highly effective process of marketing that encompasses pre-campaign activities such as forecast analytics, list compilation, creation and implementation of the campaign relevant to the target audience, and post-campaign endeavors such as fulfillment and marketing analytics. This helps us learn and fine tune future initiatives to make them more strategic.

Today most of the world's leading charities use direct marketing and most employ an advertising agency to conduct their direct marketing work. Direct marketing is about return on investment, relevance, responsibility and results.

It is a way of reaching out and building solid, mutually rewarding relationships with numerous donors, without ever meeting them face-to-face.

The best description of direct marketing is **Salesmanship in Print**. It has been in existence since the Middle Ages, yet when you mention direct marketing many think of it as just *selling via the mail.* Some confuse it with *a channel of distribution,* like mail order. And now that the Internet is an integral part of direct marketing, it has also been referred to as *contact in real time.*

Despite its existence for centuries, it is only in the past thirty years that direct marketing has really matured, expanded and become one of the leading methods of marketing.

PAST, PRESENT...

Today direct response in Canada generates billions of dollars for charities. The direct response industry provides thousands of jobs in Canada.

What is most significant today is that direct marketing along with interactive methods of marketing, an arm of direct marketing, now represent 54,3% of total marketing expenditures and growing.

Allocation of all marketing dollars in 2008

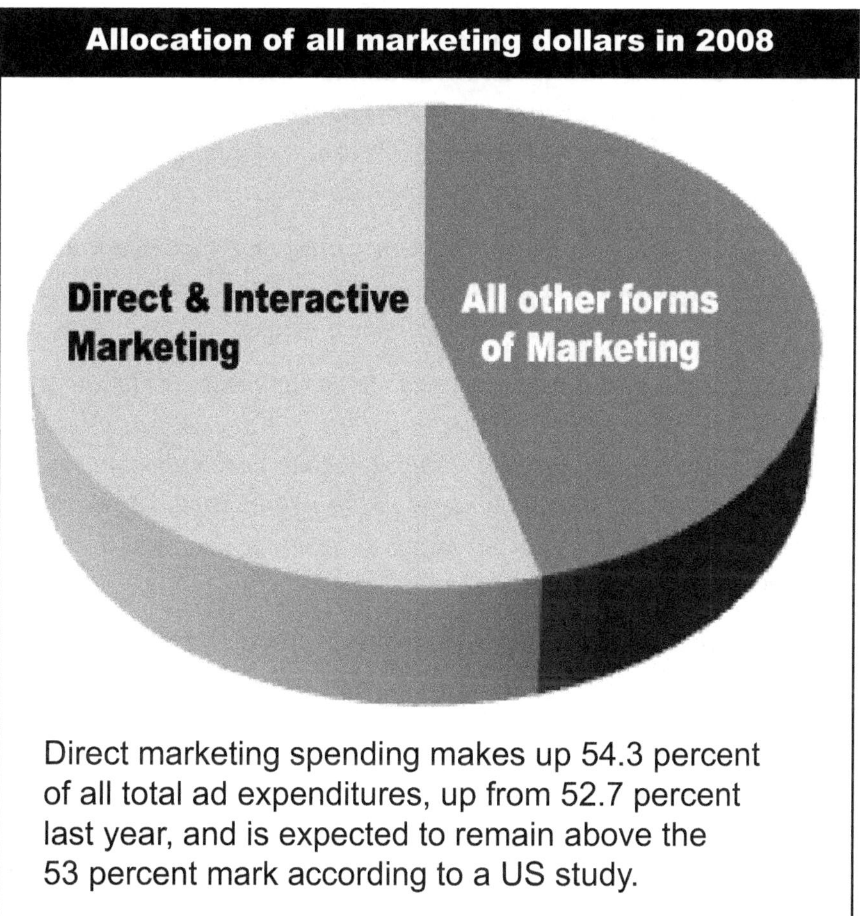

Direct marketing spending makes up 54.3 percent of all total ad expenditures, up from 52.7 percent last year, and is expected to remain above the 53 percent mark according to a US study.

...FUTURE

Growth will continue to rise in all media segments of the industry as the direct marketing industry continues to grow and mature. Today we see evidence of this with many direct marketing agencies recording over one billion dollars in sales each year and expanding internationally from their head offices to many parts of the world.

SO WHAT'S IN IT FOR YOU?

Direct marketing is becoming increasingly relevant to marketers. As a result, agencies and clients are placing a premium on people who have a broad range of skills in advertising, direct marketing, promotions and brand imaging. Demand is high for those who understand the implications of all the media channels.

Budgets are also shifting from mass marketing to direct and micro-marketing because marketers want to see a return on investment now. As a result, retaining talented marketers will become increasingly essential as agencies and clients shift their focus to integrated methods of marketing.

Charitable giving in Canada in 2007

1. Over $10-billion donated—up from $8.9-billion in 2004;
2. 23 million Canadians—84% of the population, aged 15 and over—made a financial donation to a charity;
3. The average donation size $437 is up from $400 in 2004;
4. The biggest beneficiaries include: religious organizations (46%); health charities (15%) and social services organizations (10%);
5. 10% of donors contributed 62% of the total dollars;
6. Volunteers contributed 2.1 billion hours, the equivalent of 1.1 million full-time jobs in unpaid labour;
7. 12.5 million people volunteered—46% of the population aged 15 and over;
8. 25% of volunteers contributed 52% of total volunteer hours.

Source: Statistics Canada

In one of my ***"Direct & Personal"***, articles in the publication ***Direct Marketing***, talent recruiter **Barbara Morris** said: *"I can tell you right now that we're heading for a talent crisis because of three reasons. First, there will be pent-up demand for talent in the future from companies that have held off on hiring decisions.*

Secondly, baby boomers have been retiring in big numbers, leaving a void that will have real significance in years to come. So the best talent will have even more power and employment options.

Most people think about retention as the third part of the hiring-developing-retention equation. They look at it as step three in the workplace continuum, the thing you bother with only after the employee has reached a certain level in the organization. My experience has led me to invent a new paradigm. It looks like this:
Retention = hiring + development.

Another key indicator is how the leading direct marketing agencies have fared recently. This is a good indicator of growth potential for those who are contemplating direct marketing as a serious career."

THE EVOLUTION OF DIRECT MARKETING

- In the 1700s direct marketing was called *Mail Order;*
- During the '60s and '70s it was changed to *Direct Mail* or *Direct Mail Marketing, Direct Response* or *Direct Marketing;*
- In the '80s it began to be called *Junk Mail* by consumers;
- By the mid '80s, three more names evolved - *Database Marketing, Relationship Marketing* and *Loyalty Marketing;*
- By the 1990s *One-to-One Marketing, Customer Relationship* or *Customer Bonding* became popular names;
- Today new names are being added and books written on *Participation Marketing* and *Permission Marketing* largely due to the popularity of the web and viral marketing and new privacy laws.

1700s
MAIL ORDER

1960s - 1970s
DIRECT MAIL
DIRECT MAIL MARKETING
DIRECT RESPONSE
DIRECT MARKETING

1980s
JUNK MAIL
DATABASE MARKETING
RELATIONSHIP MARKETING
LOYALTY MARKETING

1990s
ONE-ON-ONE MARKETING
CUSTOMER RELATIONSHIP
CUSTOMER BRANDING

TODAY
PARTICIPATION MARKETING
PERMISSION MARKETING

HISTORICAL REASONS FOR THE GROWTH OF DIRECT MARKETING

Although direct marketing can be traced back to the ancient times of the Babylonians and Persians who are credited with the first known envelope—a clay wrapper from 2000 BC—the biggest strides were made after the invention of moveable type. Since then many other factors have made important contributions to the growth of direct marketing.

GUTENBERG'S PRINTING REVOLUTION

Printing with moveable type was one of the most important advances in history. Invented in the 1450s by **Johann Gutenberg**, a German from Mainz, his printing press made it possible to print many copies of the Bible. This soon led to printing of other books, newspapers and periodicals and finally catalogues. Credit for the oldest existing catalogue (1498), which gave prices for the books offered, goes to Aldus Manutius of Venice.

BIRTH OF THE CATALOGUE

During the mid 1600s seed and nursery catalogues came on the scene in Europe. A popular slogan at that time was *"Eliminate the Middleman"* because farmers were upset by the high profits that others made on the goods they produced.

Franklin's Satisfaction Guarantee

"Those persons who live remote, by sending their orders and money to said B. Franklin, may depend on the same justice as if present."

One of the most famous direct marketers who published his own catalogue in the early 1700s was **Benjamin Franklin**. He has also been credited with incorporating the first **satisfaction guarantee** in his catalogue.

THE INTRODUCTION OF THE FIRST POSTAGE STAMP

It was not until May 6, 1840 that Great Britain introduced the first adhesive postage stamp called the 'Penny Black' and thus began a chain of events that was to change how the world communicated. Two days later they also introduced the 'Tuppence Blue' and soon the world copied Britain's example and began issuing their own stamps to pay for mail delivery.

A NEW WAY TO GET THE MAIL THROUGH

In the 1860s the Pony Express and the stagecoach became vehicles for mail delivery.

Ranked among the most remarkable feats to come out of the American West, the Pony Express was a service whose primary mission was to deliver mail and news between St. Joseph, Missouri and San Francisco, California.

WHAT'S SO GREAT ABOUT DIRECT MARKETING?

Direct marketing can be anything you want it to be.

Unlike other media—print, television, websites, etc.—there are few constraints on how you can present your ideas.

You can mail practically anything that Canada Post will allow.

Another great thing is that it is interactive; in fact it is the original interactive medium.

And talk about branding – it can be three-dimensional and tactile. It is the ultimate vehicle to enhance brand experience in a way no other medium can match. It involves all your targets' senses.

No other form of marketing allows you to test to find the best solution. Nor does any other provide so much data that can be used in the future or give you the means to calculate your ROI.

IN THE 1900s THE TYPEWRITER STARTED A NEW TREND

- 1926 Start of The Book of the Month Club
- 1930 Specialty catalogues (Spencer Gifts, Hanover House)
- 1950 Reader's Digest started its direct mail operation
- 1950 Publisher's Clearing House offered many magazines
- 1950 Columbia House started Columbia Record Club

1950-1960 THE BIRTH OF DRTV (DIRECT MARKETING TV ADS)

In the 1950s and 1960s, broadcast emerged as a direct response medium. The first DRTV ads were heavy-handed 'pitchmen' style presentations that sounded like traveling salesmen trying to sell snake oil. They soon improved in quality and were used to sell everything from books to merchandise, to generate leads and as a support medium for direct mail campaigns.

Other forms of DRTV include infomercial and fundraising appeals. The success of **The Jerry Lewis Telethon** for so many years proves the power of selling to a captive and receptive audience.

Today there is a channel devoted only to selling products on the air – **The Shopping Channel.**

1970-1980 BIGGER AND FASTER COMPUTING POWER

But it wasn't until the 1970s and 1980s that direct marketing really exploded due to several factors:

- Huge increase in computing power
- Drop in computing costs
- Information technology's ability to enable companies to more accurately select suitable targets for direct marketing and telemarketing

By the late 1980s two other factors had a huge impact on the growth of direct marketing: the fragmentation of television with an explosion of channels and the ease of shopping using credit cards; toll-free numbers and new methods of delivery – **FedEx** and **UPS.**

Today the Internet, a twentieth-century revolution, is propelling the direct market industry. This new response-marketing weapon continues to lead direct marketing in sales, ad spending and employment growth.

REASONS WHY DIRECT MARKETING WILL CONTINUE TO GROW IN THE FUTURE

Today no business or company can survive without computers. Technology has always been a great catalyst that has helped boost the direct marketing industry.

DIRECT MARKETING HAS THE ABILITY TO TARGET MORE PRECISELY

Unlike other forms of communication, direct mail targets only those who are prospects or potential donors. *For example*, a University's best source for fundraising is its students, so there is no circulation waste. This is an advantage that lets the advertiser have total control over the quality of the message and quantity of circulation. It not only allows marketers to reach and understand who their best customers are, but it also allows them to contact them or reward them to ensure repeat donations.

GEOGRAPHIC FLEXIBILITY

The marketer or advertiser can select their prospects by specific geographic locations by their postal codes. This offers them a demographic advantage because they can focus on those regions where they believe their best prospects or donors reside.

DIRECT MARKETING IS TOTALLY PRIVATE

This one-on-one exchange not only allows closer contact between the donor and the marketer but also provides the capacity to build ongoing loyalty. This is invaluable to direct marketing's success and will help contribute to its unprecedented growth in the future.

DIRECT MARKETING IS MEASURABLE

Since obtaining a response is the key element in direct marketing, the number of donations or leads generated by any direct mail campaign can be easily measured. This knowledge enables direct marketers to fine-tune future plans to ensure greater success.

DIRECT MARKETING'S ABILITY AND FLEXIBILITY TO MICRO-MARKET

This flexibility allows a marketer to provide different groups different offers based on their past response behaviour. It can also target specific audiences and learn who responds to what, when and how—an enormous factor in future growth potential.

WHAT'S SO GREAT ABOUT DIRECT MARKETING?

(continued)

You know from personal experience how wonderful it feels to get a loved-filled letter from your son or daughter, grandchild, parent or a friend.

Letters have magical powers. They give us joy on special occasions like weddings and births; strength when we are dealing with sadness; hope when we are weary and delight when we hear from a long lost friend.

Direct Mail lets you talk one-on-one with your donors and show your appreciation. This is so much more effective than advertising to some amorphous mass.

A SURVEY THAT REVEALS WHAT THE PUBLIC THINKS OF CHARITABLE DIRECT MAIL

A survey of over 2,000 people in UK that focused on the recipient's perception of charitable direct mail revealed the following:

1. Mail addressed to recipients is likely to be read completely or in part by up to 75% of people
2. The content of direct mail matters
   - One third of people give because of what is written in the letter
   - Three quarters give when they have a personal or family relationship with the cause
3. People are now concerned more than ever about the environmental impact of direct mail
   - 80% of donors want their charities to be more environmentally friendly

Source: nfpSynergy

LIST AVAILABILITY AND BETTER SEGMENTATION TECHNIQUES

More strategic ways have been developed to target, measure, model and analyze data and behaviour. These analytical tools and methods have led companies to lift response rates and to improve profitability.

THE INTRODUCTION OF NEW PLAYERS CONTINUES TO PROPEL GROWTH

New people entering the business with both improved technical and creative abilities have bolstered the science side and the art side of the business.

REFINED TRACKING METHODS

Direct marketing is constantly monitored to track demographic and lifestyle changes. These changes allow users to reliably predict future responses and extend opportunities.

IT IS THE ONLY TACTILE MARKETING METHOD

Since branding is important, direct marketing is the best way of getting your customers to smell, touch or experience your product first hand. It allows the marketer to send material easily by mail or by shipping overnight via a courier service.

<u>There are also many external factors that will help direct marketing flourish in the future</u>.

DIRECT MARKETING IS FUELED BY TECHNOLOGICAL ADVANCEMENTS

As technology continues to grow, direct marketers find new methods to develop in many areas. The cost and time of computing has rapidly decreased as the technology has accelerated. New technologies, especially the Internet and its social marketing channels like FaceBook, MySpace, Twitter, etc. are all contributing toward direct marketing's growth today

NEW SHIFTS IN WORK PATTERNS

More single, one-parent and dual income families have drastically changed the work model. Women in the workplace have more money but less time, so their time has shifted from hours in the mall to time on the Internet to browse, buy, get informed and donate.

THE EVER-EXPANDING 'BABY BOOMER' GENERATION

This new generation of 50+ has enormous buying power and

they are quite familiar with computers. They are becoming the most important source for commerce in general and for fundraising organizations in particular.

THE SKYROCKETING COST OF SALES CALLS

It is estimated that it now costs an average of $200+ to make a sales call. This does not mean that each call is successful. It is merely the cost of maintaining a sales person on staff to make regular sales calls. This is another reason why there is a lack of staff in a department store. The profit margins make it prohibitive to maintain large sales or service staff especially when competing with companies that offer the same goods on the Internet.

EASE OF SHOPPING

Not only is shopping by catalogue or on the Internet a great convenience but also other innovations like credit cards, toll-free numbers and overnight delivery have helped make shopping and donating easier.

THE CONSTANT FRAGMENTATION OF CONSUMER MARKETS

Multiple channels and media options have made it harder to capture audiences by traditional advertising means such as mass media. This in turn has forced companies to divert funds from mass media marketing to more targeted marketing.

GROWTH AND THE IMPORTANCE OF OTHER INTEGRATED MARKETING METHODS

From call centres to the Internet, many of these new methods help marketers grow and become channels for collecting valuable data and information.

However, the most important reason why direct marketing will continue to grow is that marketers want to see a return on investment, not in some distant future but now. Direct marketing has the capacity to deliver that promise.

Today direct marketing is booming because it is accountable. Tomorrow, as consumers turn increasingly to new media for information and demand relevance and value, marketers must keep pace and provide quantifiable results.

The popularity of direct marketing is evident in the fact that it boasts four Canadian organizations associated with it.

- The Association of Fundraising Professionals (AFP)
- The Canadian Marketing Association (CMA)
- The Direct Marketing Association of Toronto (DMAT)
- Association of Internet Marketing and Sales (AIMS)

THE POWER OF DIRECT

United States direct marketing figures:

- Sales of more than $1.93 trillion
- Each dollar spent on direct marketing yields on average an ROI of $11.65. By comparison each dollar spent on non-DM advertising yields an ROI of $5.29
- Direct marketing employs 1.7 million people
- Collective sales efforts support 8.8 million other jobs, and 10.5 million US jobs in total
- Direct marketing generates 10.3% of the US Gross Domestic Product
- 1,478,149 public charities registered in the US in 2006

** Source: ROI, Sales, Expenditures and Employment in the US, 2006 – 2007 Edition*

THE ASSOCIATION OF FUNDRAISING PROFESSIONALS (AFP)

Represents more than 30,000 members in 200 chapters throughout the world, with 1,000 members in Canada.

THE CANADIAN MARKETING ASSOCIATION (CMA)

Formerly known as the Canadian Direct Marketing Association (CDMA), it now represents people in the marketing field with:

- 3,000 members
- 750 organizations

DIRECT MARKETING ASSOCIATION OF TORONTO (DMAT)

Represents direct marketers in Toronto and has:

- 500 members
- 275 organizations

ASSOCIATION OF INTERNET MARKETING AND SALES (AIMS)

Represents Internet professionals in Canada with:

- 2,000 members
- 600 organizations

A CANADA POST SURVEY

In spite of the negative connotation of direct marketing as junk mail, people like receiving mail. Here are the findings from Canada Post:

1. Seven out of ten people like receiving mail.
2. Many people feel that getting mail is like receiving a 'Birthday present'.
3. People tend to spend an average of 3-1/2 minutes sorting their mail – often over the wastebasket.
4. Retail store catalogues, free samples, coupon books are most popular, while sweepstakes are the least popular.

THERE IS NO SUCH THING AS DONOR FATIGUE, ONLY FUNDRAISING FATIGUE

How much can be raised is not limited by how much people are willing to give but to what extent you can make the giving experience as rewarding as a holiday or an extra indulgence at the supermarket.

Donors are also consumers. They live complex, rapidly changing lives, so understanding them and new trends that influence them is important.

Trend 1: The population is aging.
People are living longer and the population continues to get older. Baby boomers are not just a spike in numbers, they are also about a change in attitudes. This is not one homogenous group; there are differences among them:

- Having matured in the swinging sixties, when women burned their bras and men abandoned three-piece suits and wore their hair long, they break rules;
- They hold positions of power and are involved as board members;
- They don't consider donations as charity but as an investment in a cause;
- They are ready to pay for services that make their lives easier.

Trend 2: Today society is more culturally diverse.
A quarter of Canada's population is now made up of immigrants. The largest group comes from the People's Republic of China, followed by people from India. They are:

- Most comfortable with others whose background they share;
- Best reached through their own associations, places of worship and community leaders;
- Family and community oriented.

Trend 3: Family structure is shifting.
Half a century ago a child was part of a family unit made up of parents, grandparents, uncles, aunts, cousins and siblings. There was 'horizontal growth'. Now as people live longer, move more often, divorce and remarry and have fewer children, the family has changed to 'vertical growth'. Children may know their grandparents but fewer know their uncles, aunts, etc.

- Married couple households are decreasing in number;
- Single-parent households are increasing and many are headed by mothers and older women.

Trend 4: More choices are at hand.
Choice is growing in every area of people's lives. This growth in choice is a result of market driven competition, but is also due to deregulation of many services:

- More TV channels are available;
- Land lines have been deregulated;
- Number of mobile phones has grown astronomically;
- Number of Internet providers have sky-rocketed.

Trend 5: New technology is changing the ways we do things.
The Internet and mobile phones have changed the way we work and conduct our personal lives:

- Internet options have steadily climbed;
- The majority of people, of all ages, now own a mobile phone;
- Millions now engage in social interaction with friends via Twitter, Facebook, MySpace, LinkedIn, etc.

CASE STUDY

BREAKFAST FOR LEARNING

Background: Breakfast for Learning is a national charitable organization dedicated to relieving child hunger and supporting quality education through the support of community child nutrition programs.

Their aim is to ensure that every child in Canada attends school well-nourished and ready to learn.

Objectives: In 2008 with back-to-school fast approaching, it became important to remind their current donors that their support was needed once again to help provide breakfasts, lunches and snacks to the children across the country.

Solution: One person who was eager to help was Sally Horsfall Eaton, past Breakfast for Learning Chair and Honorary Board Member. On her behalf donors were encouraged to join her in the 'SALLY HORSFALL EATON MATCHING GIFT CHALLENGE.'

For each donation made to Breakfast for Learning, Sally volunteered to match, dollar for dollar, every donation of $1000 or more by 100%, and donations under $1000 by 50%.

Another very important message that had to be relayed was the disastrous effect on children who go to school hungry. A simple device was used; the letter was folded in such a way that it became an interactive device. Readers had to lift up a flap to reveal the disturbing effect on children who go to school without a proper breakfast.

Outer envelope

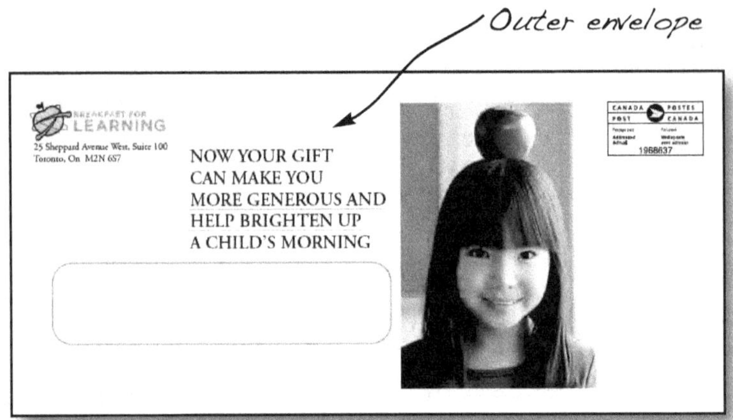

Letter with lift-up flap closed

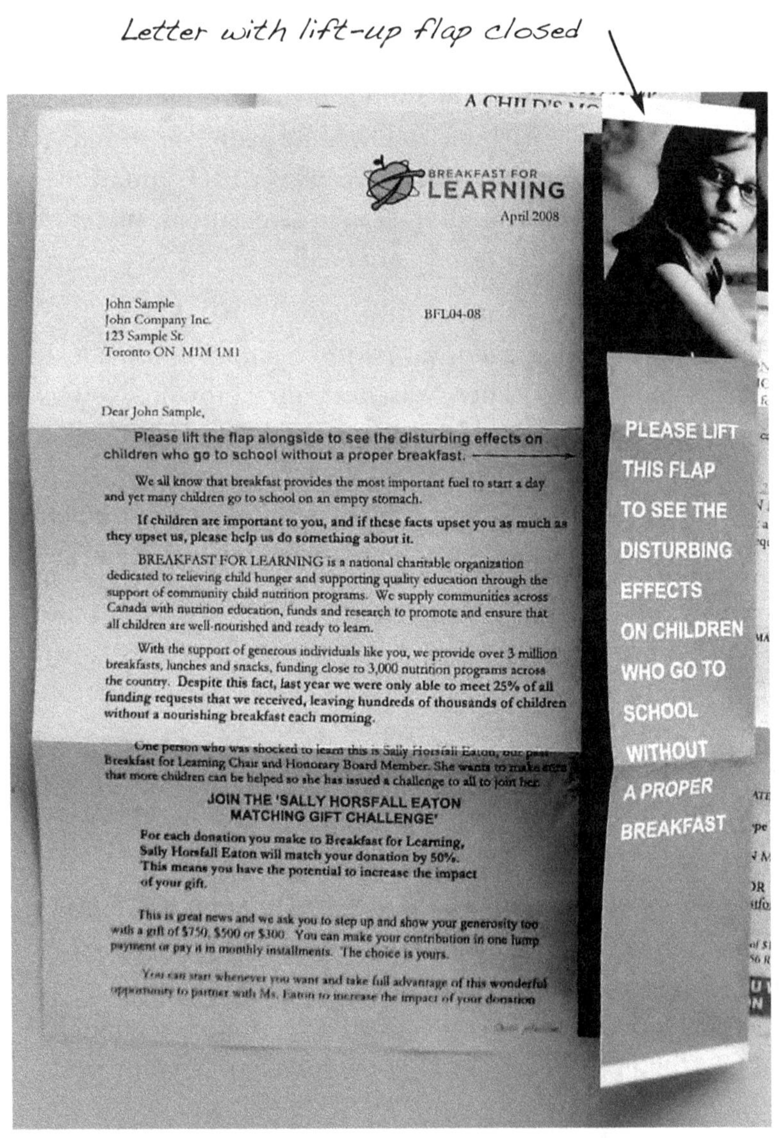

BREAKFAST FOR LEARNING

April 2008

John Sample
John Company Inc.
123 Sample St.
Toronto ON M1M 1M1

BFL04-08

Dear John Sample,

Please lift the flap alongside to see the disturbing effects on children who go to school without a proper breakfast. →

We all know that breakfast provides the most important fuel to start a day and yet many children go to school on an empty stomach.

If children are important to you, and if these facts upset you as much as they upset us, please help us do something about it.

BREAKFAST FOR LEARNING is a national charitable organization dedicated to relieving child hunger and supporting quality education through the support of community child nutrition programs. We supply communities across Canada with nutrition education, funds and research to promote and ensure that all children are well-nourished and ready to learn.

With the support of generous individuals like you, we provide over 3 million breakfasts, lunches and snacks, funding close to 3,000 nutrition programs across the country. **Despite this fact, last year we were only able to meet 25% of all funding requests that we received, leaving hundreds of thousands of children without a nourishing breakfast each morning.**

One person who was shocked to learn this is Sally Horsfall Eaton, our past Breakfast for Learning Chair and Honorary Board Member. She wants to make sure that more children can be helped so she has issued a challenge to all to join her.

JOIN THE 'SALLY HORSFALL EATON MATCHING GIFT CHALLENGE'

For each donation you make to Breakfast for Learning, Sally Horsfall Eaton will match your donation by 50%. This means you have the potential to increase the impact of your gift.

This is great news and we ask you to step up and show your generosity too with a gift of $750, $500 or $300. You can make your contribution in one lump payment or pay it in monthly installments. The choice is yours.

You can start whenever you want and take full advantage of this wonderful opportunity to partner with Ms. Eaton to increase the impact of your donation

A large donation form was also provided so that donors could either make an individual gift or pool their resources with friends and family and make a larger group donation.

Results: Both the 'Matching Gift' challenge and the simple interactive device worked extremely well. This Back-to-School package was mailed to in-house list of 1454 donors. Over 117 responded (8.05% response) and netted an ROI of 80.47%

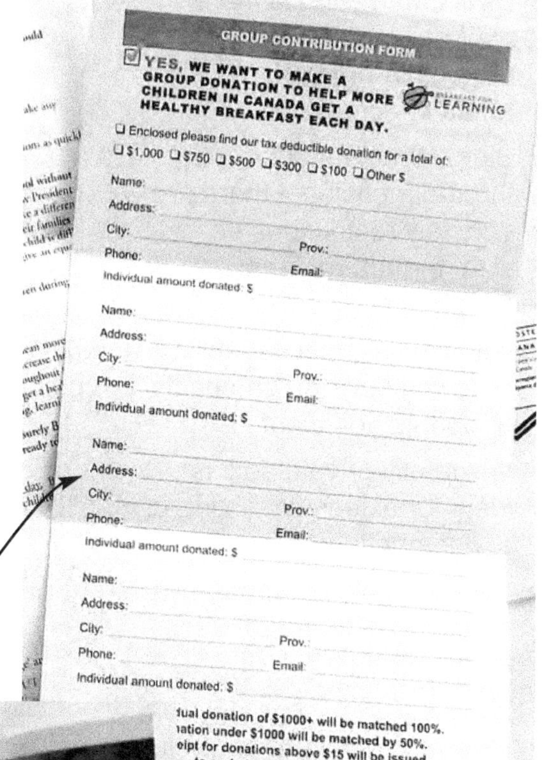

GROUP CONTRIBUTION FORM

YES, WE WANT TO MAKE A GROUP DONATION TO HELP MORE CHILDREN IN CANADA GET A HEALTHY BREAKFAST EACH DAY.

BREAKFAST FOR LEARNING

☐ Enclosed please find our tax deductible donation for a total of:
☐ $1,000 ☐ $750 ☐ $500 ☐ $300 ☐ $100 ☐ Other $

Name:
Address:
City: Prov.:
Phone: Email:
Individual amount donated: $

Name:
Address:
City: Prov.:
Phone: Email:
Individual amount donated: $

Name:
Address:
City: Prov.:
Phone: Email:
Individual amount donated: $

Name:
Address:
City: Prov.:
Phone: Email:
Individual amount donated: $

ual donation of $1000+ will be matched 100%.
ation under $1000 will be matched by 50%.
eipt for donations above $15 will be issued
to each donor listed above.

Donation form: One side of the donation form allowed an individual to make a donation while the other side encouraged donors to pool their resources in groups and make a donation.

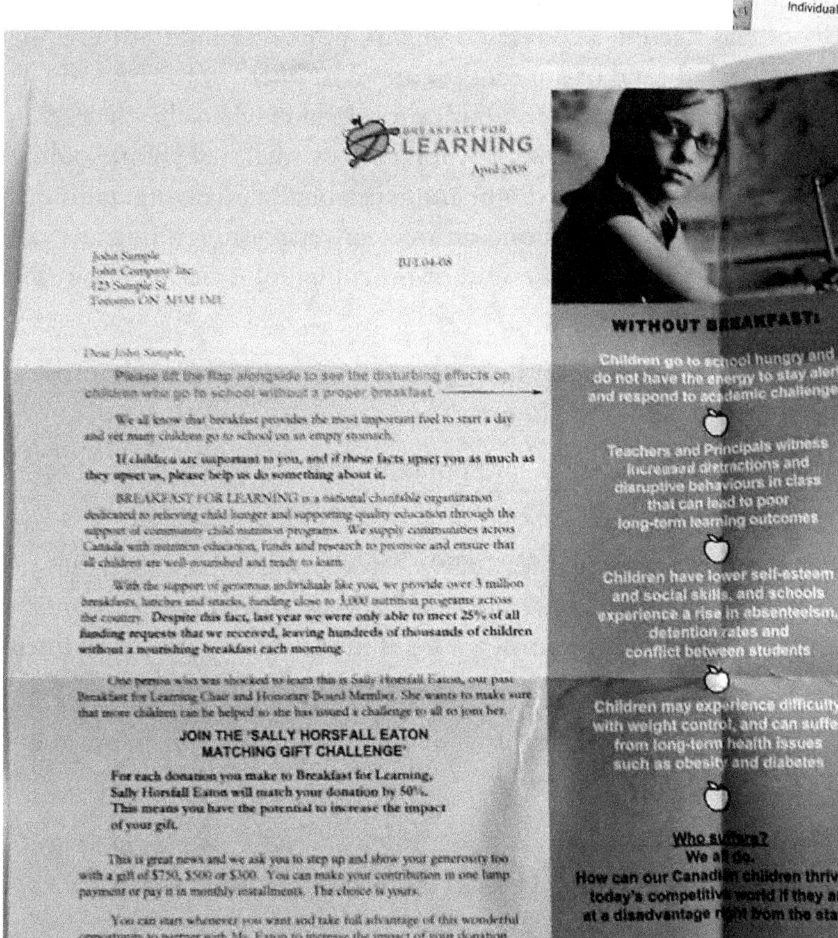

BREAKFAST FOR LEARNING

Dear John Sample,

Please lift the flap alongside to see the disturbing effects on children who go to school without a proper breakfast.

We all know that breakfast provides the most important fuel to start a day and yet many children go to school on an empty stomach.

If children are important to you, and if these facts upset you as much as they upset us, please help us do something about it.

BREAKFAST FOR LEARNING is a national charitable organization dedicated to relieving child hunger and supporting quality education through the support of community child nutrition programs. We supply communities across Canada with nutrition education, funds and research to promote and ensure that all children are well-nourished and ready to learn.

With the support of generous individuals like you, we provide over 3 million breakfasts, lunches and snacks, funding close to 3,000 nutrition programs across the country. **Despite this fact, last year we were only able to meet 25% of all funding requests that we received, leaving hundreds of thousands of children without a nourishing breakfast each morning.**

One person who was shocked to learn this is Sally Horsfall Eaton, our past Breakfast for Learning Chair and Honorary Board Member. She wants to make sure that more children can be helped so she has issued a challenge to all to join her.

JOIN THE 'SALLY HORSFALL EATON MATCHING GIFT CHALLENGE'

For each donation you make to Breakfast for Learning, Sally Horsfall Eaton will match your donation by 50%. This means you have the potential to increase the impact of your gift.

This is great news and we ask you to step up and show your generosity too with a gift of $750, $500 or $300. You can make your contribution in one lump payment or pay it in monthly installments. The choice is yours.

You can start whenever you want and take full advantage of this wonderful opportunity to partner with Ms. Eaton to increase the impact of your donation

WITHOUT BREAKFAST:

Children go to school hungry and do not have the energy to stay alert and respond to academic challenges

Teachers and Principals witness increased distractions and disruptive behaviours in class that can lead to poor long-term learning outcomes

Children have lower self-esteem and social skills, and schools experience a rise in absenteeism, detention rates and conflict between students

Children may experience difficulty with weight control, and can suffer from long-term health issues such as obesity and diabetes

Who suffers?
We all do.
How can our Canadian children thrive in today's competitive world if they are at a disadvantage right from the start?

THEY NEED OUR HELP

Letter with lift-up flap open

Direct Marketing Facts:

- Direct Marketing is more expensive in terms of reach, but more efficient in terms of acquisition.
- Since direct marketing is three-dimensional there are very few restrictions on size, format, material or length of message.
- It is highly selective—reaching only the prospects or donors you want.
- It is totally private so it is ideal for extensive testing or experimenting.
- As it is highly personal, you can send different offers to different groups of donors.
- It permits accurate analysis.
- It enables you to control the lifetime value of a customer.

CHAPTER 2

DIRECT MARKETING: DEFINED

Just like it is hard to describe all that direct marketing does, a succinct definition of direct marketing has been equally hard to pin down. Different books have defined it in various ways. I prefer to stick to the Direct Marketing Association's definition:

Direct marketing (DM) is an interactive system of marketing using one or more advertising media to generate a measurable response or transaction at any location.

This statement raises four important points:

1. DM is interactive, not a monologue. This could be as simple as starting a conversation with prospects and finding out: what kind of appeal they are most likely to respond to positively; what amount they donate; when they like to donate; and how they donate—by mail, telephone, online or fax back. Or it can be more personally involving: telling a story; starting a one-on-one conversation; sending an invitation to an event; or providing information about the charity.
2. It can use more than one medium for a targeted approach to prospects and donors;
3. It must generate a response, hence the alternative name, Direct Response;
4. Responses are measurable because you know exactly how many pieces have been sent and can measure that against the number of responses. This is invaluable for planning future campaigns.

Direct marketing is primarily accountable, but more about that later in the book.

HOW DIRECT MARKETING WORKS

Consider the universe of all the people within your boundary as the 'Market' in general.

Those that you wish to target, the ones you determine have a preference for or relevance to your charity, are called Suspects.

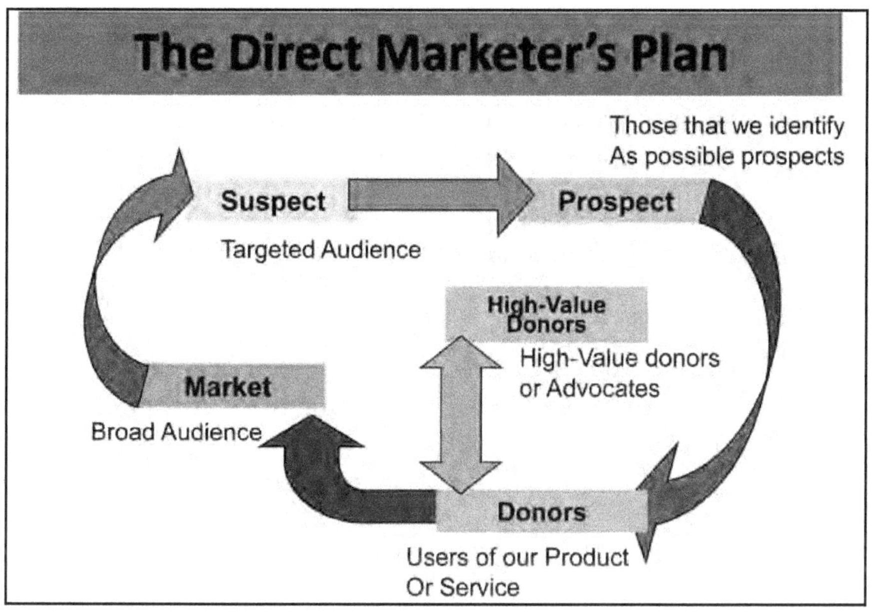

Among this group, those that respond to your initial communication are called Prospects. It is only after they commit by making a donation that they become Donors.

Those Donors with whom you have an on-going relationship and who stay loyal can then be considered as Core Donors and finally those who give you large donations are your High Value Donors or Advocates.

THE DIRECT MARKETER'S PLAN

In its most basic form this consists of the following steps:

1. Reach out to a mass market to identify and select as Suspects all those who you think may show some interest in your cause or mission;
2. Those who respond to a DM appeal the first time are then considered as Prospects;
3. Make special plans for stewardship and try and move Prospect to become regular Donors;
4. Donors who give repeatedly are considered as Core Donors while those who give large gifts are High Value Donors.
6. Analyze why and which kind of Prospects responded positively and go back to the marketplace and find more people that fit the same profile.

THE SPECIAL ATTRIBUTES OF DIRECT MARKETING

- Precision targeting
- Flexibility
- Invisible strategies
- Measurability
- Interactivity
- Personalization
- Call to action
- Few restrictions
- Accountability

Key steps in direct marketing:

1. Identify, isolate and reach your target group.
2. Learn more about them by their response or even their non-response behaviour.
3. Classify and correctly catalogue your customers on your database.
4. Initiate a plan to retain best customers.
5. Build a mutually profitable long-term relationship.

PRECISION TARGETING

Reaching the right donors for your cause is the key to success in direct marketing. Few other forms of communication can be as accurate in determining your most relevant Prospects.

Once you have determined the type of people your main Prospects are, you should target only those that fit this profile.

PERSONALIZATION

The ability to speak one-on-one with your Suspects, Prospects, Core Donors or High Value Donors is a big plus. This benefit extends beyond just addressing them by name. It allows you to tailor your communication based on who they are and on their past behaviour. *For example,* if 10% of your donors contribute $500 or more, while 15% give between $80 and $490 and the balance contributes between $15 and $75, then obviously each group belongs in a different category and should be treated according to their level of giving.

FLEXIBILITY

The ability to vary your offer or appeal to different sectors is a big advantage. Sending different offers to different groups, based on their past response patterns, allows you to test what worked best. When a direct mail package consistently performs well, it is called a 'Control Package.'

CALL TO ACTION

As indicated before, direct marketing is accountable. The entire focus is to generate a call to action. Even a no response in direct marketing provides valuable information because it tells you that the solicitation piece has flaws that need to be improved.

INVISIBLE STRATEGIES

The strategies and tactics of direct marketers are less visible because they do not use mass media as a vehicle.

This lack of visibility provides the direct marketer with an edge over the competition, which becomes all the more important when testing various strategies.

FEW RESTRICTIONS ON FORMATS OR DIMENSIONS

A direct marketing piece can come as a poster or a postcard. It can be three dimensional such as a product or a box. It can include gifts, tokens, sweepstakes or other elements as part of the package.

You can send anything that is safe to mail and which can be packaged.

The package below, for **Interval House**, had a toothbrush visible in the lower window of a double window envelope. *(See more details about it as a Case Study on page 162)*

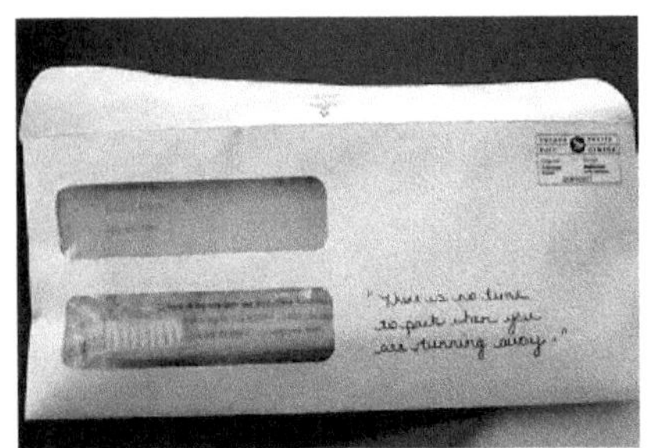

MEASURABILITY

All direct marketing activities are measurable and can be constantly monitored. Tracking demographic and lifestyle changes allow direct marketers to reliably predict future behaviour (predictive modeling) or opportunities.

- Focus on newer trends of donation behaviour;
- Provide answers as to what worked best and for who, when, where and how;
- Use response as key to future learning;
- Avoid wastage by printing only the amount to be mailed.

One of the biggest advantages to large charities (hospitals, universities, international charities and museums and symphonies) who house extensive data about their customers is their ability to micro-segment their donor base into variables like:

- Risk factors
- Current and projected profitability
- Life-stage changes or family growth or reduction

This allows them to identify and understand their donors more precisely and profitably by making available offerings that are closer to their specific needs and behaviour.

ACCOUNTABILITY

Evaluation and analysis are part of ensuring that the campaign was successful. This accountability and analysis give DM an edge over other forms of marketing.

Everything can be calculated:

- Cost per sales
- Cost per package
- Acquisition costs
- Cost per response
- Break-even cost
- ROI (return on investment)
- Response rate
- Lifetime Value of a customer

INTERACTIVITY

As the name implies the greatest asset of direct marketing is the ability to create a two-way conversation and not just a monologue. It is this capacity which allows direct marketers to understand their target audience, listen to their concerns and reward and retain their best donors. They can keep tabs on the trends in the marketplace and react quickly to changes.

It is the ideal method for building lifetime value of donors through sustained loyalty.

DIRECT MARKETING ANSWERS THESE QUESTIONS

- Did my investment in advertising actually work?
- How well did it work?
- Who are my best donors?
* Where can I find more of them?
- What did they respond to, what was it that made them donate to one package vs. another?
- What was my 'Return on Investment' (ROI)?
- How can I improve results?

THE SEVEN AIMS OF DIRECT MARKETING

Targeting: Clearly identifying your most likely 'Prospects'

Lead generation: Initiating a prospect contact via any of the various direct marketing media – direct mail, print, broadcast, telemarketing or the Internet

Lead qualification: Ensuring that the Prospect is a qualified responder to your cause.

Acquisition: Converting Prospects into Donors

Retention: Keeping Donors and moving them up to become regular givers or Core Donors

Relationship Building: Developing a one-on-one dialogue with your best 'Donors' to understand their needs and build a long term relationship that converts them into High Value Donors

Loyalty: Retaining and rewarding your best High Value Donors so they remain with you.

THE SIX VARIABLES OF DIRECT MARKETING

Just as advertising has four important variables—product, price, promotion and place—direct marketing has six. While different DM books have placed different values of importance on the first five, the last variable 'Donor Stewardship' has often been overlooked.

Donor Stewardship is as important an activity as acquiring donors in the first place and should be rated separately.

The six variables in direct marketing in their order of importance are:

1. THE LIST
2. THE OFFER
3. THE CREATIVE
4. THE MEDIA SELECTION
5. TIMING AND SEQUENCE
6. DONOR STEWARDSHIP

1. THE LIST

Also known as a 'Database,' it is a collection of names and addresses of Suspects, Prospects and Donors. It is by far the most important variable because targeting the right person in direct marketing is critical. **The right list accounts for over 50% of the success of any direct marketing initiative.**

2. THE OFFER

The offer is the proposition made by the marketer to the prospect. In fundraising, an offer usually includes either premiums or suggestions of gift amounts. For example, if a prospect gave $50 in the past, then the amount requested in the gift ladder in a follow-up mailing should be close to that amount: $50, $55, $60, other $ _________.

The offer is the next most important element in soliciting a response and is accountable for at least 20% of the success.

3. THE CREATIVE

This includes all the elements, from copy to art direction, needed to create a direct marketing package or a campaign.

Its importance is valued at 20% of the overall success.

4. THE MEDIA

These are the various channels of distribution and include direct mail, print, broadcast (radio and television), telemarketing, newsletters and the Internet.

The selection of the right media accounts for 5% of the success of any DM initiative.

5. TIMING & SEQUENCE

These are functions of delivery. A clear advantage that direct marketing has over advertising is the ability to decide exactly who to mail to, when to mail and which media to use.

Selecting the right timing and sequence account for another 5% of the success of any initiative.

The sixth and the most critical variable is:

6. DONOR STEWARDSHIP

The way you treat your donors is just as important as acquiring them. It has a big bearing on their future behaviour and their continued commitment.

One cannot exist without donors. Donors regard how you use their money as the most important factor in their giving, but running a close second is how you treat them. The quality and promptness of how they are treated has a huge impact on ensuring a donor's loyalty.

As an after-acquisition function, donor stewardship should be rated separately and should be valued at 100%.

CASE STUDY

CANFAR (Canadian Foundation for AIDS Research)

Background: Every so often the non-profit organization, CANFAR (Canadian Foundation for AIDS Research), tests at least two mailings to see which one performs better. They hope to keep current donors, lure lapsed ones back and acquire new ones.

Objectives: In May 2006, CANFAR decided to:

- Test a new creative strategy against the current 'control package' and to try and beat it;
- Produce two variations of the same test package, one that addressed the Global HIV/AIDS problem (John Doe Global version) and another that focused on the problem at home (Jane Doe Canadian version);
- Raise awareness of and educate prospects about the HIV/AIDS epidemic;
- Make the audience aware that new HIV/AIDS victims in Canada are often young adults;
- Raise funds and procure new donor prospects.

Solution: Test a radical new concept against the control package, since the HIV/AIDS message was not getting through to the general public and donations had stagnated.

It was necessary to have a message that was hard hitting and direct since there was a lot of misconception among young adults who think that HIV/AIDS is curable. Also parents needed to know that many new AIDS sufferers are young adults, 40% of them women.

The tactic was to pull no punches and to chide readers for their lack of concern.

Strategy: The creative strategy was to combine outrage expressed in the letter with a factual testimonial to tug at the hearts of the prospective donors.

The outer envelope informed recipients that AIDS victims had changed. By covering the eyes of the new victims with the address label on the outer envelope and hiding their identities, a sense of mystery and urgency was created.

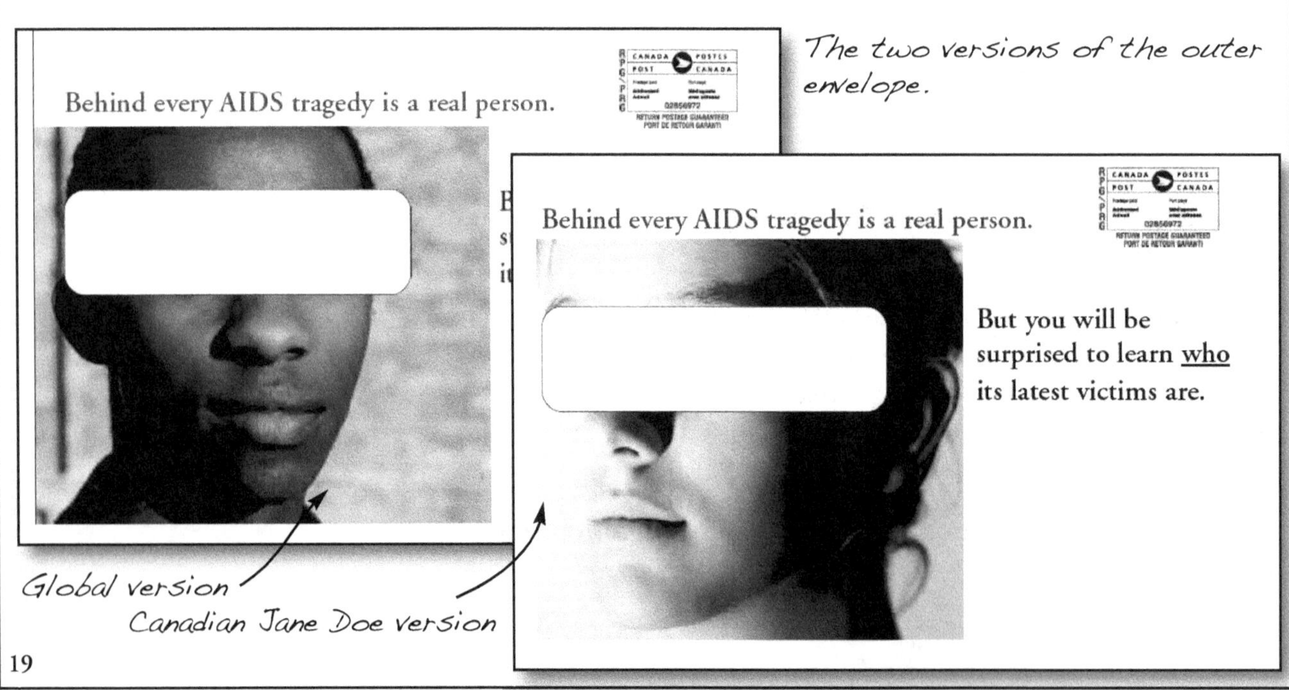

The two versions of the outer envelope.

The letter chided the target audience with a blunt message that informed them that new HIV/AIDS victims are younger and chastised the respondents for not doing more to save our youth. As one copy line stated, "*We teach our little ones never to go with or accept candy from a stranger, but we don't know how to tell our teenagers about the dangers of unprotected sex.*"

The Lift Note was a testimonial from a teenage victim.

Result: Both the new creative packages beat out the control package handily.

The new Global version got a 9.5% response, edging out the control package by 0.27%.

The new Canadian Jane Doe version did even better by almost 100% with a 16.67% response. It generated over 60% more funds than both the original control and the Global version.

Had the Global and Canadian Jane Doe versions not been split and had just the Canadian version been mailed, it would have generated a huge 26.4% response (combined total of the two versions) and beaten the control package by over 300%.

The letter

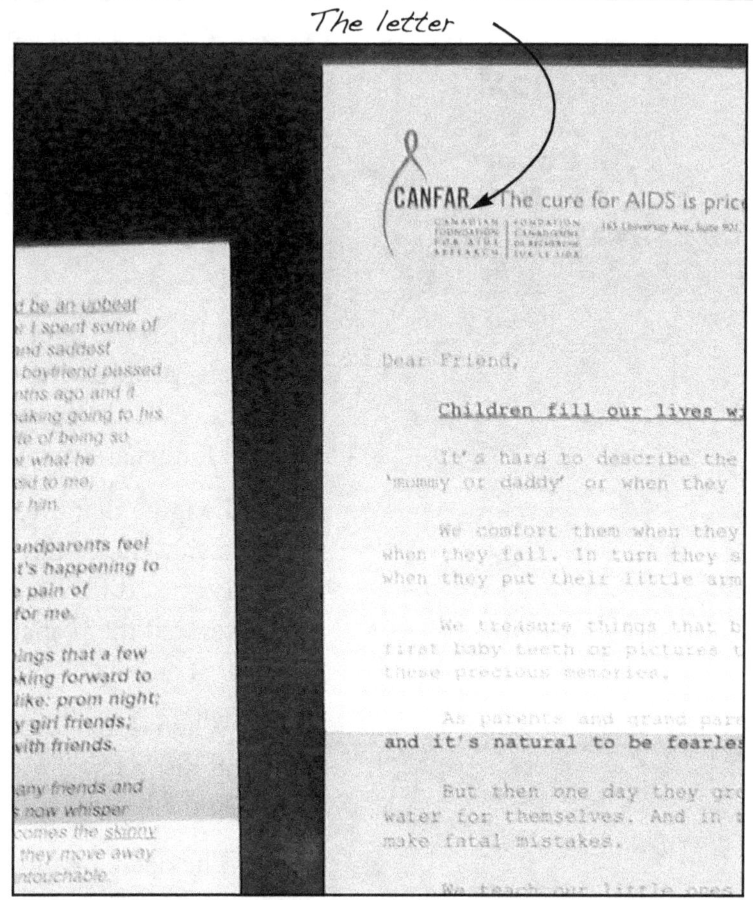

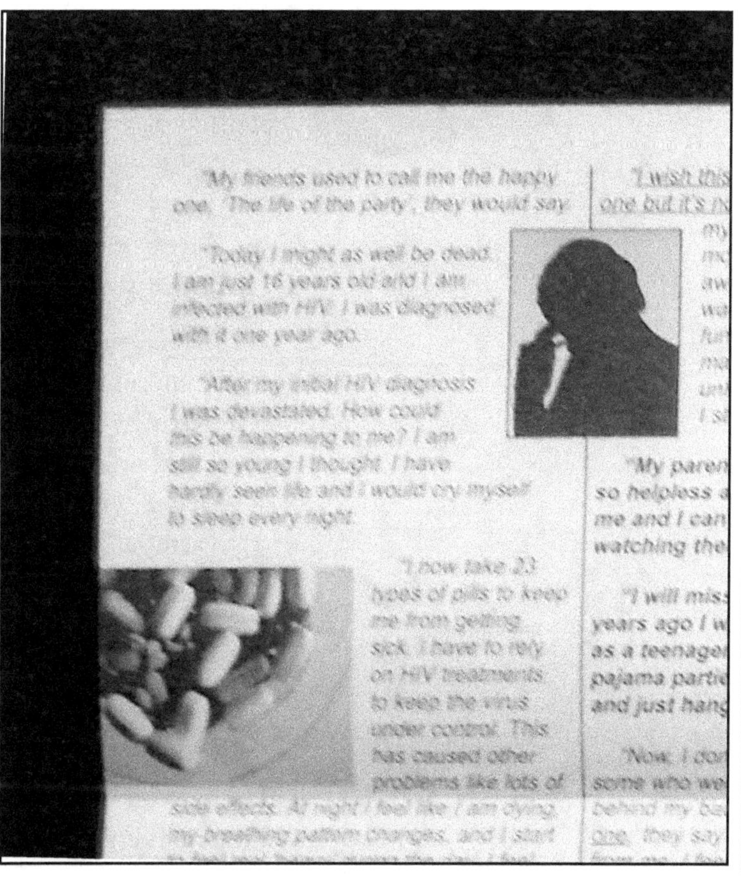

Lift Note from teenager with HIV/AIDS

DIRECT MARKETING WISDOM

All Donors Are Not Created Equal

CHAPTER 3

LISTS: TARGETING THE RIGHT PEOPLE

A list is the names and addresses of people and can consist of Suspects, people who would most probably have an affinity for your cause, and who you would like to convert to Donors, then Core Donors and finally Advocates.

Imagine that direct mail is a medium like a television show and its viewers are the list. This group will have many similarities and also vast differences. A list is compiled to capture these nuances, tell them apart and also tell which groupings of people are similar. The role of a list is therefore vital.

When does a list morph into a Database? When it grows beyond just a few hundred names and has a store of information that can be segmented to identify individuals more precisely.

The database of prime prospects can be used to send them information, solicitations or incentives that will appeal to them to respond.

An effective database contains vital information that has been collected over a period of time and should be updated constantly.

REASONS FOR USING A DATABASE

There are many different reasons for using a database. Some of the most significant ones are listed below:

- Generating new or repeat donations
- Trend analysis and forecasting
- Testing
- Program evaluation by response or medium
- Better profiling of donors
- Faster and more accurate processing and fulfillment
- Better targeting
- Lead generation and relationship building
- Market research
- Customer relationship management (CRM)

However, the primary reason for using a database is to identify your best donors, understand who they are and then go out in the marketplace and find more like them.

THE LIST RENTAL PROCESS

Usually when a company rents a list, it is done through a list broker, a listing house or a listing agent. Because the process of list compilation is quite involved due to constant updating, inputting, scrubbing and maintenance, the entire process is complex and specialized. There can be up to eight different players or partners involved in the list rental process.

The key players include:

List Renter. The person or company that wishes to mail and needs to rent a list to solicit new prospects.

List Owner. A company or individual that owns the list and rents it for a fee. List owners usually employ a list manager to manage their files. *For example,* while ***Reader's Digest*** owns their own list they use a company like **Cornerstone** as their list manager.

List Broker. Similar to a real-estate broker, a specialist works on behalf of both the list renter and the list owner and just charges a fee to the list renter as a commission. This highly-specialized individual has a wealth of knowledge and experience.

He knows exactly what kind of lists are available in the marketplace, how each has performed in the past and can advise the renter which lists would give the best results. They base their advice on the type of mailing, size of mailing, timing and funds available.

List Compiler. As the name suggests this individual is responsible for compiling a list. There are two ways that lists are compiled. The first uses all information that is openly available like names and addresses from telephone directories, government census data, trade sources, associations, etc. Next, the compiler can segregate this information into specific slots such as all individuals who are self-employed or own a business.

The second and newer approach works in the reverse order where the list compiler uses massive master files in his possession to select individual names and addresses of people who fit certain common criteria, e.g. all individuals who own a Lincoln, who are between the ages of 35 and 50 years old, and have a dog but no cats.

List Manager. The list owner employs a list manager to manage and interact with list brokers and to keep track of all aspects relevant to maintaining, negotiating and managing the list and rental fees or contracts.

Service Bureau. A service bureau provides data processing and merge/purge services using many list files. They also run **Canada**

The importance of lists and precision targeting cannot be stressed enough.

Imagine if you did not own an animal and you received a great direct mail piece offering cat or dog food at rock bottom prices. The mailing would be completely wasted.

Direct marketers are at fault for creating 'junk mail' when we target people for whom the direct mail has no relevance.

Yves Blain of **FCB Direct** believes that the big distinction that the target audience makes when they receive mail is whether the piece has any added value for the recipient. All mail becomes junk mail in their eyes if it does not add value.

He cites his own experience with Aeroplan miles:
"I receive a lot of mail – my mailbox is always crammed but there is one type of mail I open first. I want to see the goodies. I want to see the value of my reward miles. Give me value and in exchange, I will give you all the permission in the world to talk to me. What will emerge are smart marketers who will offer value to their customers to build relationships."

Use the talents of List Brokers and Compilers. They are a storehouse of valuable information and expertise.

"It costs you no more than the list rental price to pick the minds of experts who manage or have compiled the lists in the first place.

Think of the Broker as the 'bus driver' and the Compiler as the 'mechanic'. They know the strengths of their lists and how well to maneuver them. They have subtle information as to the inherent strengths of the list, which are not apparent in the 'broker list data cards'.

They know who used it last, how well it performed, how it is segmented, etc. Spending the time upfront with them will save you the extra cost and time trying to plough through reams of information that you may not be fully familiar with."

Mona Sharkway

Post's National Change of Address (NCOA) files.

The accuracy of addresses is increased with this step. With the rapid expansion of lists and the constant maintenance necessary today, service bureaus are highly specialized facilities that can perform these tasks rapidly and precisely to ready the file for lasering onto letters and envelopes.

TYPES OF LISTS

The two most popular types of lists are **consumer lists and business lists**. These are further broken down into the following:

Your own list is called a 'House List.' A House List is composed of current Donor of the organization and of Prospects, people who have had some relationship with the group but are not active Donors. This list is by far the most useful for two obvious reasons. First, it contains your own past supporters and next it also contains valuable information about them: previous donation patterns, size of gift, etc.

Rental lists could have been constructed in a variety of ways:

Response/Self-Reported Lists. As the name suggests they contain information about people who responded by mail in the past. They include catalogue buyers, inquirers, controlled circulation recipients, direct responders and questionnaire and survey responders.

Compiled Lists. These lists consist of names and addresses of individuals who have common characteristics and therefore fall in certain categories, like the earlier example of all individuals who own a Lincoln, who are between the ages of 35 and 50 years old, and have a dog but no cats. These characteristics include age, occupation, household income, length of residence, credit cards or mortgage data, neighborhood data, geographic information, socioeconomic status and census demographics.

Vertical Lists. These lists usually have a very narrow focus and are typically subscribers to specialty magazines or publications.

Psychographic/Life Event Lists. These are lists of people who have life style similarities – married, own residences or recreational properties, have children, have changed jobs or started a new businesses, are graduates or retirees.

Transactional Lists. These lists can include number of transactions, buying affinity groups, donation category data and dollar amounts.

Profiled/Modeled Lists. These are typically selected from a customized, analytical profile of customers/prospects, or from a custom-built model.

E-mail Lists. Opt-ins list are the names and information of people who have voluntarily supplied personal information when visiting, browsing or enlisting on a website. One of the greatest assets of dot.com companies that flourished before the meltdown was the vast database of information that they had collected from people who had logged on and given them their personal information. However unverified information is a major drawback with most e-mail lists. It could be false. Also in many cases, there are no physical addresses so merge/purge will not be as 'perfect' as in the postal world.

Finally, no e-mail house ever ships their list to an outside Lettershop for merge/purge and that can create duplicates and other problems.

HOW LISTS ARE SUPPLIED

Below is a typical sample of a list.

List Name: PUBLICATION OR RENTER LIST

CLASSIFICATION	TYPE	LIST SIZE	MIN.ORDER	BASE COST/M
PRODUCTS	CONSUMER	472,411	5,000	$125.00 CDN.

Description of list: This is a list of former active members and subscribers who have purchased products during the last five years. Of the above list 77% are buyers of products or services and 23% are requesters of the cataloque.

Sample Count Breakdown:
8,141 Males
38,420 Females
34,000 Direct Mail Sold
6,090 2004 Records
7,200 2005 Records
5,300 2006 Records
8,000 2007 Recards

This list is updated once a year

Age Ranges selectable include: 18-24; 25-34; 35-40 and 40+

Average Unit of Sale: $50.00

Cancelled orders are subject to charge of $25/M

Sample mailing piece required.

Payment terms: 30 days after mail date

SELECTS	COSTS
Male	$10.00/M
FSA	$10.00/M
Province	$10.00/M
Nth	$0.00/M
Key Records	$0.00/M
Year Joined	$15.00/M
Female	$10.00/M
Change of Address	$15.00/M
Multi-Buyers	$15.00/M
Age Range	$15.00/M
Fundraising Rate	$100.00/M
3 Month Hotline	$15.00/M

FORMATS	COSTS
Tape 1600BPI	$30.00 F
3.5 " Disc	$30.00 F
Cheshire	$10.00/M
Peel Off	$10.00/M
E-mail	$30.00 F
CD-ROM	$30.00 F

SORTING	COSTS
POSTAL	$0.00/M
NDG	$0.00/M

PROVINCIAL BREAKDOWN

NL 3%	NB 3%	MB 5%	BC 13%
NS 6%	QC 5%	SK 4%	YK 1%
PE 2%	ON 46%	AB 11%	NT 2%

* A minimum of 1,000 names applie to all re-use orders

List Owner asserts that this list is subject to and compliant with Chapter 5 of the Statutes of Canada 2000
Status Recorded: October 20, 2000

The List Broker makes its best efforts to ensure the accuracy of its media profiles. However, we receive information theo third-parties and cannot guarantee our profiles' accuracy or completeness

Our research shows this list was last updated: December 15, 2006
Print Date: February 20, 2006 **CLB Profile Updated: January 26, 2006**

Data mining is the analysis of information that establishes relationships between the various pieces of information in a file to identify and implement more effective direct marketing and communication strategies.

Data mining is a technique to locate and isolate informational patterns of behaviour of individuals within a database.

The aim is to isolate those prospects, based on their past behaviour: who are most likely to donate and to identify how best to communicate with them.

LIST HYGIENE

Keeping your house file up-to-date is crucial for maximum effectiveness, reducing mistakes and keeping costs down. It is also reduces costly returned mail.

1. Update your list regularly
   - Clearly spell out donor options, adding new information the moment you get it;
   - Record who gave when, how much and for which mailing, incentive or event;
   - Identify those who have donated online or who prefer to receive electronic mail.
2. Maintain a detailed suppression file
   - Identify donors who wish to keep their names private;
   - Keep a do-not-mail list of those who have indicated so, remove duplicates and the names of deceased people;
   - Adhere to people's wishes as to number of mailings and time of year;
   - Update your list when mail is returned as incorrect or no longer at this address;
   - Follow postal rules of address accuracy.
3. Ask donors to notify you of duplicate mailings and incorrect addresses
   - Contact donors for clarification if you feel you have a false negative or a false positive name on your list. (***see page 34***) It will save you the embarrassment of looking incompetent in the eyes of your donors.

Note: Although lists are available in a variety of ways, they are now usually supplied in an FTP format and shipped by email.

THE LIST RENTAL AGREEMENT

Lists are generally rented for a one-time use. The renter cannot hold on to or copy any name from the list for future use. However if anyone from the rented list responds to the renter's mailing, then the renter can add this new name to their own house list.

Prior to renting a list the renter must fulfill all conditions including specifying the date of the mailing, the size of the mailing and getting approval of the mailing itself from the list's owner.

The cost of list rentals depends on the size of the mailing, usually priced on a per-thousand basis. There is also a minimum number of names as part of the condition. The average minimum is 5,000 names.

Prices generally range from $50 to $150 per thousand for compiled lists and increase according to fine-tuning or segmentation options. *For example*, if only certain area codes are needed, or only males who have a small businesses are needed, <u>or only hotline names</u> – names of people who have donated in the last 30 or so days – are selected, costs will go up accordingly.

Responder lists cost from $80 - $250 per thousand with a $10 - $20 per thousand charge for special selection.

All shipping, GST/PST and customs brokerage charges apply. Each list is different and has its own minimum number of names that must be purchased when renting that list.

MERGING AND PURGING LISTS

The various lists, including house lists or any rented lists for a particular DM mailing, are first merged and purged to ensure a clean final mailing list. Merge/purge is a process that:

- Removes duplicate names
- Ensures address accuracy
- Divides mailings into test cells

A Note Of Caution when Merging and Purging. When a duplicate name is found while processing two or more lists, the errors can sometimes be hard to decipher.

For example:

John Doe
20 Richmond Drive
Toronto, ON
M4N 2N2

John J. Doe
20 Richmond Drive
Toronto, ON
M4N 2N2

If the decision is made that that one of the duplicate names should be purged or removed and not mailed to, then that is called a **false positive.**

If however the decision that both names are not duplicates and both should be mailed to, then that is a **false negative.**

How one uses a false positive or a false negative duplicate name has different consequences.

If a duplicate name is found while processing two or more rented lists then:

- A false positive is not to mail to that name, which may be a legitimate potential donor
- A false negative is to mail to the same name twice (or as often as the duplicate name appears)

Next, if a duplicate name is found while processing a rented list with the house list:

- A false positive is not to mail to that name, which may be a legitimate prospect
- A false negative is to mail to the same name twice. This can be even more harmful because as a current donor, they may wonder about the efficiency of your company

LIST SUPPRESSION

Another important consideration when merging and purging rented lists to remove duplicate names is to get rid of incorrect addresses that would be returned by the post office. Conscientious list handlers seek change of address notices from the post office and update their lists.

List suppression means removing names of those who have specifically requested that their names not be rented to another company. In addition, names of individuals with past undesirable characteristics, like a bad credit rating, are suppressed.

Finally, all names that appear on your house list must be suppressed from the rented list to ensure that they do not get a repeat mailing or a mailing unsuitable for a current customer. The

PIPEDA (The Personal Information Protection and Electronic Documents Act) came into effect January 2001 and sets out ground rules for how private sector organizations may collect, use or disclose personal information in the course of commercial activities.

Based on universally recognized data protection principles, the PIPEDA is a well-balanced law that recognizes the rights of consumers to protect their personal information and provides flexibility for organizations to use customer data to grow their business. Quebec has an Act respecting the protection of personal information in the private sector, and several other provinces have proposed similar provincial privacy legislation.

The Canadian Marketing Association (CMA) is a leader in self-regulation and ensures all members comply by protecting consumer privacy through its comprehensive Code of Ethics and Standards of Practice, which include specific guidelines on fulfillment procedures, Internet marketing, consumer privacy and marketing to children and teenagers.

For more information visit the CMA website: http://www.the-cma.org

A good Direct Mail strategy, as opposed to a tactical one, depends on building and using a database intelligently. The information enables marketers to recognize who people are and talk to them appropriately. It is crucial to know the preferences of your donors and prospects: how often they say they want to be contacted; how they wish to be contacted (by mail, email, etc.); how much they generally give; what time of the year they like to donate.

Intelligent use of such data prevents wasting precious marketing dollars through irrelevant mailings and prevents you from alienating your donors.

house list in this case is called a '**Kill File.**' You must be scrupulous in the way you treat your own house list lest they wonder about your company's efficiency.

DATA OVERLAY AND ENHANCEMENT

To increase the amount of information and enhance your house list, you can hire a special list enhancer to further enrich each name.

The enhancer runs your house list through his proprietary database of millions of households. Each time a matching name is found with the same address and postal code, any new psychographics, geographic and demographic information is added to the house list, information like occupation, household value, income, age, education level, length of residence, credit card info, mortgage data, socioeconomic status, telephone numbers, or other meaningful attitudinal information.

Data enhancement, when done on an individual level, is more expensive. However, when data may not be available about a certain individual then a 'surrogate' value is applied. *For example*, if the value of the individual's house is unknown then a similar appraisal is made of a like property in that neighborhood. The accuracy of applying a 'surrogate' value depends on how well it matches other properties.

HOW TO SELECT A LIST

Your mailing list should consist of prospects who are the best suited for your organization and its mission.

We have all heard the DM slogan: *"Identify your best prospects and then find more like them."* So if you are renting a list remember that if the demographic and psychographic profiles match the most loyal donors on your own house list, then they may be your best prospects to target.

Many of these decisions are logical. *For example:* If you are a charity like The Royal Conservatory of Music, then you need a list of music lovers.

However, in many cases it is not that easy to identify the best prospects so the next logical step is to check three important aspects of behaviour of people in a list. These three factors are referred to as (RFM) or Recency, Frequency and Monetary value.

RECENCY, FREQUENCY AND MONETARY VALUE

Recency refers to the time that passes between an individual's purchase, an inquiry or a donation.

Traditionally, those who have transacted by mail within the last three to six months, and no longer than a year ago, are considered ***hotline buyers.***

Frequency is the number of times a person on that list has purchased, donated or transacted with the company that last rented the list. The more often the better.

Monetary Value is the amount in dollars that a person has paid to purchase a product or service or donated to a cause from the last list renter. The more often and higher the monetary value of the transaction the better.

MARKET SEGMENTATION

Market segmentation is a grouping of people into smaller subgroups or segments which are homogeneous with each other, i.e. the people in this segment display similar attitudes about certain issues or have similar behavioral patterns. They are more likely to respond similarly to a given marketing strategy or direct mail solicitation then those who have not shown similar patterns.

Many variables can be used to segment these groups. Patterns of response can be based on:

Demographic data – personal characteristics such as young singles, families with children, affluent empty nesters, age, gender, sexual orientation, family size, family life cycle, income, occupation, education, socioeconomic status, religion, nationality, etc.

Psychographic data – attitudinal characteristics such as personality, life-style, values, attitudes, etc.

Behavioural data – refers to a donor's giving history and past preferences. Do they prefer to give to particular types of causes— the environment, cancer, children, faith based groups?

Geographic data – area or region of residence including city, urban, suburban or rural area, identified by postal code.

When numerous variables are combined to give an in-depth understanding of a segment, then this is referred to as '**depth segmentation.**'

When a clear picture emerges from adequate information of a typical person within a segment, then this is called a '**buyer profile.**'

Every member of the Canadian Marketing Association must abide by a code of ethics as published by the Association.

LIST SEGMENTATION

Segmentation is the process of targeting a stratum of a list to achieve a higher rate of response. Many mailers have discovered that certain clusters of area codes produce better responses than others to certain types of offers or mailings. People who choose similar life styles are more likely to respond in similar ways.

By mailing only to 50% of the ***hotline buyers,*** rather then the entire list, it is possible to get a 60% or 80% response and save money.

A Final Note: The importance of database content cannot be stressed enough. The cardinal rule of database collection should be to capture, record and detail every contact information with an individual on your list.

PRIVACY ISSUES

The fear of loss of privacy may be unjustified because database collection among different organizations is recorded and used differently to suit their own purposes.

For example:

- Retail records are scanned at the point of purchase to facilitate accounting, inventory control and profitability analysis;
- Financial services data is more complex with the same customer sharing multiple products. These institutions seldom share their files with others;
- Business-to-business (B2B) data records detail only customers and sales;
- Direct marketers capture name, address, sales or donor information (history, pledge amounts, acquisition record, profile, demographic, psychographic data, etc).

Therefore, any chance of these organizations swapping or selling information among themselves is highly unlikely. Besides, a database is too important a resource to any organizations. Also the Canadian and Provincial government legislation now dictates that all organizations have to get prior permission from their customers before they can trade or rent their names. This applies even to non-profit organizations.

<u>Remember that the best list is only as good as the people who use it</u>. It requires a trained eye to use a list most effectively. *For example,* if you are a children's charity and you wish to trade your list with other charities, which one should you pick? Or should you

trade with all of them because each one has a proven record of donors? What about the fact that many charities have a donor base of individuals quite different from yours like younger people or more male donors unlike your database of predominately older females?

Population redistribution can also influence an entire group's behaviour. The response from a previously lucrative area of rural donors can change suddenly with the introduction of a big shopping mall in the area or the installation of new roads or highways.

In the event of drastic changes in your response rates, before you blame your direct mail piece, analyze external factors first.

RENTING METHODS

This only applies to people who rent lists in the millions.

Renting on net name basis: This allows you to pay for only unduplicated names from the total volume. If 15,000 names were duplicates in a 100,000 file, then you only pay for the 85,000 names used.

Renting on a net-net basis: Only names mailed are paid for. If you selected 50,000 names from a 100,000 file then you only pay for the 50,000 names used, as long as you do not go below the minimum order.

TRADING LISTS

Many charities trade their lists with other charities because they contain a segment of the population of charitable donors. Not everybody is generous.

(*See list alongside of who donates.*)

Remember that if you are going to trade names, you need to get prior permission from your donors before you trade their names.

SEEDING A LIST

List renters include names and addresses of their key staff to ensure that they can track every list they rent. Renters too do the same, planting names in to ensure that a DM piece arrives as planned and in the way it was intended.

This also allows the renter to track delivery dates and discover unforeseen problems.

WHO GIVES?
A host of surveys have found:

- More women donate than do men.
- Very young people are less likely to donate because they usually have the least disposable income.
- As people get older the propensity to give drops off, most likely because of reduced income.
- Those who are separated or divorced are more likely to donate. This group has shown the largest increase in giving recently, bumping married people from the top spot.
- Parents with children donate more than those without children.
- Regular worshippers donate more than non-worshippers.
- Volunteers donate more than non-volunteers.
- The percentage of giving and the size of donations rises with income level.
- The proportion of income to donation is highest in the lowest income bracket.
- Donors involved in their local communities are more likely to be involved with clubs and associations. Those who know their neighbours by name are more generous than those who keep to themselves.

HOW TO SEGMENT YOUR MOST VALUABLE DONORS

Here is a tip for the non-profit segment. While data experts see a house list as a record of transactions, try and view it as a record of customer behaviour and it will provide you with important insights into how past donors may respond to future incentives

This behavioural perspective becomes more important when used effectively in trying to decipher whom to select for your next donor appeal and how not to lose your best donors.

Consider the old **RFM (Recency, Frequency and Monetary value) formula.** Although it is not a sure-fire formula, as any data expert will tell you, it can be used quite effectively by non-profits in deciding whom to select from the house list for their next mailing.

Donors who fall under the **'Monetary Value' category**, i.e. those who give large amounts, display a certain pattern of behaviour. They usually give once or twice a year and should not be approached too often.

Since they are your premium donors, you should pay close attention to their giving patterns and to the kind of mailing they responded to in the past. Check to see if it was a special mailing, a year-end appeal, an annual membership drive, a camp or a house appeal, etc.

Verify if they gave at the end of the year or during a certain month.

All these factors are very important in deciding when and how much and how often to ask them again. Also, don't hesitate to ask them for the same amount they gave previously.

Donors who give smaller amounts either belong to the **'Recency or Frequency' segment**. A quick check on their past transactions should give you a clue as to where they fit.

If they give frequently you know they are loyal donors who believe in your cause. Ideally, you should try to convert them to monthly giving if possible. By all means you should include them in most mailing cycles, but it is equally essential to allow them to choose their donation timing.

A good example of providing donors the option of selecting their donation timing is the case study for The Royal Conservatory of Music ***(see page 39).***

Another way to keep your loyal donors up-dated is to send them your regular newsletters containing response cards. This is a soft-sell technique that allows them to decide when to give.

You could also give them the option to donate on-line, by phone or by fax. The more choices you give them the better.

If they gave recently they are considered '**hotline candidates**' and you should cross-sell them to attend an event, a speaking engagement or to even become a volunteer. In other words, get them more involved right away.

Hotline candidates are those people most recently added to the file—in the last three to six months or so.

Experience indicates that these new donors usually are more receptive than those who have been on the file for years and give once in a while.

Keep in mind that all lists deteriorate, some by about 20% each year, others by as much as 50% each year.

Before you remove lapsed donors from your files, it may be cost-effective to try and contact them by phone, because obviously sending them more mail has not worked. If the file of lapsed donors is too large, you may consider hiring a reputable telemarketing non-profit organization rather then a commercial one.

If you do contact them by phone you may get some valuable information: why they have not responded; whether they still consider your charity to be of value; if they intend to donate again in the future.

Clearly one of the best ways of reducing defection is to make each of the above categories of donors more loyal to your cause in the future. Your data is your best source of behavioural information.

Often Development Directors feel that sending as many as four to six mailings a year to their frequent donors may be too much However, research shows that many people like the attention that direct mail and newsletters provide. Besides, no one is suggesting that you ask for funds with every mailing; just keeping them involved is important.

Many 'pros' agree with **Bob Stone,** who wrote in his book ***Successful Direct Marketing Methods*** that, *"Mail is acceptable more often than you think."* And **René Gnam** said, *"I have not seen a single case of over-use of a customer file by the owner of the file."*

CASE STUDY

SPECIAL OLYMPICS ONTARIO ACQUISITION TEST

Background: Special Olympics Ontario is always looking for new ways to acquire new donors, so when one of their strongest supporters, Air Miles Reward Miles offered to share a small list of their members to test the viability of their lists as a new source of revenue, Special Olympics Ontario was delighted and jumped at the opportunity.

Objectives: To raise funds from this new source of Air Miles donors and compare the response against the traditional way of acquiring new donors by trading a list with other charities.

Solution: Two very similar direct marketing pieces were created. The only difference was the following:

- **The one aimed at Air Miles members offered an incentive of ONE Air Mile reward for every $5 they donated to the charity.**
- **The other, mailed to a traded list, did not include any incentive.**

Results: The results were quite surprising from the two groups:

- **The Air Miles members mailing generated a low 0.6% response;**
- **While the traded list generated a 3.3% response.**

This 550% difference between the two lists showed clearly that whom you mail to has the biggest bearing on results. **Why did the Air Miles membership do so badly?**

Because Air Miles members had joined the program simply because they wanted to get something free — these were takers and not givers.

Glenn MacDonell, President & C.E.O of **Special Olympics Ontario** expressed it best, when he said. *"It just goes to show you that you simply cannot convert non-givers to become givers. Your message is the best lure."*

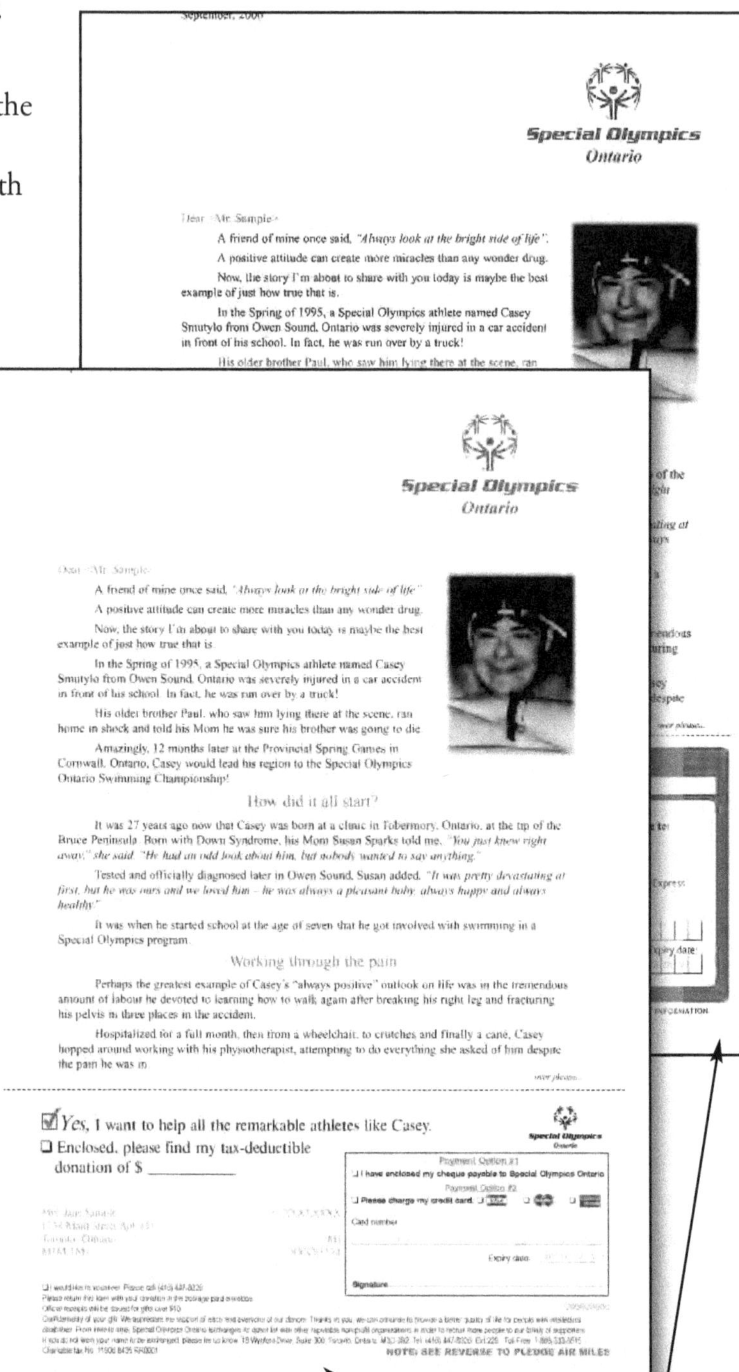

Special Olympics
Ontario

Dear Mr. Sample

A friend of mine once said, *"Always look at the bright side of life"*

A positive attitude can create more miracles than any wonder drug.

Now, the story I'm about to share with you today is maybe the best example of just how true that is.

In the Spring of 1995, a Special Olympics athlete named Casey Smutylo from Owen Sound, Ontario was severely injured in a car accident in front of his school. In fact, he was run over by a truck!

His older brother Paul, who saw him lying there at the scene, ran home in shock and told his Mom he was sure his brother was going to die.

Amazingly, 12 months later at the Provincial Spring Games in Cornwall, Ontario, Casey would lead his region to the Special Olympics Ontario Swimming Championship!

How did it all start?

It was 27 years ago now that Casey was born at a clinic in Tobermory, Ontario, at the tip of the Bruce Peninsula. Born with Down Syndrome, his Mom Susan Sparks told me, *"You just knew right away," she said. "He had an odd look about him, but nobody wanted to say anything."*

Tested and officially diagnosed later in Owen Sound, Susan added, *"It was pretty devastating at first, but he was ours and we loved him – he was always a pleasant baby, always happy and always healthy."*

It was when he started school at the age of seven that he got involved with swimming in a Special Olympics program.

Working through the pain

Perhaps the greatest example of Casey's "always positive" outlook on life was in the tremendous amount of labour he devoted to learning how to walk again after breaking his right leg and fracturing his pelvis in three places in the accident.

Hospitalized for a full month, then from a wheelchair, to crutches and finally a cane, Casey hopped around working with his physiotherapist, attempting to do everything she asked of him despite the pain he was in.

over please...

☑ *Yes*, I want to help all the remarkable athletes like Casey.

❑ Enclosed, please find my tax-deductible donation of $ __________

Payment Option #1

❑ I have enclosed my cheque payable to Special Olympics Ontario

NOTE: SEE REVERSE TO PLEDGE AIR MILES

Air Miles letter

Traded list letter

CHAPTER 4

OFFERS: HOW TO MAKE ONE YOUR CUSTOMERS CAN'T REFUSE

An Offer is a proposition made by the marketer to a prospect or donor. It is a combination of benefits that may exist in a product, a service or a social program that can satisfy a real or an inner need.

The main function of direct marketing is to get people to respond. Unlike advertising that tries to create an image to entice a mass market, the basic goal of direct marketing is **to generate a response.**

The best way to evoke this 'Call to Action' is by making people an offer that will motivate them to purchase a product (buying a goat from Oxfam to help a family in Africa) or making a donation when they are offered something by a charity (Christmas cards, Calendars, etc.)

An offer does two important things: grabs the recipients' attention but more important, tempts many of them to act.

WHAT IS THE PURPOSE OF AN OFFER?

The writer **Denny Hatch** proclaimed: **"Without an offer, it's not DM."**

According to most authors there are two kinds of offers that many charities use: tangible items like premiums and freebies that can include things like address labels, nickels and dimes, personal notepads, etc. These are called front-end premiums. Back-end premiums promise to send a promotional item once the prospect makes a donation.

Some consider the suggested donation amounts that a charity asks its prospects to give as an offer. Denny Hatch even feels that the method of donation, e.g. cheque or credit card, is an offer. *(See what he had to say alongside.)*

IS DENNY HATCH RIGHT WHEN HE SAYS THAT, 'WITHOUT AN OFFER IT'S NOT DIRECT MARKETING'?

While researching for this book, I went straight to the source via email:

Hi Denny,
I teach direct marketing at two colleges in Toronto and quote your observation, "Without an offer it's not direct marketing".

This statement baffles my students when it comes to the non-profit segment that uses direct marketing to solicit funds. Where is the offer in such a case?

Perhaps you can help me give them a good answer.

Billy

He very kindly e-mailed me back, saying:

1. *How much will you give? Check one: $5 - $15 - $50 etc. etc.*
2. *How to pay. Cheque? (Made out to whom?) Credit Card? Monthly automatic deduction from credit card? Monthly automatic deduction from chequing account?*
3. *What premium would you like: Tony Bennett for $50? All Beethoven Symphonies for $150? The Umbrella? The Tote Bag? Etc.*

Denny Hatch

MAKE SURE THE OFFER IS A GOOD MATCH

A mailing for the **University of St. Michael's College** featured a special commemorative metallic bookmark celebrating its 150th Anniversary, resulted in a huge response. The **'Faith, Hope & Charity'** year-long campaign was a big success.

Here is another good offer. It is a autographed copy of the book ***ZOOM*** by **Robert Munsch**

(For more on this see **AN EASTER PACKAGE WITH A DIFFERENCE** *featured on page 78)*

EMOTIONAL TRIGGERS THAT PROMPT PEOPLE TO ACT

- Fear
- Greed or Lust
- Power
- Flattery
- Revenge
- Love
- Anger or Envy
- Guilt
- Pride
- Bargains
- Pleasure
- Fame/Discovery
- Patriotism
- Danger

The well known psychologist, **Abraham Maslow**, first formulated a hierarchy of human needs then developed a theory to explain how and why people react in a certain way.

In his book ***Motivation and Personality***, he identified five basic human needs which he called the 'Hierarchy of Needs.' He postulated that as each need is met, it disappears to be replaced by the next progressive need.

MASLOW'S HIERARCHY OF NEEDS

Level 1	**Physiological Needs.** The need for basic survival. (Food, Water, Sleep)
Level 2	**Safety Needs.** The need for security. (Shelter, Protection)
Level 3	**Belonging.** The need to belong. (Love, Friendship, Acceptance)
Level 4	**Ego Needs.** The need for praise. (Prestige, Status)
Level 5	**Self-Actualization.** The need for achievement. (Self-fulfillment, Enrichment)

These needs fall largely into two categories, utilitarian needs and emotional desires. Many direct marketers have learned that the satisfaction of utilitarian needs can be fulfilled with basic tangible rewards, while emotional desires are satisfied with more motivational, demonstrative or rational rewards.

THE SECRET OF CRAFTING A GOOD OFFER

We can learn a lot by simply looking at the best-seller list of books. It provides a key to the popularity of various motivations that spur people to act. The top eight categories:

Aspiration to make more money
- Improve job skills, increase pay
- Learn new skills, get better jobs
- Make more outside spare-time income

Wish to save money
- Sales, close-outs, discounts, factory-direct, introductory offer, special member offers
- Longer wearing, lower replacement cost
- Do-it-yourself, reduce overhead or consumption

Yearning to win praise
- Improve self (diet, exercise)
- Improve skills (gardening, cooking)
- Earn awards or rewards

Eagerness to help children, family and others
- Health appeals
- Education
- Recreation
- Helping those less fortunate then ourselves

Aspiration to save time and effort
- Reduce physical drudgery
- Get instant results, overnight benefits
- Carefree maintenance

Ability to impress others
- Obtain special status (possessions)
- Indirect status (be part of a special group, membership)
- Gain knowledge (education, travel, speech, art, books, music)

Desire to have fun
- Traveling
- Family outing, picnics
- Nightclubs, race track, movies, bowling, dancing

Need for self-improvement
- Physical (exercise, hair care, clothes, make-up, sex appeal)
- Mental (self help)
- Financial (how to pick stocks, investing secrets)
- Developmental (dummies guide books)
- Get better grades

There are over 161,000 registered charities and nonprofit organizations in Canada*. One of the key reason why so many survive is because people like to help others.

It is estimated that 88% of all donations to a charity on average come from individuals donors.

** National Survey of Nonprofit Organizations (NSNVO) report 2003*

Although these basic wishes hold true in general, in reality multiple motives can simultaneously affect the final decision.

TYPES OF OFFERS

In the commercial world there are many types of offers. One book describes well over a hundred different ones, ranging from freebies that include information, trials and gifts to continuous rolling offers including those based on price. Offers can also be based on length of commitment. While a gift in the commercial world is regarded as an 'offer,' in the non-profit world the 'offer' can just be the good feeling that comes from knowing that certain philanthropic objectives will be achieved: the satisfaction that refugees will have shelter, children will be helped, abused mothers will find a haven, etc.

What is important to charities is that an offer should either aid membership or facilitate donations.

WHAT TO CONSIDER WHEN PLANNING AN OFFER

The offer must have added value for the recipient. It is important to remember that it is not the actual worth of the offer but its perceived value in the eye of the beholder that is crucial. Think of **MasterCard's** 'priceless' television campaign. It's not what things actually cost but what we get out of them that is priceless.

Sometimes the satisfaction of just helping others is enough. Even a simple thing like providing information can be valuable to the recipient.

If your offer is a tangible item that is hard to get anywhere else, make it exclusive. Uniqueness is key.

If the benefit derived is more ethereal, like helping feed starving children, then the offer has to be more emotional or inspirational.

It should have some connection to your product or services main benefit. Offers that do this will certainly be more memorable.

Test a wide selection of offers to see which has the broadest appeal.

If the offer is 'free,' then say so, not subtly but shout it out. The word 'Free' is the most powerful word when it comes to grabbing attention in advertising and direct marketing.

Remember, you cannot win hearts and minds without engaging your audience.

The last thing you want your package to do is to provide information and not get a response.

Here's one way to do it if you have an offer of importance to your donors.

START WITH THE OUTER ENVELOPE

Your message should start to make that all-important one-to-one connection right away with your target group.

For example: This teaser for the **Osteoporosis Society of Canada** read:
Your copy of a special report on osteoporosis studies conducted recently in Ontario.

The reason it worked was because it used the words '**<u>Your copy</u> of a special report...**'. Give your donors a good reason to open the package. Remember, the first thing that goes through their mind is (WIIFM) What's-in-it-for-me?

The response was: 8.21% in the first three weeks.

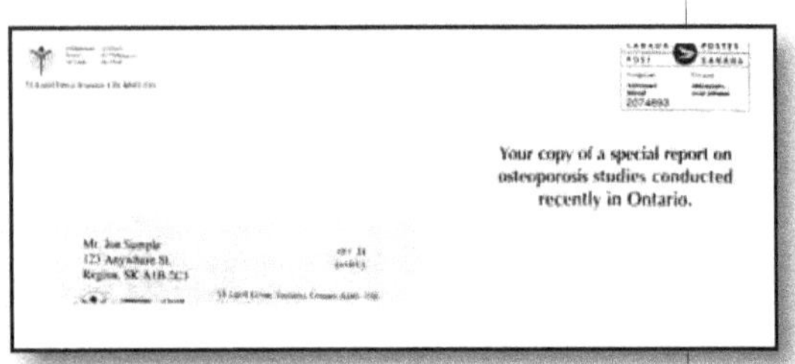

If the offer is pegged with a deadline then don't make an offer with too long or too short a deadline. Too short a deadline will reduce participation for people who never act quickly, while too long a deadline will make the respondent procrastinate.

Show the premium or product being offered through a clear window of the envelope. Tests show that the visual appearance of the premium can lift response by as much as 50% compared to just stating that a premium is inside.

Get the audience involved. Sweepstakes, tokens, stamps, stickers, scratch and win, lift-off tabs all help lift responses as long as they are relevant to the organization offering them.

Early Bird specials and limited time offers compel people. Deadlines induce quicker action and out-pull conventional offers. They dispel inertia and prod the recipient to act.

Credit card privileges or bill-me later plans tend to outperform strictly cash offers.

A yes/no offer will out-pull an offer that doesn't differentiate.

Installment payment terms for items or appeals over $15 tend to increase response.

CASE STUDY

THE ROYAL CONSERVATORY OF MUSIC

Background: When the new marketing director at The Royal Conservatory of Music was hired, she discovered that the house list of over 100,000 members had been dormant for several years. As a result many previous members had lapsed, addresses had changed and giving patterns had altered.

Objective: To reactivate membership using the house list.

Solution: The first priority was to check the house list. A data expert was commissioned to go through the entire list and select only the most likely members to be approached.

Outer envelope: One of the best ways to get the reader's attention is by revealing half a statement on the outer envelope.

From 100,000 previous members he identified just 5,789 as targets for the initial mailing. Of these 5,586 were in the membership range of \$100 to \$999 range while 203 were high-end members in the \$1,000 to \$25,000 range.

Strategy: Since these members had not been contacted for so long, it was necessary to start from scratch. The new direct mail package had to state the great advantages the Royal Conservatory provides members in particular and the community in general. The ultimate purpose was to encourage members to renew their membership.

The package provided various incentives: members could select the month they wanted to join; they could give the membership to someone in their family or to a friend. The goal was to activate as many lapsed members as possible.

Two page letter.
In today's environment of diminishing returns, it is important to get the maximum results from loyal supporters on one's house-list.

Writing for a good cause is not listing reasons why the cause is so great, but rather telling the prospect what their money can accomplish.

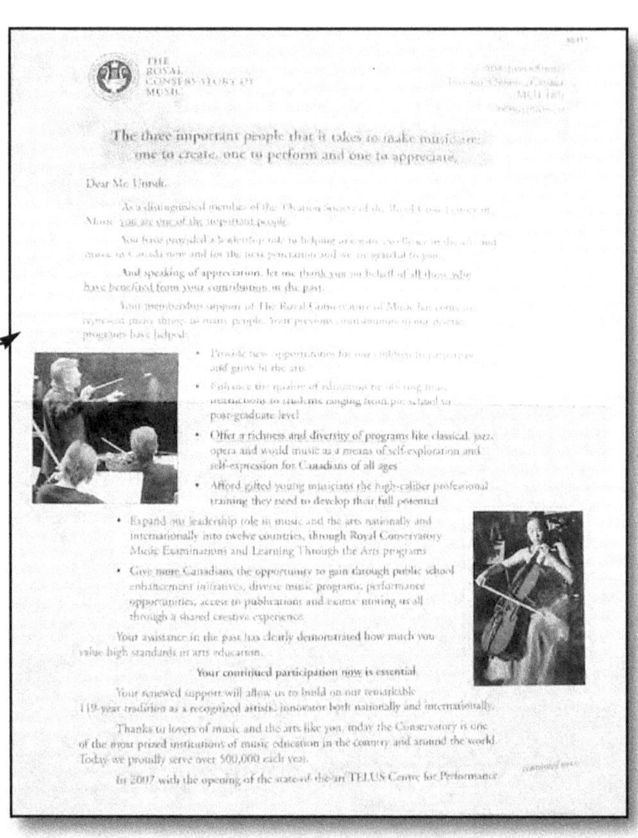

THE ROYAL CONSERVATORY OF MUSIC

The three important people that it takes to make music are: one to create, one to perform and one to appreciate.

Dear Ms Unruh,

[illegible]

And speaking of appreciation, let me thank you on behalf of all those who have benefited from your contribution in the past.

[illegible]

- [illegible]
- [illegible] post-graduate level
- Offer a richness and diversity of programs like classical, jazz, opera and world music as a means of self-exploration and self-expression for Canadians of all ages
- Afford gifted young musicians the high-caliber professional training they need to develop their full potential
- Expand our leadership role in music and the arts nationally and internationally into twelve countries, through Royal Conservatory Music Examinations and Learning Through the Arts programs
- Give more Canadians the opportunity to gain through public school enhancement initiatives, diverse music programs, performance opportunities, access to publications and exams uniting us all through a shared creative experience.

Your assistance in the past has clearly demonstrated how much you value high standards in arts education.

Your continued participation now is essential.

Your renewed support will allow us to build on our remarkable 119-year tradition as a recognized artistic innovator both nationally and internationally.

Thanks to lovers of music and the arts like you, today the Conservatory is one of the most prized institutions of music education in the country and around the world. Today we proudly serve over 500,000 each year.

In 2007 with the opening of the state-of-the-art TELUS Centre for Performance

Result: The initial package was very well received bringing in $75,960 and generating an 9.85% response.

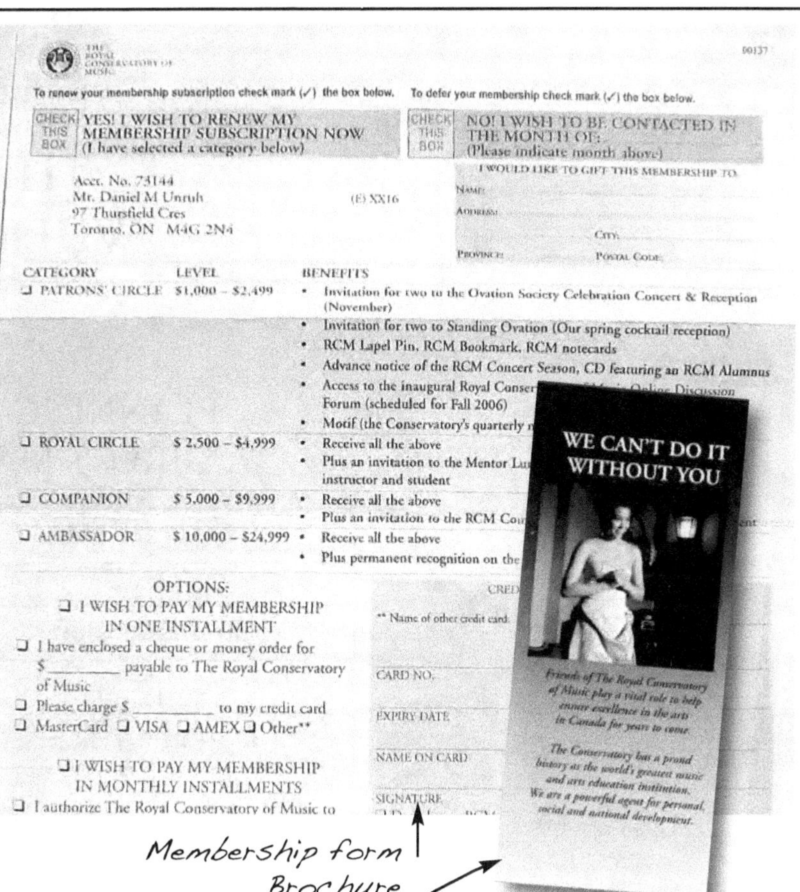

THE ROYAL CONSERVATORY OF MUSIC

To renew your membership subscription check mark (✓) the box below. To defer your membership check mark (✓) the box below.

CHECK THIS BOX — YES! I WISH TO RENEW MY MEMBERSHIP SUBSCRIPTION NOW (I have selected a category below)

CHECK THIS BOX — NO! I WISH TO BE CONTACTED IN THE MONTH OF: (Please indicate month above)

Acct. No. 73144
Mr. Daniel M Unruh
97 Thursfield Cres
Toronto, ON M4G 2N4

(E) XX16

I WOULD LIKE TO GIFT THIS MEMBERSHIP TO:
NAME:
ADDRESS:
CITY:
PROVINCE: POSTAL CODE:

CATEGORY	LEVEL	BENEFITS
❑ PATRONS' CIRCLE	$1,000 – $2,499	• Invitation for two to the Ovation Society Celebration Concert & Reception (November) • Invitation for two to Standing Ovation (Our spring cocktail reception) • RCM Lapel Pin, RCM Bookmark, RCM notecards • Advance notice of the RCM Concert Season, CD featuring an RCM Alumnus • Access to the inaugural Royal Conser... Online Discussion Forum (scheduled for Fall 2006) • Motif (the Conservatory's quarterly n...
❑ ROYAL CIRCLE	$ 2,500 – $4,999	• Receive all the above • Plus an invitation to the Mentor Lu... instructor and student
❑ COMPANION	$ 5,000 – $9,999	• Receive all the above • Plus an invitation to the RCM Co...
❑ AMBASSADOR	$ 10,000 – $24,999	• Receive all the above • Plus permanent recognition on the...

OPTIONS:

❑ I WISH TO PAY MY MEMBERSHIP IN ONE INSTALLMENT

❑ I have enclosed a cheque or money order for $_________ payable to The Royal Conservatory of Music

❑ Please charge $ _________ to my credit card
❑ MasterCard ❑ VISA ❑ AMEX ❑ Other**

❑ I WISH TO PAY MY MEMBERSHIP IN MONTHLY INSTALLMENTS

❑ I authorize The Royal Conservatory of Music to

** Name of other credit card:
CARD NO.
EXPIRY DATE
NAME ON CARD
SIGNATURE

Membership form

Brochure

Twenty-five members specified the exact month when they wanted to be contacted.

The reminder mailing alongside, sent a month later, secured another 2.5% new members.

THE ROYAL CONSERVATORY OF MUSIC

90 Croatia Street,
Toronto, Ontario, Canada
M6H 1K9
www.rcmusic.ca

YOU MATTER

A month or so ago we sent you a renewal letter when your membership lapsed but we have not heard from you. If our letters crossed in the mail and you have already sent back your renewal form then please ignore this letter. If however you set it aside to deal with it later, we fully understand because it might be a busy time for you.

In any case, here's another membership form that you can act on immediately. The sooner you renew your membership, the less likelihood of missing many of the wonderful events planned for this year and the special privileges that your membership provides.

MUSIC MATTERS

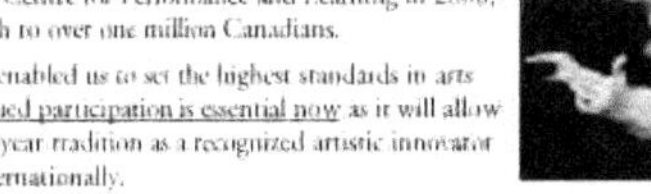

As a distinguished member of the 'Ovation Society of The Royal Conservatory of Music' you play a crucial role in helping ensure excellence in the arts and music in Canada. Thanks to music and arts lovers like you, today we proudly ...00 participants each year. With the opening of the ...ELUS Centre for Performance and Learning in 2008, ...r reach to over one million Canadians.

...rship enabled us to set the highest standards in arts ... continued participation is essential now as it will allow ...r 120-year tradition as a recognized artistic innovator ...nd internationally.

YOUR MEMBERSHIP MATTERS

...sier for you to renew now. You can do so with a single pledge or ...e as a monthly supporter. In either case, your contributions are tax-... completed form in the postage paid envelope or fax it back to us. You ...rcmusic.ca

...bership as a gift to a family member or a friend who would appreciate ... You can even decide when to start your first payment. It's that simple

...nefits listed on the membership form, knowing that the greatest ...nowledge that you are helping talented musicians realize their dreams.

...ld saying is true: "What you give to others ...o you." The young musicians you help today will ... and all of Canada tomorrow.

Sincerely,

Barbara Sutton, CFRE
Vice President, Development

For the reminder mailing the outer envelope to the members in the upper bracket of $1,000 to $25,000 was hand written and had a live postage stamp.

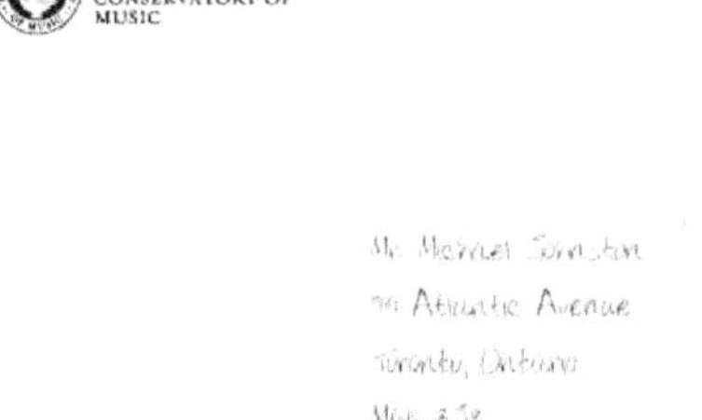

The reminder letter was a single page. and the original membership form.

CHAPTER 5

THE PROCESS: WHERE TO START?

PLANNING AND POSITIONING A DIRECT MARKETING PROGRAM

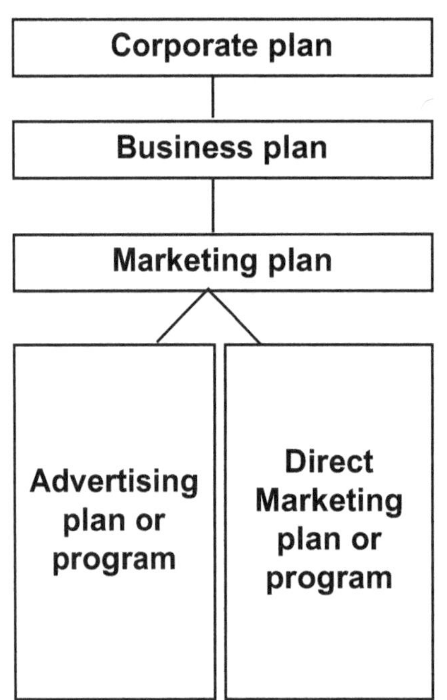

A **direct marketing plan** along with an **advertising plan** is based on an organization's **marketing plan.**

The **marketing plan** is in turn based on the **business plan.**

The **business plan** evolves out of the organization's **corporate plan.** A **corporate plan** is the direction the organization intends to pursue for the foreseeable future. It is usually a vision of the CEO or the President and is instigated by the marketing manager. It looks ahead to what the company wishes to achieve in the next three to five years.

The **business plan** shows how the goals will be met strategically and is usually broken down according to various departments or services the organization provides. It is a more specific plan and covers one to three years.

An organization's **marketing plan** is further broken down to reflect what each department has to achieve and how tactically each goal should be reached. An entire year's program is outlined and is broken down into individual activities including: advertising activities; direct marketing drives; PR activities and any other program which is part of the mix. It specifies the time when each activity should happen.

INITIATING A DIRECT MARKETING PLAN

A direct marketing plan should define your objective, identify the audience, position your organization, map your strategy and establish a budget.

The final materials that the creative and production department produce should be the embodiment of that plan.

STEP ONE

Answer these questions:

- Did my investment in direct marketing actually work?
- If it did, then how well?
- Who are my best donors?
- Where can I find more of them?
- What did they like about a particular mailing?
- What made it different from other mailings?
- What was my return on investment (ROI)?
- How can I improve results?

STEP TWO

Time your direct marketing activities to be most effective:

- When you can clearly identify your target market. This form of direct marketing is generally referred to as prospecting.
- When you can trade or rent a list of new prospective donors and ask for the first gift. This is referred to as an acquisition mailing.
- When you have much to say or explain. This can be done in the form of megalogs or newsletters either through mail or the Internet or both.
- When you need to hold on to your best donors. This is called retention.
- When you want to welcome or reward donors. This is called building loyalty.
- When you need to tailor your communications to different segments and to build a one-on-one relationship with each segment.
- When you find a direct mail piece that out-performs others consistently over time. This becomes your control package.

The most important step in direct mail fundraising is conducting a thorough cost analysis and getting a clear idea of your break-even response rate before mailing. Only then can you make adjustments to ensure you do not lose money.

Donors usually spread out their support to several charities. Very few give to just one organization.

Keep this in mind and offer donors different ways to give and different programs to support.

WHAT IS IMPACTING CHARITIES TODAY?

There are several things that have been pulling and pushing charities today:

- The Internet and digital economy have brought profound changes to the charitable sector and this affects how we contact many of our donors and suppliers.
- Many charities have downsized or resized, often moving many functions internally that were once handled for them by their advertising agency or outside suppliers.
- Major shifts away from mass to segmented marketing approaches have fueled a growth of new players including consultants, freelance individuals or small boutiques who specialize in one or more of the following areas: direct marketing; database marketing; creative services (copy or design); production; website development; door-to-door; email and viral marketing. Many of the above now function as separate entities either within a charity or from outside suppliers.

STEP THREE

Determine how to use the five basic direct marketing components most strategically:

1. LISTS
2. OFFER
3. CREATIVE
4. MEDIA
5. TIMING & SEQUENCE

All five are essential and how you combine them will affect the outcome.

STEP FOUR

Follow a pre-planned program that goes out as scheduled. This should include the complete series for the year: all your communication pieces; direct mail; newsletters; emails and reminder mailings.

- Giving your donors the right number of opportunities to support your organization is important and although this can vary from organizations to organization, depending on its size, one should never feel discouraged with low responses from one singular effort.
- Patience and persistence is key, because what is important is the total income generated annually. Asking your donors too often for funds may increase the rate at which they lapse, but not sending enough appeals each year is worse because they are more likely to lapse even faster.

THE ROLE OF A FUNDRAISING DIRECT MARKETING AGENCY

If you are a large charity and have to deal with a direct marketing agency, remember that agencies are idea-based cultures and that is what they should bring to the table. It is tempting for them to introduce services not attuned to your organization's mandate so question any proposal that doesn't seem relevant.

If you are a small charity and cannot afford the services of a fundraising direct marketing agency, then the many functions they can provide which are listed next, will have to be conducted internally.

THE WORK FLOW

1. PLANNING

- Defining campaign objectives
- Auditing current market/competitive conditions
- Confirming the overall budget
- Gaining donor insight
- Selecting the right target audience for each mailing
- Database/list selections
- Considering testing opportunities
- Selecting campaign elements

2. IMPLEMENTATION

- Developing campaign messages/themes
- Defining response channels
- Developing production schedule
- Briefing all parties involved: creative team, data personnel and supplier/printers
- Briefing fulfillment house/response handlers/research agency
- Specifying the mail pack/response elements

3. EVALUATION

- Assessing response data
- Evaluating research feedback
- Reporting on campaign objectives
- Quantifying donors/life time value implication
- Evaluating list performance

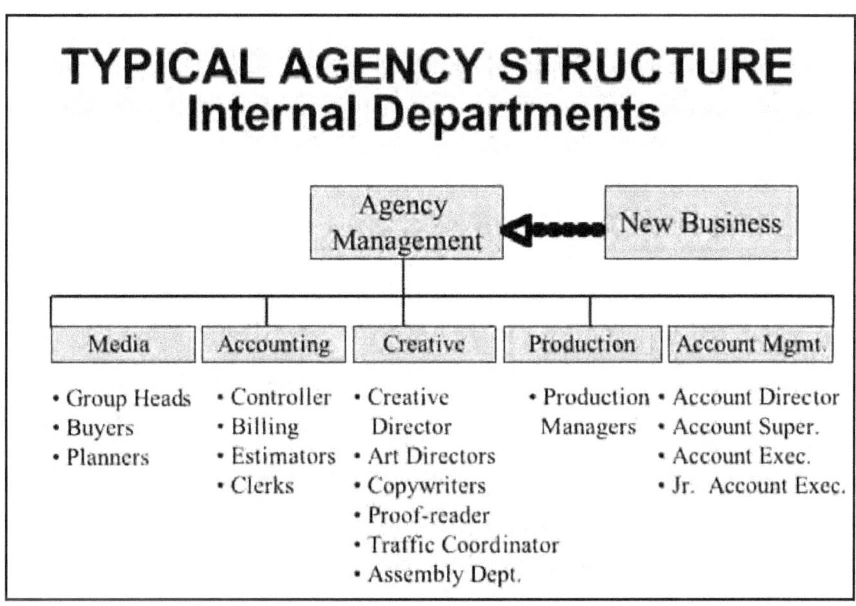

AGENCY STRUCTURE: ROLE OF VARIOUS DEPARTMENTS

ACCOUNT SERVICES DEPARTMENT

The client management function falls to the account executive (AE). The good news is that account services take a day to learn; the bad news is that it takes a lifetime to master.

What the job involves:

- Getting to know and understand the client's business (mission, people, competition, etc.)
- Mirroring and matching the client levels of reporting from junior account levels to the top-most rank.
- Servicing the client as well as representing the interests of the client and the agency.
- Preparing briefs, reviewing the work and presenting it to the client.

Today's AE must:

- Be a multi-disciplinarian
- Work quickly in the digital economy
- Add value to the agency/client relationship
- Be able to work from both sides of the brain
- Have a mix of academic and real-world experience
- Be proactive, outgoing and sociable
- Appreciate the creative process
- Be a skilled project manager
- Know the client's business 'cold'

What skills must an AE develop?

1. Job skills
2. Relationship skills
3. Judgment skills
4. Presentation skills
5. Selling skills

Other tasks that an account executive must perform are:

1. Creating **Contact Reports** – these are regular updates of client meetings and discussions
2. Providing the Client with an **Estimate** for every job before proceeding
3. **Billing** the client after tabulating all the costs
4. Providing **information** about the competition and market updates

STRATEGIC PLANNING

Many account executives are also strategists. Working in concert with the client, they ensure agreement on all details before proceeding with a direct mail piece or campaign and update the client at all stages, attending meetings with the client, internal staff and outside key players. They must issue information to all agency participants via a **Contact Report.**

When initiating a project the key elements are:

- Setting specific goals and objectives
- Commissioning market research
- Establishing the minimum response rate needed to determine the break-even mark
- Deciding what tests to conduct
- Determining how success should be measured
- Developing a critical path
- Procuring lists
- Setting up list management process
- Collecting competitive material

Account executives must also make arrangements for postage (indicia, meter or stamp) which is usually pre-paid by the client. As well they must insure that all seed names, final quantities for each cell and types of samples required by the client are supplied to the lettershop. Seed names are important to ensure that a DM piece turns out the way it was intended. Agencies seed the list by adding clients and agency names.

Seeding also helps track delivery dates, points out unforeseen problems and acts as a check that the recipients do receive the DM piece as planned.

Account executives also supervise list rental and data work, lettershop and fulfillment. If a list is being rented or traded with another charity, the account executive must also provide the charity's house list which is used as a 'kill file' to ensure that the piece does not go to a current donor whose name and address may also be in the rented or traded file.

Analyses of the results are either conducted in-house by the agency or by outside professionals.

HOW TO CREATE A STRATEGIC BRIEF

One of the most important functions of the account executive is creating a **Strategic Brief** for every assignment. This brief is the backbone of any direct mail promotion and is crucial to its success. It is sometimes also referred to as the **marketing plan.** The strategic brief outlines the client's goals and objectives and sets guidelines to be followed. There is no magic formula for this detailed document as each agency has its own version. However, one rule applies to them all: A good **strategic brief** should be exactly that—brief.

IMPORTANT POINTS
A STRATEGIC BRIEF COULD COVER:

1. Opportunity

   A. Clear, tangible, measurable goals

   - Increase membership or donations by X%
   - Seize opportunity to capitalize on recent news
   - Communicate the charity's key advantages

   B. Marketing Objectives

   - Create awareness of the needs
   - Test effectiveness of certain concepts
   - Educate the recipient about new findings, studies, etc.
   - Create excitement about new reports, results, etc.

   C. Creative Objectives

   - Design direct mail package including outer envelope, letter, order-form, BRE, folder

   D. Marketing Tactics

   - Budget
   - Plan

2. Background

   A. Market Environment

   - Prevailing market situation, peoples' attitudes
   - Current market share
   - Historical data
   - Competition info
   - Trends

   B. Current/Previous Marketing Approaches

   - Past direct mail outcomes
   - Media used
   - Communication channels
   - Advertising stance, imagery
   - Telemarketing outcomes
   - Other marketing programs or activities currently in operation
   - Internet site info
   - Strategic alliances in the past and outcomes

C. Barriers Encountered

- Historical
- New challenges

3. Marketing Strategy

A. Details of what needs to be communicated

- Names, statistics and facts
- Details of how and when

B. Donation ladder

- Based on past gift of each donor
- Suggested increase or 'whatever donor can afford'

C. Main benefits/features
- Provide details

4. Target Audience

A. Targeting Objectives

- Primary focus
- Secondary focus
- Demographic, geographic and psychographic profile of potential recipients or past history
- Past or current behaviour patterns

5. Strategic Approach

A. Positioning

- Current position
- Mission

B. USP (Unique Selling Proposition)

- Key advantage or selling points

C. Other Advantages

- Convenient donation options (cheque, Amex, MasterCard, VISA, etc.)
- Convenience of donation (donate on-line, by phone, fax, one-time gift or monthly option)

D. Premium incentive or offer included

- Show or describe
- Available from when to when (start date and end date)

E. Timing/Seasonality

- Critical period
- Timing with other media blitzes or promotions

My favourite definition of 'a brand' comes from online permission marketing pioneer **Seth Godin**, who once said: *"Your brand is what people say about you when you're not in the room."*

Not testing enough.

The odd thing about charities is that on the one hand they are overly cautious but on the other they are guilty of being risk-takers and gamblers.

One of the biggest advantages of direct marketing is testing and yet very few charities ever test a concept, a list or important items before launching an initiative.

Testing is all about making sure a package works; it replaces guesswork with facts.

6. Tactics/Creative Direction

A. Tone

- Type of appeal

B. Branding

- Mandatory elements for consistency with past or current efforts

C. Call-to-Action

- Modes of response: cheque using business reply envelope (BRE), fax, phone, email, web site, coupon or application form
- Locations for replies
- Website or toll free numbers

D. Delivery Channels

- Mail, radio, TV, email, newsletter, web site

E. Current Media mix

- Advertising or promotional offers

F. Mandatory

- Tracking devices
- Number of languages (English, French, bilingual)
- Inclusions (logos, signatures, legal copy, disclaimers, terms & conditions, trademarks, copyrights)
- Web site inclusion
- Specs: colour, sizes, paper-weight, stock
- Bindery: perfs, glue, folds, inserts
- Personalization
- Postage
- List any other items to be included in package

G. Testing Options

- Number of cells
- Number of versions

MEDIA AND TIMING

Selecting the media depends on two factors. First, which media presents your charity or particular appeal in the best light and secondly, the size of the budget available for this project?

EVALUATING CREATIVE

Another very important task that an AE must be trained to do is to evaluate the creative itself.

Here are some important guidelines for evaluating creative copy. Try to be objective rather than subjective as you work through your check list:

1. Is it on strategy?
2. Is it targeted to the most relevant people?
3. Does the envelope have stopping power?
4. Does the piece focus on the recipient and explain why it is being sent to him or her?
5. Is the language easy to read or is it jargon-filled?
6. Does the piece sound as though a person rather than a corporation wrote it? Is the message focused, convincing, believable and worth considering?
7. Is there a logical sequence to the way the proposition is presented?
8. Is the appeal emotional rather than rational? Does it pull at the heartstrings?
9. Has the writer included compelling reasons to respond? Would you respond to this package?
10. Does the opening paragraph of the letter contain too many words? (No more than eleven words should be used for maximum effectiveness.)
11. Does the opening draw you in?
12. Are the sentences short? (The average should be about 14 words per sentence. A one-word sentence is just fine.) Every paragraph should contain one thought which should not require more than seven lines of copy.
13. Does the letter close with impact?
14. Is there a P.S. in the letter? (4 out of 5 people read a P.S. before they read the letter.) The postscript is often referred to as one of the direct mail 'hot spots,' a place where copywriters have the last chance to drive home their point.
15. Does it follow the five-second rule? Can you immediately figure out what they want you to do?
16. Does it persuade the reader to write out a cheque, get on the phone or donate online right now?
17. Is there a clear call to action?
18. What is the overall impact of the piece?
19. Does it need other items to make it stronger, like case histories, statistics, performance figures, names, dates, quotes, facts, testimonials, Lift Notes, brochures?

When judging design, ask these questions:

1. Does the design help make reading effortless? The function of design is not art. It must communicate the message.
2. Has the designer used a serif typeface? Serif typefaces are the kind with little feet, with hooks at the end of the letters.

STAGES OF CREATIVE EXECUTION

1 Writer and art director brainstorm and create thumbnails of various ideas.
2 They then select the best ideas and create headlines and rough layouts.
3 These various concepts and ideas are presented to the creative director as rough drafts.
4 The creative director approves the strongest concepts and shows them internally to the different departments.
5 After internal discussion on the merits of each concept usually three are chosen and final mock-ups and copy developed. A creative rationale is prepared for each concept and all are presented to the client.

Like this typeface, compared to this one, which is sans serif. Serif faces are much more readable.

3. Is the type size big enough to read comfortably?
4. Do the colors reflect the product, service, or market?
5. Have starbursts and other devices been used to highlight important points? (Bursts, corner cuts, underscoring and other devices add punch to direct mail.)
6. Is the design active? (Active designs make the piece feel alive and therefore spur action.)
7. Do graphics or images lead the reader's eye into the copy? (Are the people in photographs facing toward the copy or away from it?)
8. Is the call to action clear? Is it easy to fill out and return?
9. Does the letter look like a letter? Most letters use a serif or typewriter face and a 1-inch margin or more, with short paragraphs that are indented with single spacing between lines.
10. Is the copy broken in the middle of a sentence to force the reader to turn to the next page?
11. Has the artist kept sight of the need to sell the message or has it become an extravagant creative exercise?

CREATIVE DEPARTMENT

This department traditionally consists of one or more creative directors, copywriters, art directors and assembly artists.

The creative director's role. Creative development is the responsibility of the creative director of the agency. He or she decides which art directors and copywriters should be used for the job and is the final authority on which strategy to present to the client. Responsibilities include:

- Getting briefed, reviewing strategic plans, background information, competitive material, contact reports
- Reviewing final copy and layouts
- Preparing a creative rationale for each version
- Presenting final versions first internally and then to the client

The art director and copywriter's joint roles. Many agencies have specific teams of writer/art director while others have a less rigid setup.

The art director and the copywriter must ensure that the direct mail piece is produced in accordance with the strategic plan approved by the client.

The copywriter's responsibility includes:

- Writing different concepts
- Ensuring that all the different versions have been proofread and completed and that all legal copy is accurate

The art director's responsibility:

- Producing rough layouts, thumb nails and concepts for the creative director's approval
- Designing final layouts
- Supervising photo shoots or illustrations
- Selecting formats and paper stocks
- Approving final mechanicals and art work done by the assembly artist

The art director also specifies the typeface, size and colours, position for lasering of the various pieces, gives folding instructions and the sequence of the elements to be inserted in the envelope.

A thumbnail.

PRODUCTION DEPARTMENT

This department, headed by the production manager, is responsible for producing the final printed pieces.

The production manager usually decides who will print the job based on price, availability of the press, quantity, competence and specialty of work of the press and the reputation and trustworthiness of the printer.

The production manager decides if the job needs prepress colour separation, film or plates, folding, die-cutting and binding, if it can go directly from disc to digital printing and then checks which printer can do the best job.

The production manager works with the printer and lettershops to ensure proper size, weight, stock and scheduling. They ensure the outcome by testing a dummy mock-up for proper fit of all elements as per the client's approved version.

There may be more people in production with various other jobs as assistants. The entire production department is responsible for:

- Procuring production estimates
- Selecting the appropriate suppliers
- Ensuring that mechanicals and art work match specs approved
- Reviewing printer's film proofs and chromalins along with the art director, creative director and client
- Attending press approvals and lettershop work

Today just about any colour can be printed. Designers can pick a colour from 100s of Pantone selections from their swatch book or on the computer. They can even choose to screen back a colour. Expensive looking stock such as granite or parchment often leaves recipients feeling like they've received something exclusive. While these specialty papers can be effective, they are also expensive because they require special mill runs.

One can print a background colour or a texture on plain white stock and save both time and money.

- Ensuring list rental and data files are with the appropriate suppliers

EXTERNAL SUPPLIERS

Many of the functions listed below are usually provided by external sources or vendors.

LIST RENTAL AND DATA WORK

These are outside the agency functions so it is prudent to meet and strategize with list brokers and consultants as to what the job requirements are. List rental and data work usually include:

- Identifying the primary and secondary sources for names
- Renting mailing lists
- Pulling all the lists together in one usable format
- Performing sophisticated data extracts and overlays
- Segmenting and predictive modeling
- Testing the data output
- Merging and purging all lists to ensure a clean final mailing list that has no duplicate names and addresses, accurate addresses and mailings divided into test cells.

PRINTING

Two methods are available, film separation or digital imaging. The art-work produced by the agency is first sent to either a film-house or an output bureau to produce the final film for printing.

The art director and production managers supply the specs to the film house. They also check the final chromolins for colour fidelity, tonal value and for registration, to ensure that none of the colours have shifted. The approved chromolins are sent to the client who signs off on all materials before they are sent along with a dialux or colour keys to the printer.

Most envelope manufacturers carry an assortment of sizes and styles from window envelopes to bangtails. Specialty envelopes can be obtained from printers or manufacturers and include:

- Self-mailers
- Inserts
- Snap-packs
- Closed faced kits
- Postcards
- Boxes and tubes

LETTERSHOP

Lettershop and fulfillment activities are independent operations, conducted by professional services outside the direct marketing agencies.

The two departments within an agency that deal directly with the lettershop are the account services department and the production department.

Their work includes:

- Selecting the right lettershop
- Confirming mailing specs and equipment capabilities
- Creating a 'dummy' package to test equipment
- Ensuring delivery of printed material to lettershop on time
- Pre-arranging for postage, indicia and BRE numbers
- Approving and receiving samples

Most lettershops can handle the duties above. However when hand sorts are needed or extras elements have to be inserted in the envelope or self-mailer, then specialty mailing houses take over.

Lettershops also provide a complete inventory of the pieces mailed, as well as warehousing and maintaining lists and preparing subsequent follow-up mailings.

FULFILLMENT AND CUSTOMER SERVICE

Once a mailing has 'dropped' and people start responding, there is a ton of additional work still to be done. This consists largely of 'Caging' (processing the information that can be gleaned from the returns) and 'Cashiering' (processing the donations themselves).

It is rare for a DM agency to handle these tasks in-house so usually this is farmed out to a specialized computer service bureau, often the same place where its customer list is maintained.

(*More about Fulfillment and Customer Service in Chapter 11.*)

ANALYZING RESULTS

Analyzing the results of a mailing is the 'back end work' and helps to improve subsequent mailings by:

- **Testing** – exploring untried lists or the effect of tweaking some element in the letter's copy or design;
- **Caging** – massaging and manipulating the information from the responses in hopes of finding a productive new mailing list that will marginally improve the results even by a few pennies.

(*More about Analysis in Chapter 11.*)

Paper plays a huge role in branding and in response because of its tactile nature. Hence, while organizations of repute deem it important that all their printed material be on high quality stock, non-profits are overly cautious to ensure that they do not come across as being extravagant.

Paper comes in different weights that are usually determined by weighing 500 sheets (one ream) of paper of a standard size. The standard size of bond paper is 17" x 22" and the standard size for offset paper is 25" x 38".

A recent test mailing of 65,000 pieces with half on textured stock vs. half on plain white stock resulted in a 24% gain in response for the textured stock.

The colour of a stock also plays an important role. In a test of white vs. cream stock, the cream stock out-pulled the white by 46.25%.

DIRECT MAIL PRINTING IS GENERALLY A TWO-STEP PROCESS

In step one the printers print all the common elements of the DM package that do not require lasering or personalization like logos, signature, etc. Creating a blank shell.

In step two the blank shell to be lasered is sent to the lettershop. The lettershop lasers the names and addresses on the various versions and then sends it on to the bindery for trimming and folding.

The fulfillment house collates all pieces and inserts and sorts them by LCP (postal code), seals, bundles, bags and delivers them to Canada Post.

Printing involves simply putting ink on paper or on any other surface. There are many options and combinations of equipment one could use.

The four most common methods of printing include LETTERPRESS, GRAVURE, SILK-SCREEN PRINTING and OFFSET LITHOGRAPHY.

The rule of thumb is that the best price is usually obtained on the smallest press that can handle the job. The exception is a printer with a larger press that is not busy, because even a small job on a big press is better than no job at all.

SILK SCREEN PRINTERS have the capability of printing on any surface. Largely used for point-of-sale material, banners, etc., the cost is generally dependent on the kind of material and surface that needs printing, the square foot area to be printed and the number of colours to be printed.

LABEL PRINTERS produce mass stickers, labels and tags of the same kind either in rolls or sheets.

SHORT RUN AND SPECIALTY PRINTERS. Digital technology allows four-colour digital printing where the data and the printing files are sent directly to press, bypassing the traditional steps of film separations, film stripping and plate burning for digital 4-colour printing.

Today some printing presses also have the capacity to personalize each piece separately making it cost effective for very small runs. This printing technology uses direct computer disc to printer hook-up (Heidelberg press, Indigo). IBM and Indigo presses can even match offers to response with the data received.

CASE STUDY

(Formerly EDUCATION WIFE ASSAULT now SPRINGTIDE RESOURCES)

BAND-AID Brand Adhesive Bandages and Poster

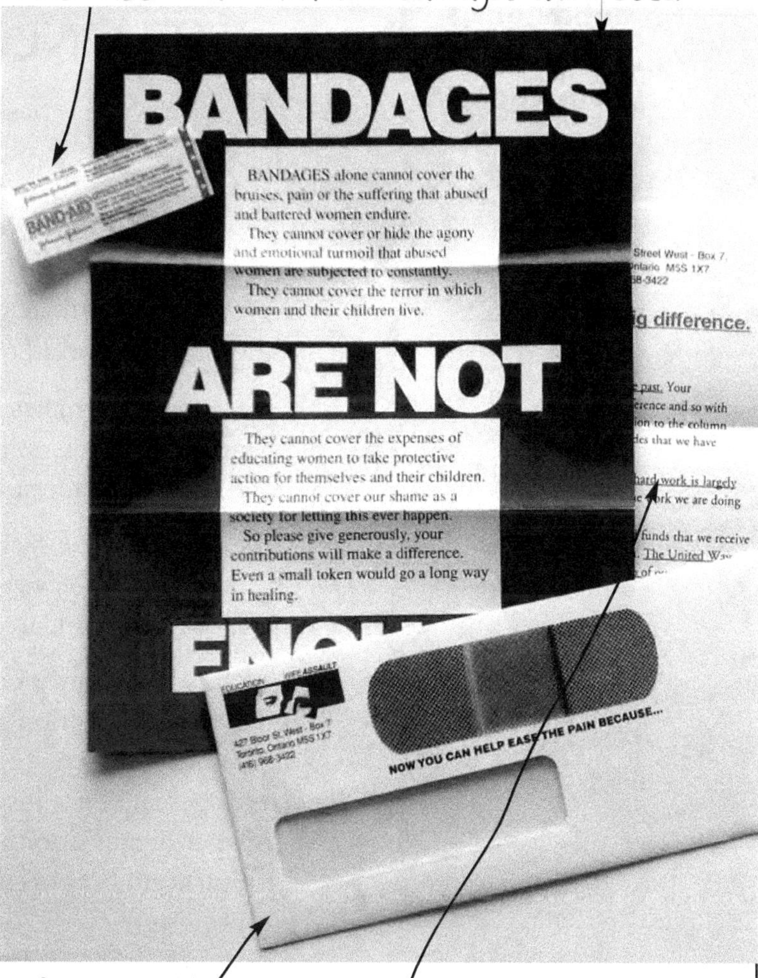

Outer envelope and letter

Background: Education Wife Assault (EWA) is a charity that provides kits, referrals and life saving information to abused women and their children.

They also train teachers, social workers, doctors, lawyers and judges to identify and respond to abused women and their children.

Objective: To raise funds to:

- Compensate for the reduction in government funding;
- Educate and inform the target audience about the seriousness of the issue;
- Acquire funds for essential services;
- Emphasize the important work and role that EWA plays as an educator in our society.

Solution: The direct marketing piece focused on two issues:

- The plight of abused women and the pain and suffering they endure;
- The shame that 'we as a society' should feel for letting this happen.

Strategy: The outer envelope said, NOW YOU CAN HELP EASE THE PAIN BECAUSE...

The recipient opened the package to find a poster with the statement, BANDAGES ARE NOT ENOUGH. As they unfolded the poster, a Johnson & Johnson BAND-AID Brand bandage fell out. The copy addressed the issues above directly.

Results: This interactive piece made a strong point about society's neglect with regard to the prevention of the abuse of women. Johnson & Johnson were so moved by the concept that they provided their BAND-AID® Brand Adhesive Bandages for <u>free</u>.

The piece generated a 22% response.

- It collected $11,300 in the first six weeks – a record for this organization.
- Letters and calls poured in as people expressed their appreciation of the DM package.
- Donations continued to trickle in seven months after the mailing.
- The average gift was $58.00.
- The exact package has been mailed as a 'control piece' several times.

DIRECT MARKETING WISDOM

You can't change behaviour.

You can only alter a viewpoint.

Chapter 6

CREATIVITY: THE FINE ART OF PERSUASION

POSITIONING

An important creative decision is 'positioning'– a concept common to the world of advertising.

Positioning means deliberately portraying a product, service or organization as possessing a particular attribute in relationship to other similar products, services or organizations in the marketplace.

Since positioning refers to a hierarchical order, a product or an organization can be viewed as the best, better than, as good as, average or bad compared to other similar products or organizations.

It is important to understand that positioning is largely a function of perception and not reality, therefore a product or an organization does not actually have to be better than its competitor. The target audience just has to think it is. Positioning a product, service or organization in the marketplace is really positioning its attributes and benefits in a positive way in the minds of your prospects.

Positioning, a common advertising term, takes on added value when used in direct marketing because a product or organization can be defined more precisely. Two or more very different positions can be tested among different groups. The results will clearly demonstrate the better selling proposition to adopt.

POSITIONING A PRODUCT, SERVICE OR ORGANIZATION ALONG A HIERARCHICAL SCALE

There are many ways of positioning an organization or service. One can present them as having certain advantages over the competition but without blatantly saying that organization 'X' is better then organization 'Y'.

One of the best ways to position a charity is by telling its donors what makes it different, its called the charity's USP (Unique Selling Proposition).

A USP sets your charity apart from your competition. The USP provides the most compelling reason why the target audience should consider you over your competitor.

Some of the best examples of a USP are hidden in the taglines of commercial products. They not only isolate themselves but they also 'brand' the product or service in the audience's memory.

Here are a few famous ones:

AMEX: Don't leave home without it

L'Oreal: Because you're worth it

McDonald's: I'm lovin' it

And the author's two personal favourites:

United Negro College Fund: A mind is a terrible thing to waste

Nike: Just do it

Unfortunately, many charities don't even know what their Unique Selling Proposition is, let alone use it to position themselves.

Why is a USP important?

If you don't give your customers solid facts about how crucial you are to fulfilling a need, then they will think why bother? And they won't.

The great line mentioned before, 'A mind is a terrible thing to waste.' was created in 1972 by **Forest Long** as a slogan for the **United Negro College Fund.** It has remained unchanged for more than three decades and has helped raise more than $2.2 billion for the charity.

Guiding structure for using direct marketing

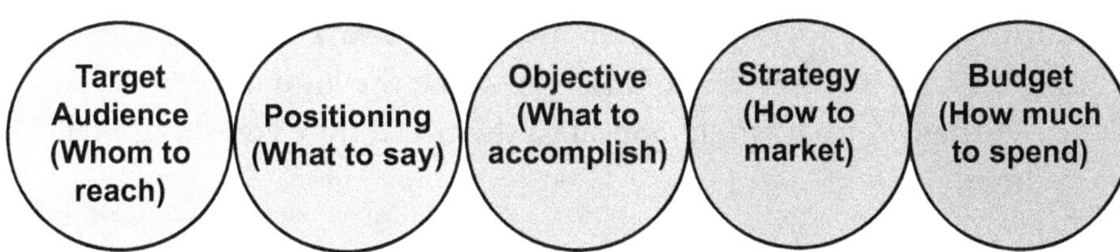

GETTING STARTED

The 'strategic brief' is the guide you must follow. Make sure you comply with every detail. Study what has worked or not worked in the past. Look at what the competition is doing. Try and determine what the USP is of your product, service or organization to set it apart from its competition.

I once read an ad that said:

When people talk to themselves we call it insanity.

When companies talk to themselves they call it marketing.

Every DM book advocates that we use the word "You" rather than "I" or "We". That's because we are intruding on the recipient.

All they want to know is WIIFM – What's In It For Me? Why should I buy your product or support you? How does it benefit me?

Telling the recipient what's in it for them is fundamental. Yet many packages contain a laundry list of attributes about themselves with little or no relevance to the recipient.

The result is "brag and boast" advertising.

THREE WELL KNOWN DIRECT MAIL FORMULAS:

AIDA

- Get Attention
- Arouse Interest
- Stimulate Desire
- Ask for Action

The AAPPA Formula

- Get Attention
- Show an Advantage
- Prove it
- Persuade
- Ask for Action

The PPPP Principle

- Picture
- Promise
- Prove
- Push

THE DIFFERENCE BETWEEN A FEATURE AND A BENEFIT

A FEATURE helps distinguish one product from another. It is a characteristic inherent in the product or service.

A BENEFIT ties the product or service's feature to the customer's needs and illustrates the advantage that the buyer would gain from it. A benefit cannot exist without a buyer.

For Example: **A FEATURE** is a goat you can buy from **Oxfam**.

A BENEFIT is the satisfaction you will have when **Oxfam** gives your goat to a poor family in Africa.

COMING UP WITH THE BIG IDEA

True creative is coming up with a solution that solves the client's problem and thinking up ideas to best accomplish the solution. There is no magic formula for creativity. What are needed are a trained mind and a wealth of experience.

David Ogilvy once said: *"The difference between a good surgeon and a great surgeon has nothing to do with their hands. A great surgeon simply knows more."*

Deciding how to approach the client's problem and recognizing how to take advantage of an opportunity is what creative is all about. Often the challenge is how to bring order to the chaotic wilderness of ideas.

The one thing we know for sure is that innovation must be at the core of creativity. One must be able to take existing objects or ideas and combine them in different ways for new purposes.

People have defined creativity as the process of using your wisdom, dreams, vision, intuition, talent and skills to combine existing substances such as matter, light, colour, sound and smell into something new.

COPY WRITING

The power of the written word is legendary and nowhere has this power been used more effectively than in direct marketing. It is a cost effective and persuasive means of influencing the reader to react and make a donation. To use it well we must understand its strengths and its potential.

Keep the target audience in mind at all times. Before putting pen to paper, know your audience. Always keep them in mind. Think 'method marketing' – imagine the kind of person you are writing to, what would appeal to them and how you should talk to them.

Next, learn about all the benefits of your product or service. Research the competition and what it is offering that is different. Then focus on the single most important benefit you have to offer your target audience and what would compel them to respond.

Good copywriting is comprised of the craft of writing and the art of persuasion. The craft consists of using all the tricks of the trade to grab attention, create interest, provide benefits, give assurances and inspire confidence. The art of persuasion means captivating, convincing and motivating the reader to respond by fulfilling a need, creating a desire and giving them compelling reasons to take action.

Start by unloading your thoughts. Cleanse your mind by randomly transcribing facts on paper. You will notice that certain phrases clearly describe and define what you want to say, while others may sound like clichés or borrowed slogans. Use only the ones that do justice to the information you wish to impart.

Go with the flow. The real creative process kicks in when one good idea sparks another and before long you are rolling along at a swift pace. Good copy suggests its own subheads. Good copy leads the reader on.

William Zinsser in his book, *On Writing Well,* states that clutter is like weeds that grow when you write, which must be removed. He maintains that, *"Writing is hard work. A clear sentence is no accident."* Editing is essential to remove superfluous words.

Sentences should be short with only one idea to a sentence. Keep it Simple Stupid (KISS).

Research on writing has revealed that the numbers of words in a sentence directly affect comprehension:

	Level	Sentence Length
1.	Very easy to read	8 words
2.	Easy to rcad	11 words
3.	Fairly easy	14 words
4	Standard	17 words
5.	Fairly difficult	21 words
6.	Difficult	25 words
7.	Very difficult	29 words+

Use the present tense and active sentences and phrases. Instead of saying, *"Children's health can be improved with your gift,"* say, *"Your gift will improve our children's health."*

State facts. Facts are more believable than general statements. *For example:*

- ***Every day 750 people die of HIV/AIDS in Kenya.***
- ***356 people die of HIV/AIDS every hour in the continent of Africa.***
- ***The World Health Organization estimates that by 2010 there will be 43 million orphaned children living on the streets of Africa due to HIV/AIDS.***

HANDY HINTS

- Write as you speak.
- Many new words are being added to the English lexicon daily. Skip the ones that are hard to pronounce. A litmus test is to try using them when you swear. Do they roll off your tongue easily? If not, don't use them.
- Use short sentences, but vary the length of your paragraphs.
- Tautology. An increasing number of words we use are redundant and contradictory but may have become part of our vocabulary by sheer repetition. Here are a few: *"It was a tall skyscraper."* Have you ever seen a short skyscraper? *"It could be a major nuclear disaster." What exactly would constitute a minor nuclear disaster?*

Other factors that work well include:

- Case histories
- Statistics
- Performance figures
- Names of personalities, especially if there is a strong believability factor
- Important and relevant dates and data
- Quotes from experts
- Facts that prove a point
- Testimonials

Use the strongest benefit in the letter. Use the less beneficial features or technical points in the brochure.

Use a McGuffen or a tangible device to tell a story or to involve the reader. Such a piece will not only make the package memorable but will also help boost response. (*See alongside*)

Other simple devices that make readers act include involvement items like scratch & win cards, a thought provoking activity, an interesting or a challenging puzzle.

Finally write and re-write until you are satisfied that you have done the best job. **David Ogilvy** once rewrote the same piece over a hundred times.

DESIGN

Design is the fine art of leading the reader to follow your trail. Imagine walking into a room with five pictures, each one the same size, shape, etc. Which would draw your attention first? Hard to say, isn't it?

Now if one of these pictures was slightly askew or one was a bit larger, which one would you notice first? Of course, the crooked one or the larger one.

That's the principle of direct mail design – get the readers' attention to focus on what you want them to see first.

The main purpose of design is to heighten communication using graphics or pictures, when words alone are not enough. The function is not to create a masterpiece but to help make reading effortless and lead the reader to act. Here are some design principles to follow:

- **The eye instantly goes to large objects and then moves to smaller ones.** Use this fact to get the reader to start at the most important part of your message.

WHAT IS A 'McGuffen'?

A '**McGuffen',** a word coined by, **Michael Johnston**, is an element that is added to the package, which captures the essence of your message and helps drive the story.

The word '**McGuffen**' originated from the movie ***The Maltese Falcon***, where the plot revolved around the chase for a statue of a falcon reported to contain priceless jewels.

Here for example, is a package of sugar that was key in this mailing for **FoodShare**. It helped tell the story of the real cause of obesity in our children today.

- **The eye travels from dark areas to light areas.** Position your contrasting elements to take advantage of this.
- **The eye moves from bold to passive colours.** Hot colours project warmth and urgency while cool colours create a muted effect. 
- **Create Stopping power.** Certain elements are guaranteed to get noticed like a face making direct eye contact with the reader, or odd sizes and shapes of images.
- **Large blocks of copy are best digested in bite-sized portions.** Long copy can be daunting to the reader. Smaller blocks look like less work.
- **Vary sections to look visually different.** Having to plow through information that all looks the same can lead to boredom and a bored reader is a lost reader.
- **The primary concern of the designer should be to create an over all impression relevant to the message.** Making the piece look beautiful should be secondary.
- **The design should be active.** Neat, tidy, linear layouts tend to make the piece feel settled, while starbursts, callouts, tilted pictures or arrows make the piece active. Use them but do not overdo it.
- **Handwritten messages stand out.** What appears to be a personal message can be effective in highlighting special segments. ← This always works
- **Photographs or illustrations should face the copy.** This leads the reader into the copy and keeps the eye focused on the message.
- **The best place for a headline is above the body copy.** Placing a headline between the copy blocks can interfere with the natural reading pattern. Also, the headline should be close to the body copy so the reader can easily move to the copy.
- **Type should be set flush left and ragged right.** We read from left to right, so don't make the readers do acrobatics by forcing them to read vertically, at an angle or upside down.
- **The length of your paragraphs should vary.** A paragraph can be any length from a single sentence to seven or eight lines. This helps prevent monotony. Space between paragraphs improves legibility.

HOW IMPORTANT IS CREATIVITY?

Although many other books have evaluated the value of creativity as barely 5% or 10%, I beg to differ.
Every company and its competitors have access to the same lists, the same premiums, the same formats, the same options, the same techniques and the same target market. The only big difference is creativity. Creativity can truly make or break how well the piece will be received.

Creativity has the advantage of setting your product or service apart from the rest. It creates that all-important magic that allows people to perceive it as being better than the competition.

HANDY HINTS

USE NUMERALS INSTEAD OF WORDS. Numbers act as icons and are not only recognized more quickly but are also assimilated much faster.
1.4 million is a quicker read than 'One point four million'

HANDY HINTS

GET THE PRODUCT IN THE READER'S HANDS. Everyone test drives a car or tries on clothes before they buy. It increases their comfort level. This does not mean giving them samples, but putting the product needed or the problem to be dealt with, up-front and central.

Two ways to do this are:

(a) Make the photograph or illustration of the product or issue as large as possible.

(b) Place the picture in the reader's perspective, e.g. show a photograph taken from the reader's point of view.

- **Pictures should be cropped tightly to reveal their essence.** Remove all parts of a picture that are unnecessary to tell the story. The reader's mind will automatically fill in missing parts. You will save space and have pictures that are more dynamic.
- **To add impact it is acceptable to** start the copy in a larger point size and then gradually reduce the size. Once you have grabbed the reader's interest you can drop the point size to a comfortable reading size type.
- **Use captions or call-outs below photographs or illustrations to explain what is being shown.** Remember there is a 50% chance that the reader may miss the benefit in the letter or start with the picture rather than read the copy from the top.

Finally, a picture is worth a thousand words but always keep in mind that nothing can replace the persuasive power of the printed word. Art direction is a fantastic tool that can enhance your ability to communicate.

Refugees returning home after fleeing from genocide

TECHNICAL ASPECTS OF DESIGN

There are many other design considerations involved in the creation of a direct mail package including format, paper stock, involvement devices, etc.

- **Don't diminish a letter's legibility by using a fancy typeface.** Use serif faces like Courier, Garamond or Times for legibility.

- **Design for actual readability.** How something looks on the computer screen is not how it will look to the reader on a printed page. Print a copy to check legibility.
- **Use wide margins so readers narrow their focus on the copy.** Short columns are easier to scan.
- **Keep your copy width down to sixty characters or less.** Beyond that the reader has to move his head back and forth, making reading more difficult.
- **Avoid large blocks of copy in reverse type on a dark background.** This is hard to read.
- **If you want to grab attention,** you can use uppercase for HEADLINES and SUBHEADS. However do not make them too long or they become difficult to read. Other ways of making copy stand out are **inserting a different typeface**, **bolder type**, <u>underlining</u> or *italics.*
- **Show your product in use.** A static illustration or tabletop photo of the product does not grab the reader's attention as readily as a picture showing the product in use.
- Use photos or illustrations to tell a story. Pictures are more than decoration, they say something words fail to convey sometimes.

DIRECT MARKETING FORMATS

Direct Mail packages come in all shapes and sizes: flyers, postcards, self-mailers, folders, tubes, boxes, etc. Anything that either goes through the mail or can be hand delivered is usually considered to be direct mail.

Printers are constantly finding new ways to increase their business and to gain an edge over the competition by introducing new and interesting formats for direct marketers. Some of the popular formats:

THE STANDARD DM PACKAGE

Also known as the classic direct mail package, this usually contains all or most of the following pieces:

1. Outer Envelope
2. Letter or solicitation piece
3. Order/Donation Form (the call-to-action piece)
4. Brochure
5. Lift letter or Lift Note
6. (BRE) Business Reply Envelope

Standard DM Package elements:

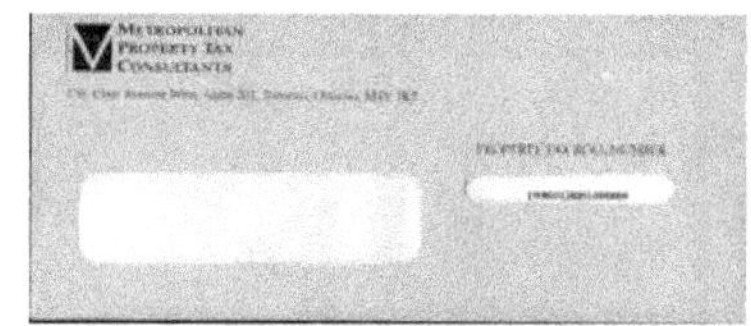

1.Outer envelope

Imagine you are a 14 year old girl in Kenya.

Now picture your daily routine in this way.

2. Letter

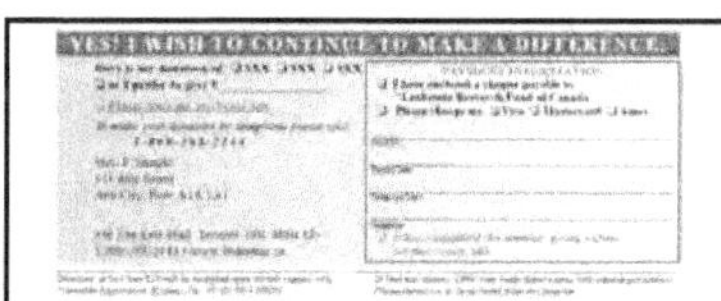

YES! I WISH TO CONTINUE TO MAKE A DIFFERENCE.

3. Order/ donation form

4. Brochure

5. Lift Note

6. BRE

Standard window envelope

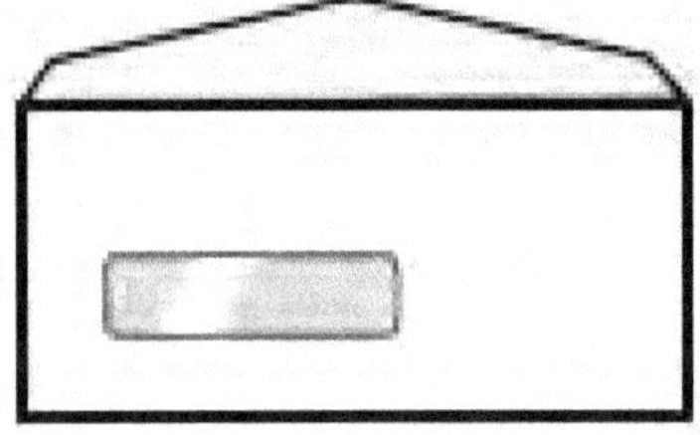

The size of the package can vary from a standard No. 10 envelope to a 9" x 12" envelope. Colours and stocks can also be varied.

SELF-MAILERS

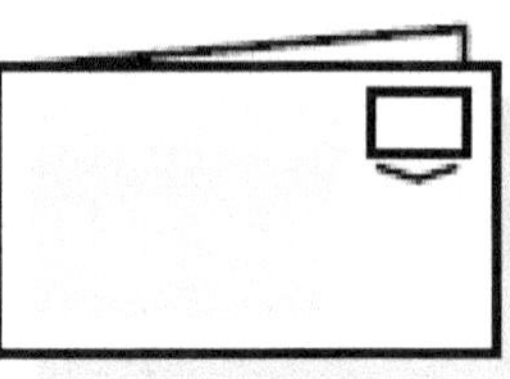

Self-mailers are self-contained packages. These highly comprehensive pieces can incorporate all the elements of a standard DM package including the letter, brochure, a reply or order card and a business reply envelope. The reply form is usually perforated and pre-glued to function as a business reply envelope. Self-mailers are more economical then the standard DM packages when the quantities are large. However, the response rates tend to drop substantially because they have the look of a mass mailing rather than a one-on-one mailing.

INSERTS

Inserts are a highly economical way to send additional literature along with tax receipts or mailings. Like mini-brochures, they piggyback with other pieces of mail at no additional postage cost. Though they lack one-on-one communication, they are great as reminders or for generating additional information.

BUCK SLIPS

HURRICANE UPDATE: Animals need a new shelter urgently

Buck slips are small inserts, usually about 3.5" x 8.5. They are used for a very specific purpose—to flag some late breaking news or to tell the recipient something important. This could be late-breaking news like an emergency, a crisis situation or even an eminent postal strike.

SNAP-PAKS

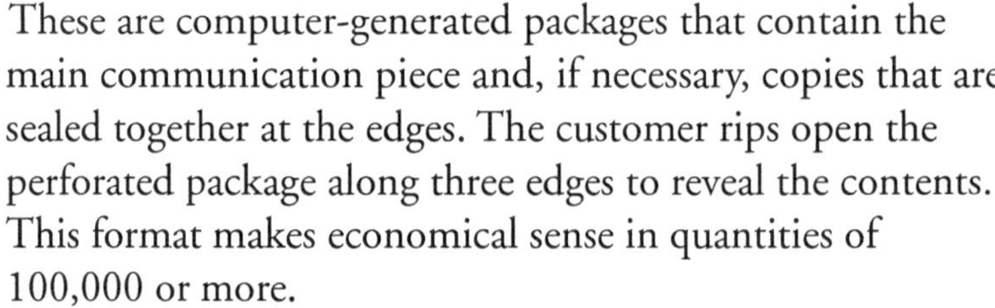

These are computer-generated packages that contain the main communication piece and, if necessary, copies that are sealed together at the edges. The customer rips open the perforated package along three edges to reveal the contents. This format makes economical sense in quantities of 100,000 or more.

CLOSED-FACED KITS OR PACKAGES

The various sheets in a kit, like the letter or order form, can be personalized while other elements like folders or other material can be added to provide more information. Kits are highly effective since pieces can be added or subtracted to fit the recipient's needs, a great leave-behind information vehicle.

POSTCARDS & DOUBLE POSTCARDS

A simple postcard with a selling proposition, return address and telephone number can be a cost-effective way of reaching people at minimal cost. They are ideal as reminders, lead generators or single product promotions. Double postcards allow the customer to tear off one of the cards and mail it back. The mail back postcard can also be personalized to minimize the work by the responder. This format is highly effective in producing high response rates at a fraction of the cost.

Dimensional Package

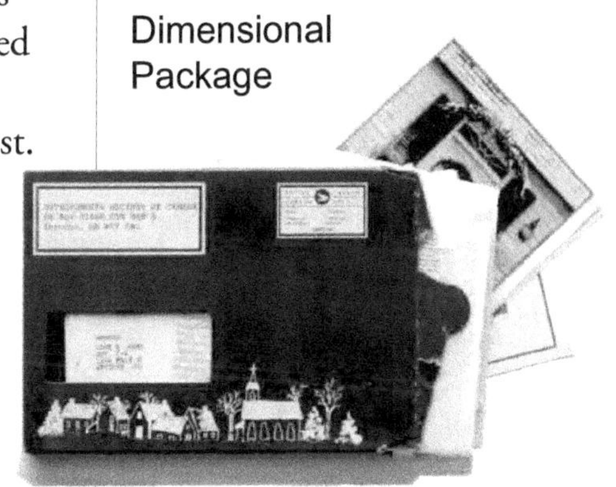

DIMENSIONAL PACKAGES

Dimensional packages range from boxes to tubes. Often intricate they are also expensive since they require hand sorting or stuffing.

POSTERS

Posters come in a variety of sizes, the most popular ones being 11"x17", 18" x 24" and 19" x 27". Posters can be highly impactful because of their colour and size.

Poster

FSI (FREE-STANDING INSERTS)

These are flyers or printed pieces that are inserted in newspapers or magazines. Since the identities of the recipients are unknown, they are not personalized. Another form of FSI is an unaddressed DM multi-package used by fast food outlets or other participants.

TAKE ONES

These are counter-top offerings in plastic holders or racks at retail, airline, bank or gas station counters. They can include credit card applications, gift certificates, information material and newsletters.

DOOR HANGERS & LEAVE BEHINDS

Door hangers help announce that you stopped by. Door hangers help you add new prospects in your local area.

Leave behinds are pieces of literature to inform and convince new prospects to donate.

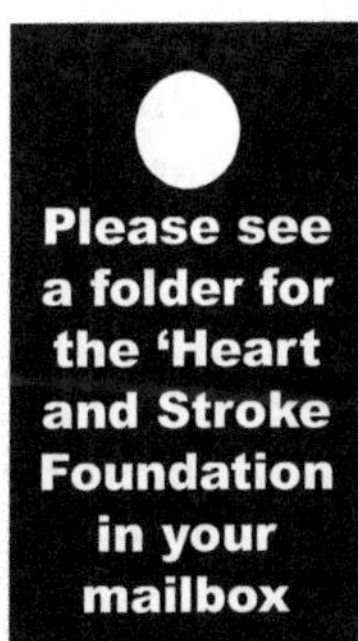

Leave behind

HANDY HINTS

ON THE ENVELOPE
Don't ask a question that can be answered with a simple "yes" or "no".
For example: Don't ask: *"Do you want to make more money this year?"*

Ask them: *"How much money do you want to make this year?"*

CATALOGUES

Many charities that sell products or services rely on catalogues to sell them. This helps them increase the income for the cause or for a special initiative.

This has become a highly effective way to generate additional funds. Often the catalogue is also displayed on the website which increases the audience for the solicitation.

THE OUTER ENVELOPE

A colourful envelope is a great way to draw attention, like the one above.

One of the hardest things to do in direct marketing is to get the recipient to open your direct mail package, therefore, the outer envelope is of prime importance. Its function is more than just holding the contents securely; it must entice the respondent to open it.

Siegfried Vögele, a research professor of direct marketing, observed that the average person spends between five and fifteen seconds scanning their mail, screening and rejecting what to open, what to discard or what to save for later, all in the proximity of their wastebasket.

If your direct mail piece never gets opened, your message never gets read. So how do you ensure that your piece survives?

Here are some simple yet effective ways to ensure that your direct mail piece is opened:

The first thing that goes through a recipient's mind is WIIFM. What's-in-it-for-me? Why is this company writing to me? What do they want from me? Remember, you are intruding on someone's time, so make sure the piece has some relevance to the recipient. Otherwise you are just producing junk mail.

Provide a hint of what is inside. Partially revealing the contents through a window can be exceedingly effective. Many books have suggested this, but the most conclusive evidence is a piece of research that tested two envelopes.

One had simply the words 'Free Book Inside'. The other had a large window that partially revealed an actual book with the same words, 'Free Book Inside'. The envelope that revealed the book

STANDARD ENVELOPE SIZES

No. 61/4	3 1/2" x 6"
No. 63/4	3 5/8" x 6 1/2"
No. 7	3 3/4" x 6 3/4"
No. 73/4	3 7/8" x 7 1/2"
No. 85/8	3 5/8" x 8 5/8"
No. 9	3 7/8" x 9 7/8"
No. 10	4 1/8" x 9 1/2"
No. 11	4 1/2" x 10 3/8"
No. 12	3 3/4" x 11"
No. 14	5" x 11 1/2"
Slim-Jim	6" x 11 1/2" or 6 1/4" x 11 1/2"

out pulled the other by 30%.

Clear polybags display the entire contents. Polybags are great for mailing unique offers, posters or several booklets or multiple pieces. Publishers and catalogues use poly bags extensively.

Capture the reader's imagination. Remember if the reader can easily decipher what you are selling without even opening the envelope, then it is a bad envelope. The best envelopes do not reveal everything – they only tantalize you to look inside.

Use teaser copy. Teaser copy can arouse curiosity and interest, either by using a provocative statement or by asking a question. The teaser can be a partial one to lead the recipient inside or it can be split on the front and back of the envelope. If it is enticing, the recipient will flip it over to get the complete message.

Envelope front

Envelope back

When targeting a very select group the message should be meaningful to the audience.

*For example, "**Your copy of a report on osteoporosis**"* is more likely to be opened by someone concerned with osteoporosis.

A word of caution when using clever headlines. Don't trick the recipient into opening the envelope if the contents inside don't live up to the clever headline outside. It could back fire and cause damage to the reputation of the company sending the piece.

Get the audience involved. Sweepstakes, tokens, stamps, stickers, scratch and win, lift-off tabs all contribute to helping lift response as long as they are relevant to the product or the organization offering them.

Early Bird specials and limited time offers. Deadlines induce quicker action. They prod the recipient to act.

Using blank envelopes with just the company logo. This works especially well for many organizations, especially when the receiver has a membership. The reason is quite simple. Recipients will open any communication from these sources to determine whether the envelope contains important information for members.

Using full-colour images on the entire envelope. This is a great way to create imagery and to show your product in its best light. It can draw attention and interest. For example, pictures of children and animals are veritable magnets.

HANDY HINTS

Many mailers use bells and whistles in the mailing to involve the reader. One simple way to do this is to use address labels with a YES/NO proposition. They work exceedingly well

Contrary to popular belief, many tests have proven that a longer letter often out-pulls a shorter letter. A good example of a long letter is this mailing about transporting hazardous material. The piece contained a six-page letter with no graphics except the photo of an executive and a strong statement on the envelope.
The result: It outperformed the control package which contained a shorter 2 page letter by 233%.

Use of manila or official looking envelopes. Government notices and municipal tax bills have a very official look and feel to them. Duplicating them has its pros and cons, so use caution.

Three-dimensional mailings. Boxes and tubes nearly always get opened. The same holds true for envelopes that are over-sized or oddly sized or shaped.

THE LETTER

There is an old saying: **"The letter sells. The brochure tells."** Years ago **Ogilvy & Mather** researched this and discovered that the most important part of any direct mail package was the letter. Over the years the truth of this has been proven repeatedly.

The secret to good letter writing is to transfer all the benefits of and information about the product, service or organization into a logical, persuasive document.

The challenge is to convert factual marketing plans, fact sheets, client briefs and research findings into free flowing conversational language.

Most of the suggestions on copy writing mentioned before apply here. Good letter writing is hard work and requires skill and practice.

SOME HELPFUL HINTS

For starters, make the letter look like a letter. Do not turn this into a design project. Effective letters usually have all or most of the following elements:

- Company or personal masthead
- Date
- Salutation (Dear…)
- Short indented paragraphs
- Sender's signature
- A P.S. (Post script)

Make the letter sound like a letter. Again, a letter's primary function is to converse intimately, privately and personally with the recipient.

Letter writing is one-on-one communication. So once again imagine that you are trying to convince just one person with your letter. How you express something has a far greater impact than what you say. Style is tone while phrases are body language.

Don't just praise your organization or service, sell the reader on what it can do for those who need it. Tell them how your organization will benefit those who need your service.

The most important sentences in a letter are the first and the last. Make it intriguing from the start and end just as strongly.

Keep the target audience in mind when selecting type size of the letter. Older people need a larger font size, while younger readers are comfortable with a smaller type size. The ideal point size, like in books, should be between 11pt and 13pt. The smallest type size one should use is 8pt.

Make your letter a dialogue, not a monologue. If your letter is only filled with 'I,' 'We,' and 'Our company,' chances are the reader will ignore the piece. Remember the 'what's in it for me' rule. Talk about how they will benefit from your product, not how great your product is. Also flattery, if used wisely, is a powerful tool to get people to act.

Involve the reader. The old saying: *"Tell me and I'll forget. Show me and I'll remember. Involve me and I'll understand."* works best. Ask probing questions and give logical answers. Make them imagine situations and show them how they can be resolved.

Remember, you only have three seconds to capture your reader's attention. One way to do this is by focusing on the reader as below:

> Dear Ms Doe,
>
> **This letter is not about us.**
> **It is about you**
>
> In the past we have sent you letters that told of the strength and courage of people who face the devastating effects of leukemia.
>
> Many of them were children who had to endure this disease themselves but ....

Limit your paragraphs to about seven lines per paragraph. (Note: this is a block of 'lines' NOT sentences.) Use single spacing in paragraphs and double spacing between paragraphs. This makes it easier to read.

Make it easy for the reader to respond. Clearly tell them what you want them to do, how and when.

Don't forget the P.S. A P.S. is more than just an afterthought. The P.S. is your last ditch effort to convince your prospects and it is often the first thing they read, so use it to highlight the main offer or advantage explained in the letter.

Finally, the age-old question – How long should a letter be? The answer – as long at it takes to do the job well. If a two-page letter can be pared down to a single page, without losing its meaning, then it is one page too long. If on the other hand it needs that extra page or more pages to do full justice to ensuring response, then it is too short.

HANDY HINTS

It has been proven that four out of five readers will read the P.S. before they read the letter, so use it to stress the main point in your letter or to repeat your offer.

THE BROCHURE

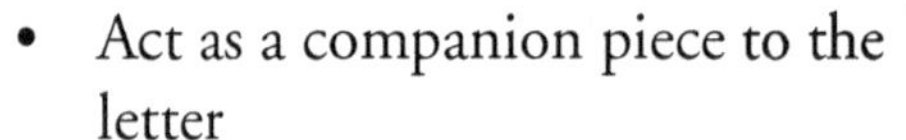

Because, the letter's job is 'to sell' while the brochure's job is 'to tell', the brochure should be different from the letter and should:

- Act as a companion piece to the letter
- Reveal other facts that may not be in the letter
- Provide additional information about the charity or service
- Support the claims made in the letter
- Highlight the main features and benefits of the organization or service
- Demonstrate technical superiority, supply proof or comparisons
- Showcase the organization in the best light
- Feature people or products to back up your claims and lend credibility.

There are no rules as to the sequence in which all the vital information should be introduced or how the visuals should be displayed in the brochure because the information in each brochure is as diverse as the organizations themselves. It is up to the art director or designer to organize the elements in the most pleasing but functional way.

TIPS ON WHAT THE BROCHURE SHOULD CONTAIN

The cover sets the tone for what is inside. Show the product or demonstrate your services in the best way on the cover.

Graphically and verbally make the main benefit exciting. Use the headline to either tell a complete story or as a teaser to drive the reader inside. This is purely subjective. Many prefer to tell the main benefit up front and not waste the cover by only revealing half a message, unless there is no other benefit to state. The reader is more informed with all the information up front and there is less danger of them not turning the page.

Next, decide where to position each element. Remember, premiums are incentive drivers while deadlines are time drivers.

Validate by comparison. Show how your charity or service is superior to that of the competition. Use photos, illustrations, diagrams, charts, tables, etc.

Make it reader friendly and legible. Use visuals to attract and copy to explain.

Highlight things of importance. Use borders, boxes and

colour. Bullet points help list miscellaneous or technical information for easy comprehension.

If the big benefit on the cover needs further explaining, then do it inside. If not, use the inside to detail and dramatize other benefits and features. Benefits sell while features attract. Use the space inside for important explanations, comparisons or clarifications, for facts, proofs, or visual and verbal demonstrations.

Use the back of the brochure to summarize and give other detailed information like company name, address, phone, fax, e-mail, web site, head office, regional offices, contacts and maps. This information is for ease of contact and order generation. Give guarantees to reduce risk and increase confidence, or repeat the main benefits in bullet form to help people who just scan to understand the key advantages.

Finally, the size of the brochure. If it is important and needs a classy look then use a folder. If it needs a lot of information to make a strong case, then use a booklet. Use a flyer if the information is simple and can be fit into a small space.

Open Side envelope

Open End with side seal envelope

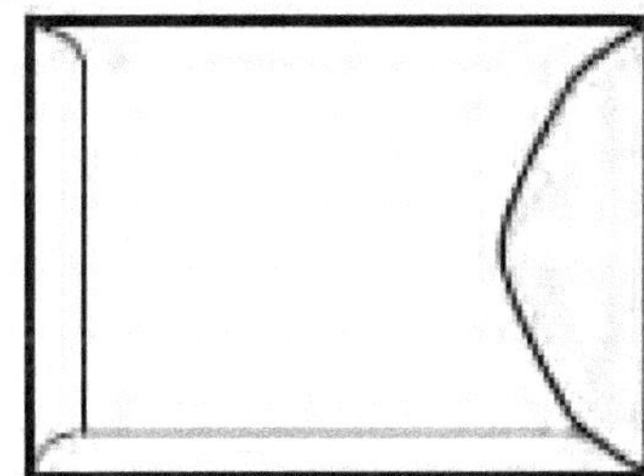

THE DONATION FORM

Why pay so much attention to the donation form? The reason is simple. You want to make it as easy as possible for recipients to respond.

YES! I WISH TO CONTINUE TO MAKE A DIFFERENCE.

Here is my donation of: ❑ $XX ❑ $XX ❑ $XX
❑ **or I prefer to give $** ____________

❑ Please send me my brass pin

To make your donation by telephone please call:
1-800-268-2144

Mrs. J. Sample,
123 Any Street
Any City, Prov. A1A 1A1

936 The East Mall, Toronto, ON M9B 6J9
1-800-268-2144 • www.leukemia.ca

PAYMENT INFORMATION

❑ **I have enclosed a cheque payable to "Leukemia Research Fund of Canada**
❑ **Please charge my** ❑ **Visa** ❑ **Mastercard** ❑ **Amex**

Card No.

Expiry Date

Name on Card

Signature

❑ I have completed the monthly giving section on the reverse side.

Donations of less then $10 will be receipted upon written request only
Charitable Registration Business No. 10762 3654 RR000

To find new donors, LRFC may trade donor names with other organizations.
Please contact us to be excluded from this program

SOME DESIGN TIPS

Make it appealing and easy to use. If a donation form looks complicated visually, chances are it will be hard to fill out too.

Leave a lot of space if information needs to be filled out by hand. Cramped space discourages response and increases the likelihood of errors in processing and tax receipting.

Keep the information logical and orderly. The layout should be compatible with and should follow the same sequence as the order entry system. This will speed up processing and reduce the possibility of errors.

Place the order form where it is easy to locate. Catalogues traditionally place the order form in the center, to avoid splitting it from the return envelope. Not-for-profit direct mail pieces place it conveniently either by itself or attached to the letter and perforate it for ease of fulfillment. The cardinal rule should be to make it easy to find.

Keep it simple in appearance and content. Make sure to enclose only pertinent information. As far as colour is concerned remember that old saying: ***'Too much colour is no colour at all.'*** Overuse of colour can distract.

Clarify the shipping addresses. Often the address for an item purchased may be different from the billing address, as in the case of a gift. So the 'ship to' and the 'billing information' should be clearly labeled. Offering a free gift card is a nice touch.

Detail Payment Information. It is important to detail cost, taxes and shipping charges in a systematic fashion. If one particular item, a packet of seeds in a catalogue, is identified as a 'Winter Special', it should be clearly separated from the rest in bold letters or colours.

Thank your donors for their gift. A little courtesy goes a long way and this gesture of appreciation makes a good impression.

Ask for a friend's name. Grab this opportunity. Use your form to ask for a friend's name in exchange for a small gift. This is a great way to build a list of prospects at no cost and to show your donors that they are important.

Don't forget to get your donor's telephone number or email address. If an unforeseen delay or question should arise or if you need to contact them you can do so.

Give your telephone number so they can contact you. This is equally important. Adding a toll free number also adds to customer confidence and security.

Ask for change of address information. Provide a separate area for corrections, should there be a mistake or a change in the name and address you have used.

Personalize your donation form. Personalizing the donation form is not only convenient but it saves the donor from hand writing his name and address which may be hard to read otherwise.

Explain your minimum donation policy. To help discourage your customers from using credit cards for small donations, clearly state your minimum donation policy on the form.

Date your prices in your catalogue. To avoid ambiguity or misconception, clearly indicate your expiry date for all items.

State your delivery time. Customers like to know when the gift they have purchased will be delivered to the needy family. Stating a delivery date not only builds credibility and trust but can also increase response.

Publish your costs clearly. State if the prices are in U.S. or Canadian dollars. Also, clarify which provinces have different tax laws and leave space in the order form to comply with those laws.

Early Bird special and other incentives. Adding discount items in the form of impulse items or Early Bird specials is good for business and prompts sales.

While the main letter in this Amnesty International package below is written by the President, a second letter or the Lift Note was written by **Robert Bateman** to lend support to the charity.

LIFT NOTES

Lift Notes are primarily used to add substance to a direct mail piece. Either they are endorsements by well-known celebrities or individuals admired in a particular field. They lend credibility by voicing their opinion.

THE BRE (BUSINESS REPLY ENVELOPE)

This is a pre-paid return envelope used to facilitate donation transaction. You want to make the recipient's response as easy as possible.

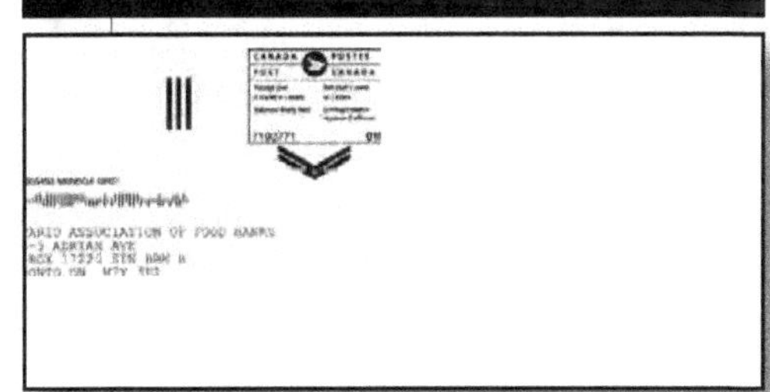

ANNUAL REPORTS

An annual report is a document produced annually by charities designed to portray a true and fair view of the company's annual performance, with audited financial statements.

Its function is a the stewardship and accountability of the charity to its partners, stakeholders giving them a accurate assessment of how funds have been collected and used.

CASE STUDY

United Nations High Commissioner for Refugees (UNHCR)

Background: When the United Nations High Commissioner for Refugees (UNHCR) decided to launch an acquisition direct mail piece for the first time in Canada, when hostilities heated up in Afghanistan, just after 9/11. They knew that it would take more than a simple appeal to get people to respond.

Objectives: To highlight the plight of refugees it became necessary to produce a direct mail package with impact. One of the best ways to do this was by using a 'McGuffen' to get the reader's attention.

Solution: A folded piece of cardboard was inserted in the package to conjure up the image of homelessness.

Strategy: On the outer envelope was a simple message that read. **Please don't ignore the cardboard included in this package...**

The outer envelope stressed the importance of the piece of cardboard inside

Cover of piece of cardboard *and the message inside*

On the outside of the folded cardboard piece were the bold words: **Refugees deserve a better shelter than this.**

Inside the folded cardboard piece, the message continued, "**Hold this cardboard over your head and imagine that it is the roof of your house. This will give you a glimpse of what it is like to be a refugee.**"

Refugees deserve a better shelter than this.

Hold this cardboard over your head and imagine that it is the roof of your home. This will give you a glimpse of what it is like to be a refugee.

Cardboard boxes, plastic sheeting, rags and tin are often the only materials refugees have to build a shelter for themselves and their families.

Having lost all their material possessions, many refugees also suffer the loss of parents, partners or children. Refugees are people just like you and me, who have been forced to flee their homes because of war or persecution. They are not a threat. They are people who are threatened, and they need our help and protection. Refugees rely on the generosity of others for their basic needs: shelter, food, water, sanitation and medical care.

Physical shelter is arguably the most pressing need of refugees. From the forests of Central Africa to the mountain ranges of Afghanistan, these people need protection from the elements. UNHCR strives to put a roof over every refugee's head.

Though sometimes this is only a temporary measure, it can make all the difference. Where possible, we also provide refugees and returnees with construction materials to build a family shelter or to rebuild a destroyed home. To them shelter is more than just a pile of bricks: it means security and the chance to bring back some normality to family life.

This winter nearly 10 million refugees and other internally displaced people will turn to UNHCR for shelter from the cold and snow. Our ability to meet these needs will rely in large part on the contributions from private individuals like you.

Please help us provide refugees with a better shelter than this. Your action today will help them rebuild their homes, their communities and their lives.

The letter included images of refugees and the costs associated with helping them

The message was simple and effective. The letter stressed the importance of helping refugees with any donation amount they could afford. It also contained pictures of refugees and told what the various donation amounts could accomplish.

United Nations High Commissioner for Refugees
1775 K Street, NW, Suite 290
Washington, DC 20006

Toll-free number: 1-800-770-1100
E-mail: info@usaforunhcr.org
Website: www.UNrefugees.org

One emergency food and shelter kit providing one refugee family with cooking supplies, food, and a canvas turpaulin for shelter.

August 2004

Dear Friend,

Please don't ignore the cardboard included in this package. It's a sample of what often is the only roof refugees have over their heads.

The fact is, you can help them right away by making a tax deductible gift of $28, $41 or $150.

A gift of just $41 will provide a returning Afghani refugee family with a building kit including the necessary materials to rebuild their home. $28 will provide a family of refugees with an emergency food kit and a canvas tent to shelter them from the cold and rain. $54 will send for a doctor to provide urgently-needed medical care in a refugee camp. $150 will deliver a truckload of supplies. Any amount you can contribute today will immediately save refugees' lives.

Most important, your generosity will demonstrate to refugees that someone cares.

One building kit to provide a returning Afghani refugee family with the necessary materials to rebuild their home – wood beams, two windows, a door, hinges, pipes, nails, and tools.

The plight of refugees

Refugees are people like you and me who have been forced to abandon their homes because of war or persecution, often at a moment's notice. They flee with little more than the clothes on their backs.

Women and children make up three-quarters of the world's refugee population and are at greatest risk. Women carry out most of the essential tasks in refugee camps - gathering firewood, collecting water and keeping uprooted families intact. Child refugees are especially vulnerable. Too many children and teenagers are separated from their families and are forced to shoulder adult burdens, such as supporting younger siblings. Many have been the victims of horrific abuse.

Your gift will help these devastated people who clearly need and deserve our support. Every day spent in exile is a day too long. If they refuse to give up hope, how can we?

continued over...

One doctor's visit to a refugee camp to provide necessary medical attention and care to refugees.

Delivery of one truckload of emergency supplies to refugees by a local driver traveling treacherous roads.

A postcard gave details of the more than 1.5 million Afghan refugees who were affected.

Result: This direct mail piece was mailed to 50,000 prospects from various rented lists. It generated $61,500 from 726 donors (1.45% response).

The piece quickly became the control package, outperforming all other pieces and was immediately adapted in the U.S. It became the control package for UNHCR.

The postcard focused on the plight of Afghan refugees.

Canada Post deems the following items as unacceptable for mailing:

- Bottle caps
- Coins
- Food items
- Glass
- Jewellery
- Keys
- Liquids
- Powdered material
- Seeds
- Fragile or perishable items
- Anything that may soil or harm other mail, postal equipment or employees
- Anything prohibited by law or considered dangerous

CHAPTER 7

THE MEDIA: OUR CHANNELS OF DISTRIBUTION

There are various ways of contacting people via direct marketing. These include the mail (either by postal service, hand delivery or by courier), print, TV, radio, telemarketing, the Internet and newsletters.

CHANNEL 1 THE MAIL

Pretty much every organization that relies on individual donors or members needs this channel. After all, there's a limit to how much information you can convey face-to-face, by phone, or even over the Internet. And an intimate lunch with every single donor is out of the question. That's why the mail comes in handy.

The postal service is by far the best method of sending mail and you have two choices as to how to send it. One is called 'addressed mail' and the other is known as 'un-addressed mail'.

The difference, as the names imply, is that one is personalized with the name and address of your prospects and the mailing goes directly to them.

Un-addressed mail goes to a group whose names are unknown but reaches those your research has shown might be good targets for your charity or service. This type of mail: includes flyers, newspapers, brochures or special promotions. This is an economical way to reach a community.

Businesses and organizations of all sizes use this medium to:

- Generate leads;
- Offer discounts, try to up-sell or cross-sell to increase sales;
- Hold contests, sweepstakes and promotions;
- Encourage trial by sending samples;
- Increase in-store traffic;
- Build a database using a business reply envelope or a card.

Mail is one of the most convenient and cost-effective ways of sending personal messages, business correspondence, invoices and billing statements. A direct mail piece must meet the conditions and requirements of **Canada Post.**

They include:

- Letters
- Postcards
- Cards
- Receipts or invoices
- Notices of voting for federal, provincial or municipal events
- Self-mailers
- Annual, semi-annual or quarterly reports or documents containing financial information
- Product/service information
- Dimensional pieces
- Tubes and cartons
- Catalogues
- Magazines
- Flyers
- Any other material that is capable of being mailed

The material can be **standard mail**, meaning it must comply with **Canada Post's** criteria of a maximum length of 245mm and a maximum height of 156mm. It must weigh 50g or less and have the correct mailing address and postal code.

It can be **non-standard mail** and not meet the criteria for standard letter mail size by **Canada Post.** A different rate applies to this category of mail.

It can be **oversized mail**, whose size and/or thickness exceeds those of standard items and can go up to a maximum length of 380mm, a maximum height of 270mm and a maximum weight of 500g.

Any item that exceeds the size or weight of oversize letter mail must be mailed at Regular Parcel prices.

A direct mail package can be mailed using a live postage stamp or in the case of most large volume mailings, **Canada Post** offers a discount on 'Incentive Lettermail™' or bulk mail by providing a postal indicia or a metered impression.

A postal indicia is the rectangular box in the upper right hand corner of an envelope or mailer. It contains **Canada Post's** corporate identity and a special customer permit number that **Canada Post** provides and which certifies in advance that payment will be made by the customer.

AN EASTER PACKAGE WITH A DIFFERENCE

Normally letters for non-profit organizations are filled with sad stories, but this package for **The Easter Seal Society of Ontario** was different. They had the endorsement of the famous children's author **Robert Munsch** and a wonderful story of a spunky little child with physical disabilities named **Lauretta**, who had inspired **Robert** to write a book about her called ***ZOOM.***

Michael Martchenko, who illustrates **Robert Munsch's** books, did the illustrations for this package. **Robert Munsch** even graciously signed and donated copies of the book to **Easter Seal Society.** As the writer of this wonderful package I remember my friend **Tony Lovell** who once said to me, *"Writing is like sweating blood."* This time it was pure joy.

All 'Incentive Lettermail™' that does qualify for discounted prices must comply with **Canada Post's** requirements.

These requirements include, but are not limited to, minimum volumes, mail preparation and presorting, address accuracy, automated mail processing equipment acceptability and readability, size and weight.

For Addressed mail:

- Bulk mail has its own indicia.
- A special indicia is required should you want undeliverable mail returned.

One must be aware of the strict guidelines that **Canada Post** has regarding the minimum and maximum dimensions of mailing pieces. Also one has to factor in the charges according to the weight of the mailer. All standard envelopes or self-mailers must have the correct mailing address and postal code and comply with the maximum weight of 50 grams or less. Non-standard pieces will cost more to mail and are charged according to weight and size.

MACHINEABLE		LENGTH	WIDTH	THICKNESS	WEIGHT
Short and Long	max. min.	245 mm 140 mm	156 mm 90 mm	5.00 mm 0.18 mm	50 g 3 g
Postcards and Cards	max. min.	235 mm 140 mm	120 mm 90 mm	5.00 mm 0.18 mm	50 g N/A
Oversize	max. min.	380 mm 140 mm	270 mm 90 mm	20.0 mm 0.5 mm	500 g 10 g

Non-Standard pieces are charged higher and can be heavier, smaller or larger but weigh up to maximum 500 grams.

CATEGORY		LENGTH	WIDTH	THICKNESS
Standard and Non-coded	max.	245 mm	156 mm	05.00 mm
Envelope and Self-mailer	min.	140 mm	90 mm	00.18 mm
Card or Postcard	max. min.	235 mm 140 mm	120 mm 90 mm	05.00 mm 00.18 mm
Other Lettermail (including non-standard and oversize)	max. min.	380 mm 140 mm	270 mm 90 mm	20.00 mm 00.18 mm

NOTE:

1. A self-mailer is an article that does not have an outer cover, wrapping or envelope in addition to the paper or material on which the communication is written.

2. Items smaller than the minimum size for Lettermail are accepted at the standard Lettermail price if paid by postage stamps.
3. Any item that exceeds the size for Oversize Letter must be mailed as Regular Parcel.

PRESORT MAIL

Presort Mail can be prepared as one of the following:

- Envelopes
- Open items
- Wrapped items – transparent and paper
- Postcards/cards

CATEGORY		LENGTH	WIDTH	THICKNESS	WEIGHT
Short and Long Both	max min	245 mm 100 mm	156 mm 70 mm	5.00 mm 0.18 mm	100 g N/A
Oversize Both	max min	380 mm 100 mm	270 mm 70 mm	20.0 mm 0.18 mm	500 g N/A
Dimensional Addressed Admail – Large	max min	300 mm 250 mm	150 mm 90 mm	35 mm 20 mm	500 g N/A
Dimensional Addressed Admail – Medium	max min	250 mm 180 mm	130 mm 90 mm	35 mm 20 mm	500 g N/A
Dimensional Addressed Admail – Small	max min	180 mm 140 mm	130 mm 90 mm	35 mm 20 mm	500 g N/A
Catalogue Mail	max min	1.1 m NA	1.1 mm NA	1.1 mm NA	25 kg 500 g

Items like catalogues and financial reports should be rectangular or square.

UNADDRESSED MAIL

Unaddressed mail includes flyers, brochures, cards, coupons, envelopes, samples, magazines, newspapers and co-operative mailings.

Co-operative mailings are cost effective because they are bundled together and they are a great way to reach customers in a specific geographic area

You can cover the entire front of an envelope with an image and print the postal Indicia on the top flap of the envelope as below.

An unaddressed mail piece is just as likely to elicit a donation as addressed mail.

Below an unaddressed post card for CAMH Mississauga

Postal Indicia

Canada Post logo

Product type addressed mail, unaddressed mail, Bulk Mail

Registration Number

CASE STUDY

SPECIAL OLYMPICS ONTARIO

Background: Prior to the National Summer Special Olympics Games, Special Olympics Ontario needed to raise funds for athletes, staff and coaches to participate in the games.

A direct mail initiative was designed for this purpose and sent to a house list of donors.

Objectives:

- Raise funds for Special Olympic athletes so that they could participate in the National Summer Special Olympic Games to be held in Brandon, Manitoba;
- Create a sense of urgency for supporting the athletes who have been training so hard to participate in the National Summer Games;
- Demonstrate the importance that donors' gifts make in transforming the lives of athletes living with intellectual disabilities and what this support means to the athletes who have been training so hard for the event.

Solution: A two-pronged strategy:

PACKAGE 1

- Highlighted the personal story of one Special Olympics Athlete, Sarah Lynn Lisi, who would be going to the National Summer Special Olympics Games for the first time to represent Ontario;
- Focused on the struggle and hardships of Sara from her mother's point of view. It captured the true essence of hard work and dedication that all Special Olympians face and what they endure because of their intellectual disabilities.

PACKAGE 1

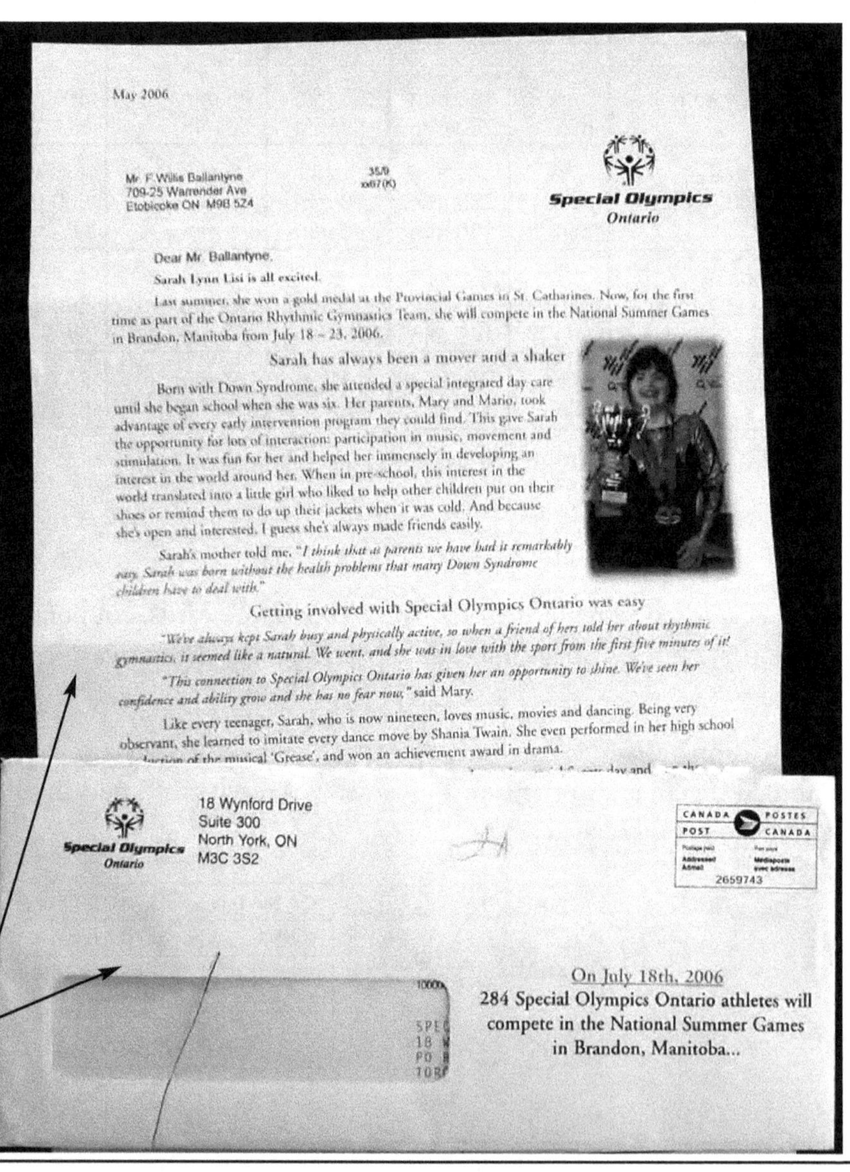

May 2006

Mr. F Willis Ballantyne
709-25 Warrender Ave
Etobicoke ON M9B 5Z4

35/9
xx67(K)

Special Olympics
Ontario

Dear Mr. Ballantyne,

Sarah Lynn Lisi is all excited.

Last summer, she won a gold medal at the Provincial Games in St. Catharines. Now, for the first time as part of the Ontario Rhythmic Gymnastics Team, she will compete in the National Summer Games in Brandon, Manitoba from July 18 – 23, 2006.

Sarah has always been a mover and a shaker

Born with Down Syndrome, she attended a special integrated day care until she began school when she was six. Her parents, Mary and Mario, took advantage of every early intervention program they could find. This gave Sarah the opportunity for lots of interaction: participation in music, movement and stimulation. It was fun for her and helped her immensely in developing an interest in the world around her. When in pre-school, this interest in the world translated into a little girl who liked to help other children put on their shoes or remind them to do up their jackets when it was cold. And because she's open and interested, I guess she's always made friends easily.

Sarah's mother told me, *"I think that as parents we have had it remarkably easy. Sarah was born without the health problems that many Down Syndrome children have to deal with."*

Getting involved with Special Olympics Ontario was easy

"We've always kept Sarah busy and physically active, so when a friend of hers told her about rhythmic gymnastics, it seemed like a natural. We went, and she was in love with the sport from the first five minutes of it!

"This connection to Special Olympics Ontario has given her an opportunity to shine. We've seen her confidence and ability grow and she has no fear now," said Mary.

Like every teenager, Sarah, who is now nineteen, loves music, movies and dancing. Being very observant, she learned to imitate every dance move by Shania Twain. She even performed in her high school production of the musical 'Grease', and won an achievement award in drama.

Special Olympics
Ontario

18 Wynford Drive
Suite 300
North York, ON
M3C 3S2

CANADA POST POSTES CANADA
2659743

On July 18th, 2006
284 Special Olympics Ontario athletes will compete in the National Summer Games in Brandon, Manitoba...

Package 1.
Outer envelope and letter

PACKAGE 2

- Two months after the event a second package was mailed as an update to the same target audience to thank and inform them about the results that Sarah Lynn Lisi had achieved.

Strategy: The creative strategy was to send Package 1 prior to the event to secure funds for athletes, staff and coaches. It featured Sarah Lynn Lisi, who would be attending the games for the first time to represent Ontario. A few months later, Package 2 would update the same target audience and inform them about the results that Sarah Lynn had achieved.

Result: PACKAGE 1, which was mailed to a house list of approximately 13,000 donors, received a much higher response than expected. It beat the projection by more than 60%, raising well over $114,500. The response rate was 17.64%.

Current donors gave the largest gifts with 57.18% contributing an average gift of $44. While 26.28% of lapsed donors gave an average gift of $50.

PACKAGE 2

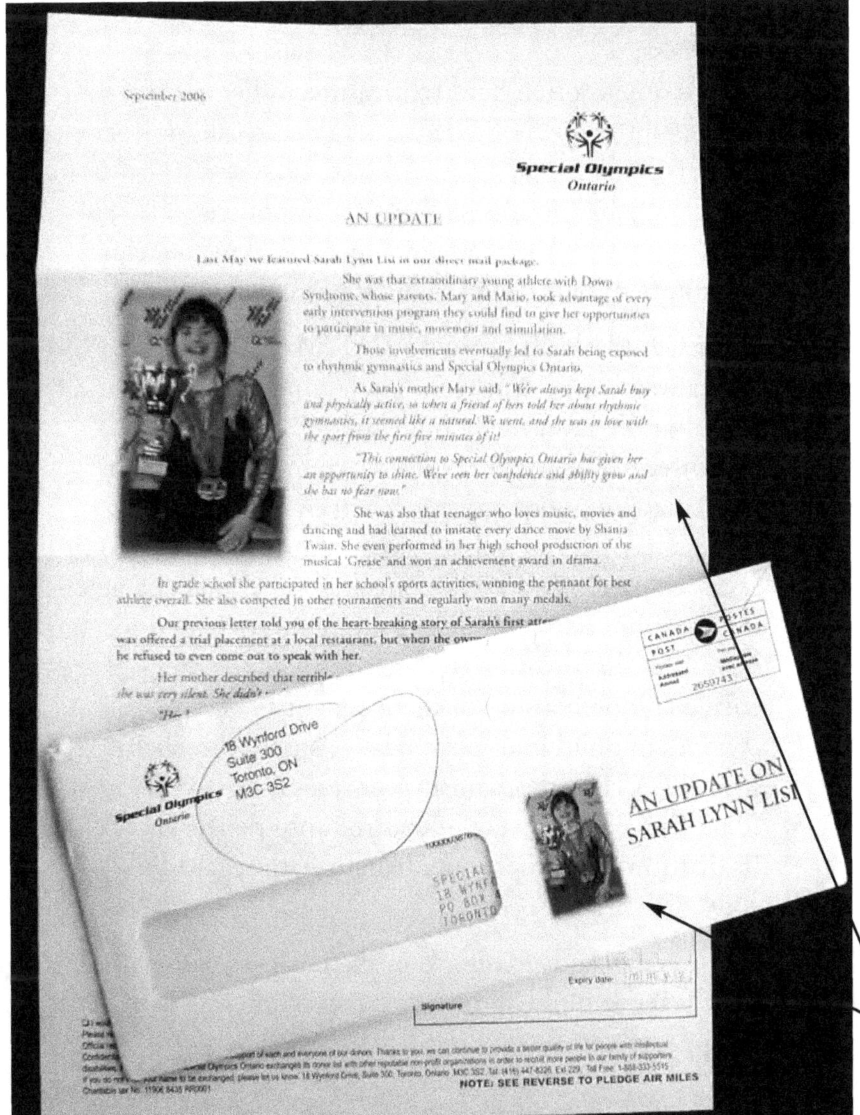

September 2006

Special Olympics Ontario

AN UPDATE

Last May we featured Sarah Lynn Lisi in our direct mail package.

She was that extraordinary young athlete with Down Syndrome, whose parents, Mary and Mario, took advantage of every early intervention program they could find to give her opportunities to participate in music, movement and stimulation.

Those involvements eventually led to Sarah being exposed to rhythmic gymnastics and Special Olympics Ontario.

As Sarah's mother Mary said, *"We've always kept Sarah busy and physically active, so when a friend of hers told her about rhythmic gymnastics, it seemed like a natural. We went, and she was in love with the sport from the first five minutes of it!*

"This connection to Special Olympics Ontario has given her an opportunity to shine. We've seen her confidence and ability grow and she has no fear now."

She was also that teenager who loves music, movies and dancing and had learned to imitate every dance move by Shania Twain. She even performed in her high school production of the musical 'Grease' and won an achievement award in drama.

In grade school she participated in her school's sports activities, winning the pennant for best athlete overall. She also competed in other tournaments and regularly won many medals.

Our previous letter told you of the heart-breaking story of Sarah's first att... was offered a trial placement at a local restaurant, but when the own... he refused to even come out to speak with her.

Her mother described that terrible... *she was very silent. She didn't...*

Package 2. Outer envelope and letter

PACKAGE 2 was mailed to 11,000 donors of the same list.

This update package also performed better than expected, beating the projected figure by over 300%.

It generated an additional $72,000. This time 63% of the total came from current donors and surprisingly 26% came from previous unknown or lapsed donors, who gave even higher average amounts of $45.

Finally, this e-mail from the client sums it up best:

"We have had the highest response ever with these two mailings. I am extremely pleased."

Lynn Miller,
Marketing Administrator
Special Olympics Ontario

CHANNEL 2
PRINT

Print includes all publications from magazines to newspapers.

THE DIFFERENCE BETWEEN DIRECT MARKETING AND ADVERTISING

ADVERTISING IS MASS MARKETING

- Its focus is to create an image and awareness for the product, service or organization;
- It sends one universal message to everyone;
- This message is repeated often for impact and to build awareness;
- Its outcome is often hard to measure. When measured it is usually in the form of aided or unaided recall, or it is not measured at all;
- It generally has no mechanisms for response;
- It does not offer the marketer any control in the retail environment or during the distribution chain.

Hincks Campaign Ad

DIRECT MARKETING IS INTIMATE MARKETING

- It creates an opportunity for a sales or a lead generation by targeting the most likely individuals;
- Its primary objective is a call-to-action. It can ask for immediate response or acknowledgement;
- It presents offers to individuals specifically tailored to fit their response patterns, lifestyles or other individual characteristics;
- It is does not rely on building awareness by repetition but the main benefits are often repeated throughout the package to ensure comprehension of these benefits;
- It hopes to build long-term relationships with clients;
- It provides clear mechanisms for response;
- It lets the marketer stay in control until delivery;
- Its distribution is a product benefit with regard to convenience and speed.

While general advertising is in the business of cutting through the daily clutter to build an image, direct marketing is the business of making people act or respond.

Since an ad is difficult to personalize and doesn't include a return device, direct marketing ads try to use one or a combination of reply devices to get a response:

- Detachable reply cards that request name, address, phone numbers, e-mail address, etc.;
- Toll free or direct dial numbers;
- Tip-in or bound-in cards (magazines);
- Fax back forms or numbers;
- Website and email address for contacting.

Good direct marketers make sure that there is more than one way for the prospect to respond, in fact the more the better.

If you want to incorporate some type of reply device in a direct marketing print ad, you have to fit all the direct mail elements into one area. The message and the reply device must be concentrated in this one area without the assistance of any other element like a brochure, a lift note, etc.

THE NEXT IMPORTANT QUESTION TO CONSIDER IS WHEN TO USE A DIRECT MAIL AD VERSUS A DIRECT MAIL PIECE

A direct mail ad is preferred over a direct mail package when a publication only caters to a specific target group.

Running a direct mail ad in these publications is more logical because there is no need to rent a mailing list when you can reach this group all at once.

Another advantage is that even non-subscribers may have access to the publication or buy it from time to time. *For example,* though not every person in an agency subscribes to ***Marketing Magazine*** or ***Direct Marketing News,*** the office copy is circulated throughout the agency and everyone has a chance to look at it.

Cost saving is an important factor in choosing an ad as opposed to producing a direct mail piece for each reader or subscriber of the magazine. The savings on postage is another important consideration.

Also ads are easier and faster to produce. You can repeat the same message in subsequent issues or change it slightly each time depending on the response. One can even produce a whole series of ads to feature and test different results.

Print makes sense when you have a new product or service to talk about but the market is not clearly defined. It would be very difficult to determine whom the product or service would appeal to the most, where it should be located and what your market potential is.

Hincks Campaign Ad

Turning to publications also makes sense when lists have been overused and you have no way to secure new prospects.

If the organization is unknown, the ads can have 'a halo effect' of giving it credibility and legitimacy. People will trust a respected publication. Many customers feel more comfortable responding to print advertising rather than direct mail.

Some products need the privacy of direct mail while others need a public forum, broader product recognition and a need to establish and/or maintain a corporate image.

Often combining direct mail with print advertising can be a very productive way of enhancing response.

Though a number of organizations and associations do not rent their lists, they do publish annuals, semi-annuals or periodicals for events and shows in which you can place an ad.

Ads are a great way to:

- Generate new leads or inquiries
- Acquire new prospect names to build your database
- Make a new sale or test a creative or a service

GUIDELINES FOR PRODUCING ADS

According to **Siegfried Vögele**, we spend between three to seven seconds scanning the pages in any publication. He determined this through extensive eye-motion experiments and by recording subtle changes in skin chemistry.

Next, he observed that people have their own set of 'filters' and 'amplifiers' when observing or interacting with something. Filters make the piece being viewed uninteresting or off-putting. On the other hand, amplifiers attract and capture our attention.

With this in mind, here are a few hints to remember when creating direct mail ads:

The Headline: It is the most important element in an ad. It must hook the reader to want to read the rest of the ad. 98% of stopping power of an ad is due to the headline. Besides, the reader's attention can be lured by other ads or information on the same page.

The visual: It is the next crucial element in an ad. An eye catching and dramatic visual that is pertinent to the message will capture the reader's attention.

The offer: A strong offer with a clear benefit to the reader will stop them every time. Tailor your offer according to what will appeal most to the particular reading audience.

For example: If you provide organic food to your clients, the readers of a environmental magazine would most likely respond quite favourably to your charity. Make the reader want to donate to your cause. Remember, you are working against reader inertia – a body at rest tends to stay at rest.

The copy: The copy is the vehicle by which you organize and present your material about your products' benefits and features.

HINTS FOR WRITING ADS

Tell a compelling story. We all love to hear a story. One of the best ways to get the reader's attention is to narrate a fascinating story. One of the most successful and oldest ads was, "**They laughed when I sat down to play the piano.**"

Provide relevant and convincing reasons. In his book ***Tested Advertising Methods***, **John Caples** identified the three most important things to consider when writing an ad.

1) *Self-Interest*: You should write in thoughts, terms, and wants that are important to your reader. Your message should trigger a desire to read the ad.

2) *News*: News always attracts and is a popular theme. A news announcement that targets your customers' current needs has a high probability of getting read.

3) *Curiosity:* Curiosity is also a key in getting the reader's attention.

Most people are always looking for things that are meaningful to them and improve the quality of their lives, their looks, their health and their surroundings. If your charity provides a service like music or products in this direction, then shout it out. And remember to talk about the benefits the reader will gain, as a member or a donor.

One of the most successful campaigns for International Paper Company was a series of ads which became so popular that they got over 30 million requests for reprints. The thirteen ads were even converted into a book published by Doubleday called ***How to Use the Power of the Printed Word.***

Offer useful information. People are inquisitive and love to get new information, secrets, tips and hints.

Make it easy for the reader to respond. Make sure that response is easy and convenient. Don't keep readers guessing. If you want them to call, make your phone number larger. If you want them to fill out a form, make it easy to fill out and mail. Use a dashed box around your response card. Everyone knows what to do with a dashed box.

Use testimonials. Nothing is stronger than an endorsement from an authority. *For example:* **Yo-Yo Ma** talking about performing a concert for the Symphony in a local magazine is more likely to get classic music lovers to respond.

Resist the temptation to use clichés that impart no actual information. People tune them out. Also avoid cleverness, jokes, puns or wordplay just to be cute or amusing because they can sometimes backfire. However, humor can be used effectively if it is appropriate for the product or if it is an integral part of a strategy to position the product or service.

CAREFULLY SELECT THE MAGAZINE TO RUN YOUR AD

Magazines are sold either by subscription or as single copies. There is also the pass-along factor or hang around factor to consider. Many prime magazines stay around on tabletops at barbershops, hair salons, doctors' waiting rooms and dentists' offices. Popular magazines like ***MacLean's*** and ***Chatelaine*** tend to stay the longest. This is important to consider especially if the objective for your ad is lead generation.

Some magazines like ***Inside Direct Mail*** are strictly sold by subscription while others like ***MacLean's*** or ***Chatelaine*** can also be picked up at bookshops, convenience stores and kiosks.

One of the important things to consider besides the makeup of the target reader group is not the number of issues they publish but the number of people who actually subscribe to the magazine on a regular basis.

Called '**controlled circulation**', this is the key factor that most media buyers concentrate on when recommending a particular publication. The controlled circulation numbers for all Canadian publications are printed in ***CARD Magazine*** (Canadian Advertising Rates and Data) while all American Magazines' controlled circulation figures are published in ***SRDS*** (Standard Rate and Data Service).

TARGETED REACH
This small space Ad for the Spina Bifida & Hydrocephalus Association of Ontario (SB&H) ran in CARP's magazine that reaches 192,905 senior subscribers all of whom are over the age of 50.

IF YOU OR SOMEONE YOU KNOW HAS DIFFICULTY WALKING, URINARY INCONTINENCE OR MEMORY LOSS,

WE MAY HAVE SOME GOOD NEWS.

Call: 1-800-387-1575
Or send for your FREE Informational booklet:

SB&H
555 Richmond Street West, P.O. Box 103, Toronto, ON M5V 3B1

These publications are monthly magazines that provide a wealth of knowledge. In addition to the circulation information, they list their data according to categories – women's publications, men's publications, business, etc. Other detailed information about the various sizes of ads available, the advertising rates for each size, the sales offices and the addresses of the publishers are also provided.

FACTORS TO CONSIDER WHEN PLACING AN AD

Editorial content and readership. Evaluate whether the publication has the right editorial voice and the kind of readership that would appeal to your charity or service. See what kinds of ads are frequently placed in the publication. This will give you a good idea if this is the right environment for your organization or service.

Size of ad. Check the size of other ads in a publication you are interested in, keeping in mind that you will be competing with them. Size alone can improve results, so determine the minimum size that would be most effective for you and that you can afford. *For example:* Symphonies or Ballet companies rarely run ads less then a full page because they have found that sells seats most successfully. Figure out what works best for you.

Position of ad. Although the publication makes the final decision as to where an ad is placed, you can request the position. i.e. the bottom or top in a half-page or a quarter-page ad.

Colour of the ad. Colour plays a vital role when used effectively. However, it costs more to use colour both in terms of the production and publication charges. Adding a second colour helps the ad stand out but some products and services demand full colour to do them justice. Think of food or clothing in black and white and you'll see why.

Inserts. Many magazines accept inserts in their publications but this costs more. You can preprint the ad according to the magazine's specifications and ship the quantity required to them. Inserts are preprinted on a heavier stock than the magazine pages and therefore provide a high probability that the magazine will automatically fall open where they are placed.

Eight, six, double or full-page inserts are bound in or blown in. Many have a pre-perfed detachable response coupon or the detachable coupon can be placed before the ad.

A birth control Ad for teenagers to prevent unwanted pregnancies and promote safe sex.

Inserts also come in many shapes and sizes. They can be smaller then the magazine page, like postcards, or can be business reply envelopes. Inserts require the lead-time to produce and add to the print costs. And they are not always effective as some readers find them annoying and rip them out before reading the magazine. One should consider the economics of inserts carefully.

Publications limit the number of inserts in each issue so much lead-time is required. If you can afford it, the position of close to the front or back cover is optimum for pulling power.

Split runs. Many publications offer to run different versions of the ad in the same issue. As the magazine is printed, different versions of the ad can be inserted in every other issue so that the audience is randomly exposed to one version or the other. Split runs are great for testing a variety of offers or creative. You can place a code number on the response device or use different telephone numbers in order to track results. The number of split runs that can be tested in each edition is either a function of total circulation or how they are split.

Availability of segmented editions. Many major magazines offer several regional editions, which give you the chance to place your ad in the province of your choice. You could even place two entirely different ads in two different regions to see which performs better. Sometimes ads act as part of a campaign in conjunction with either a direct mail or television exposure in a particular region.

The upside is that this allows you to test different options of copy or products to find what is most effective. The down side is limited control as to where the ad will appear in the regional issue.

Availability of special editions. Many magazines focus on special issues that tackle a particular subject matter that may be of special interest to certain demographic groups. Placing an ad in these issues is like advertising to a captive niche market. Just like Super Bowl TV ads, this costs more but it does reach the right audience.

Discounts. A variety of discounts are available to lure advertisers. Magazines offer many special rates such as discounted rates for frequency or multiple pages either in the same issue or over a period of time. Publishers who print a variety of magazines will also offer special discounts if the ads are placed in numerous publications. Often space in magazines is unsold and media buyers are offered a discount to fill that space.

Classified sections. Many magazines also lump small space ads in their classified section under different headings. This can be an inexpensive way of gaining exposure to a particular readership. It is also a good way to test a certain publication. There is also no need to hire a designer to copy fit your ad. The publication does that for you and charges by the depth of the ad as dictated by the number of lines in the ad.

Get Something For Nothing.

Did you know there are six ways to improve your next DM piece? Visit my Web site, click on to showcase, and see what I mean. (http://www.designersinc.ca)

Or get valuable hints monthly for free. Just e-mail me at: designersinc@sympatico.ca and get my newsletter.

Each month I reveal new ways to increase response and show you what works best and why.

1407- 99 Harbour Square,Toronto, Ontario M5J 2H2
Phone: (416) 203-9787 http://www.designersinc.ca
E-mail: designersinc@sympatico.ca

The author's classified ad in ***Direct Marketing News***

NEWSPRINT

Running an ad in a newspaper has many distinct advantages. Daily newspapers have a larger circulation than magazines.

Newspapers also offer a variety of sections, including news, lifestyle and sports. You can advertise in the Sunday editions that have an even larger readership than the daily newspaper or in their TV magazines or other supplements, which stay around for at least a week. Newspapers offer the insertion of 'Freestanding Inserts' (FSIs). They have certain weekdays that have become synonymous with retail shopping – Wednesdays for food, Thursday for fashion.

A newspaper's classified section might be a good choice for a smaller advertiser.

Other newsprint advantages:

- **Speed of Response.** Since it is a daily medium, a direct marketer can quickly gauge how fast the ad has performed;
- **Frequency.** Because newspapers usually run seven days a week, one can immediately repeat an offer that works;
- **Immediacy.** Newspapers cover current events so if an event is advantageous to the charity they can optimize on it. *For example,* if a newspaper runs a special on the environment, a charity dedicated to this issue can capitalize on it;
- **Reach.** Newspapers still command the highest household readership and have high pass along value;
- **Sunday supplements.** They allow the reader to browse through at their leisure.

Which is the ideal month to advertise? Media buyers and publishers keep track of which months have the heaviest advertising. Although this may differ from publication to publication one can spot general trends.

The best advertising months are generally January and February, followed by September, October and early November.

Other factors that affect readership and response are disastrous events, special events and the weather. Disastrous events bring out the philanthropic side of people. At the height of the 9/11 disaster people donated millions of dollars and blood to the **Red Cross.** This phenomenon is now called '**Flash Philanthropy.**'

Special occasions like Thanksgiving and Christmas see a surge in donations to charities. **It is a great time to give back to society so ads that run during these months can benefit.**

An example of advocacy advertising

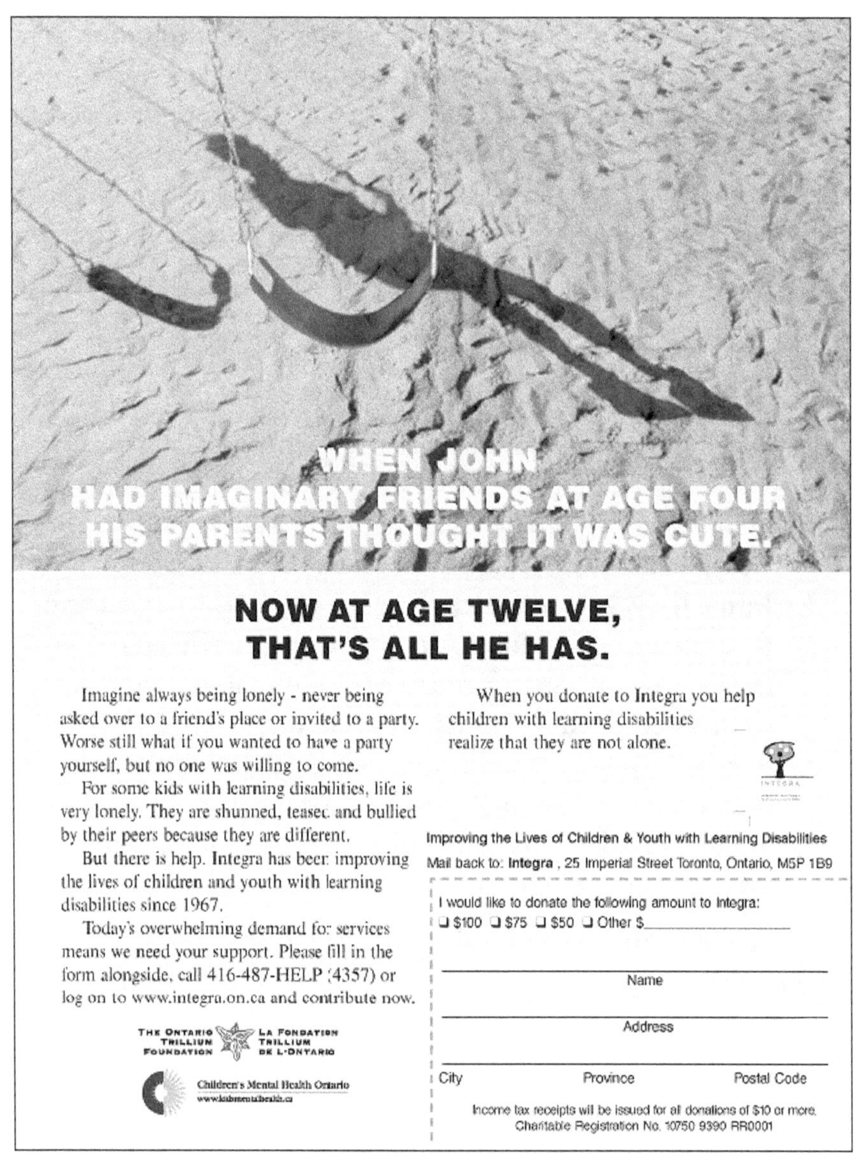

CASE STUDY

INTEGRA FOUNDATION

Background: In August 2007, Integra Foundation, along with other charities, decided to participate in a *Toronto Star* supplement for Children's Mental Health Week.

Each of the charities was allocated half a page.

Objective: To educate the general public about the importance of children's mental health.

Solution: Since there were so many charities participating in this insert, it was necessary to stand out with a message that dominated the insert.

Strategy: Since all the other charities taking part would publish articles about the mental health problems facing children, Integra decided to create an ad that focused on the solution that Integra provides featuring one child.

Result: The insert clearly dominated the supplement and got rave reviews from the other participating charities.

Sometimes it is better to zig when you know that others will zag. That sets your organization or product apart from the herd.

INTEGRA'S AD

ADVERTISING SUPPLEMENT

CHILDREN'S MENTAL HEALTH WEEK • MAY 7-11

THIS SUPPLEMENT CAN BE VIEWED ONLINE AT

ONE IN FIVE children and youth in Ontario struggles with their mental health

Although a child or youth who's depressed or angry or anxious may feel isolated, he or she is not alone. The problem is much bigger than most of us realize.

Although a child or youth who's depressed or angry or anxious may feel isolated, he or she is not alone. The problem is much bigger than most of us realize.

One out of every five children and youth under 19 struggles with a diagnosable emotional, mental or behavioural disorder. These problems are painful, serious and very real.

Any young person, regardless of age or circumstance, can experience mental health issues. Left untreated, kids in distress can turn to drugs and alcohol, become suicidal, drop out of school, become violent, or withdraw into silence and isolation.

These problems are not the fault of the child. They can affect a child or youth as easily as cancer or a physical disability. The causes are varied and

Although mental health problems among children and youth are vast and complicated, the following seven are the most common:

- Anxiety disorder
- Depression
- Conduct Disorder (bullying, vandalism, etc.)
- Attention Deficit Hyperactivity Disorder (ADHD)
- Eating Disorders
- Schizophrenia
- Bi-Polar Disorder (Manic-Depression)

The way a child or youth acts or behaves may be a sign that he or she has a mental health need. Ask yourself if the child's behaviour is unusually intense; whether he or she has been acting like this for a while, whether the behaviour is age appropriate; and

THE SUPPLEMENT

A radio campaign I once heard began with these words: *"Hi! I am Jane Doe. Help save vulnerable babies."*

What sprang to my mind was, vulnerable? Why vulnerable?

"Of all the adjectives **Webster's Dictionary** offers, why pick 'vulnerable' which draws almost no word-image?
We have wonderful words like 'helpless' and 'innocent' which might be pertinent to this message.
So why pick 'vulnerable?'

H.G. Lewis
Author, copywriter.

CHANNEL 3
RADIO

Radio is that great invisible medium that has been described as the theater of the mind. It can captivate you and practically command a response.

It touches you when you are least aware. You could be driving in a car, sitting in your living room or lying on a beach, listening to music or a talk show with NOTHING else to occupy your mind. Radio has grown and continues to grow and now ranks as the fourth largest in sales among all media.

Radio reaches about 95% of all adults on a weekly basis while certain groups of people watch less TV than ever before.

The number of listeners alone paves the way for success in direct response radio messaging.

Other reasons for its success:

- Radio gets a single message across clearly and repetitively using forms that range from strong consumer statements to jingles that stick in the mind;
- Radio allows you to grab the listener's undivided attention and present a compelling offer or urgent call to action;
- Radio gives you access to hard-to-reach demographic groups like teenagers or retirees;
- Radio allows you to use humor, drama or a tragic event to get your point across.

HOW TO PRODUCE A GOOD DM RADIO COMMERCIAL

Start with a grabber. Getting the listener's attention early is even more important than describing the benefits of your organization or service. After all, what good are all of your benefits if the listener switches stations or turns off the radio?

Provide clear benefits. State them articulately, restate them if possible and prove them to the best of your ability.

Use an appealing voice. An irritating voice will direct the listener's hand to that fateful knob.

Make your message believable. Credibility is the hardest thing to achieve and depends on what you choose to include or exclude in a commercial. Be careful how it is written but more important take care in how it sounds.

Respect your listeners' intelligence. Be honest and talk to your audience frankly. Some ads have UNTRUE written all over them.

Use humor carefully. Many radio commercials love to be witty but sometimes the attempt to be funny interferes with the selling message.

Think carefully about response mechanisms. Remember your audience may be on the move or may not have pen and paper handy. A telephone number is harder to memorize than the name of the organization. This does not preclude giving a telephone number as long as it is easy to remember.

CHANNEL 4 TELEVISION

Television is the most expensive medium and thus leaves little margin for error when it comes to generating response for direct marketing.

Once again there is a big difference between an advertising TV commercial and a direct marketing TV commercial. If an advertising television commercial turns out to be a dud, chances are that the sales of that product may dip slightly for a short period. There will still be a market for the product and many will ignore the commercial and continue to support the merchandise.

The creative director or account director will not get fired nor will the services of the marketing manager or the advertising agency be terminated.

However, because the merit of a direct marketing TV ads is judged on immediate return or response, should the commercial bomb, there is no rock large enough for the people responsible to hide under. While regular TV ads may rely on **BBM** (Bureau of Measurement) and **Nielson** ratings, direct marketing is judged by an even higher standard. The cash register has to ring or people must respond to ensure a profitable return on investment or the ad is a failure.

Television is truly a window of opportunity. You are being invited into people's homes each time they turn on the set and watch your commercial.

You have the chance to:

- Generate leads and get a donation;
- Piggy back on images already built by other forms of promotion or advertising;
- Launch new products or initiatives.

Television is a visual and verbal medium. People expect to be entertained, visually captured, transported and informed or touched when they watch television.

However, television commercials are interruptions to the shows being watched by the audience. Generally TV ads are produced in segments of:

- 15 seconds
- 30 seconds
- 60 seconds

New stats show that only 9% of television viewers can actually name the brand or product they saw on a TV commercial recently.

Most did not forget the message, just the messenger. Many people can accurately describe the commercial, but they can't seem to remember the product being advertised.

It's not that commercials are less compelling or less entertaining to watch. On the contrary, with bigger budgets and computer animation, buildings, people, animals or things spin, morph or talk. No, the real problem is that today's consumer is busier, has to multi-task and is becoming more marketing resistant. With thousands of messages hurled at them every minute, they have developed a form of 'selective intake' mechanism. So, what is the answer?

It's "TFCI" marketing: targeted, focused, creative and integrated marketing.

- Targeting because consumers can turn off that switch in their head, if the message is not for them or not important to them;
- Focused because too many mixed messages don't work;
- Creative because we still have to get their attention;
- Integrated because it must be repeated often in various media to reach the consumers and it must be consistent.

- 2 minutes

This means that you have a very limited time, ranging from 15 to 120 seconds, to show and sell your message. There are a number of ways of doing this.

EFFECTIVE TV FORMATS

The old pitchman style. Here the presenter explains a problem, gives details about the hazards, offers his magic solution and shows the happy outcome of people he has successfully treated.

By demonstration or by comparison. Here the object is to show by contrast the superiority of your organization or service over that of the competition.

By communicating details. Many initiatives or services need further explanation that is most effective as a visual and verbal demonstration. Television is the ideal medium for this. The audience is supplied with enough pertinent information to enable them to make an educated decision. These information-packed spots stem from a journalistic approach. They try and answer who, what, why, when and where within the time span of the commercial.

Use well-known personalities to do your selling. As mentioned earlier, one of the most convincing ways to talk about how your service has helped is to use a celebrity. An endorsement from a highly-recognized and respected person is an excellent way to use television.

Testimonials add an air of validity and have been used successfully by charities using celebrities like **Sarah McLachlan** for the **SPCA** and **Céline Dion** for **Canadian Cystic Fibrosis Foundation.**

Tell a story. From slice-of-life formats to live situations, many TV ads are effective because they are believable. Not-for-profit organizations that can afford to produce and air TV commercials use the medium very successfully. Using a documentary style they can show suffering people in dire need of help or conditions in desperate need of improvement.

The techniques one can use to captivate the television audience are numerous and varied. To leave a strong visual or audio impression TV ads use compelling copy, amazing graphics, catchy jingles, computer animation, fantasy, humor or a combination of them all. The bottom line, however, is never to lose sight of the reason for producing television spots in the first place – to motivate the viewer to respond.

A vital part of an effective commercial is a toll-free telephone number that stays in sight throughout the commercial. Websites and mailing addresses also enhance response.

Many direct marketers use this formula:

- Tell the audience why they should buy into your organization, service or cause.
- Tell them again.
- And finally tell them what you have just finished telling them.

Keep in mind the repetitive nature of television means your TV ad will most probably be seen many times. Be sure your message is clear but avoid repeating any one statement to the point of irritation.

DRTV (DIRECT RESPONSE TV) OR INFOMERCIAL

These ads can range from 10 to 30 minutes or longer. They are produced before a live audience or use a sound track mixed to give that appearance. This format has been used successfully to sell exercise equipment to charitable work. Usually delivered in a pitchman style, the show follows a predictable formula.

DRTV PRODUCTION

TV ads are shot on either film or videotape, and then edited. Video gives the spot a 'cinéma vérité'– documentary or live on-air feel – while film tends to give a slick movie look. Creating the right look is important, but more important is to make the TV ad believable.

Storyboards are prepared in advance to help identify the shots needed to construct the sequence. They are a combination of audio and video or animatics with a montage of key visual frames of various sizes. Storyboards can also consist of a page with no visuals and only a written description of the video.

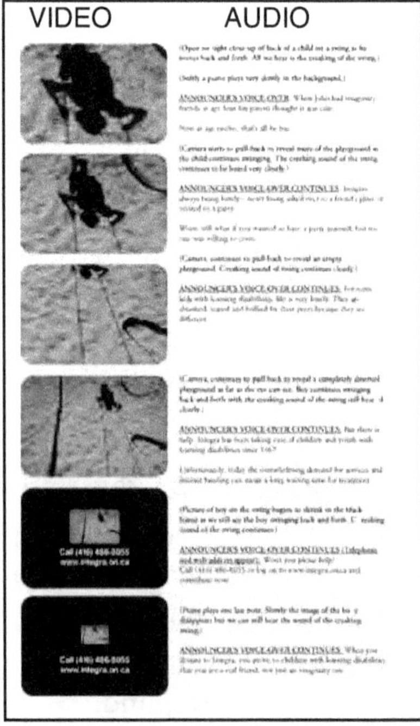

After the commercial is shot, sound effects, music and narration are mixed in at the editing stage. From a master, copies are duplicated and sent to television stations for airing.

CASE STUDY

HINCKS CENTRE FOR CHILDREN'S MENTAL HEALTH

Background: The Hincks Centre for Children's Mental health (now called Hincks Dellcrest) provides training, education and treatment to seriously disturbed children. Its activities include: fellowship, seminars, conferences, research, psychotherapy, training and treatment programs. In spite of the work they do as a charity they are relatively unknown by the public at large.

Objective: To launch a public awareness campaign that would:

- **Promote the work that this charity does**
- **Convince foundations to become participating partners**
- **Inform, educate the public, industry and government about the seriousness of the problem**
- **Stress the importance of the vital services performed by the organization**

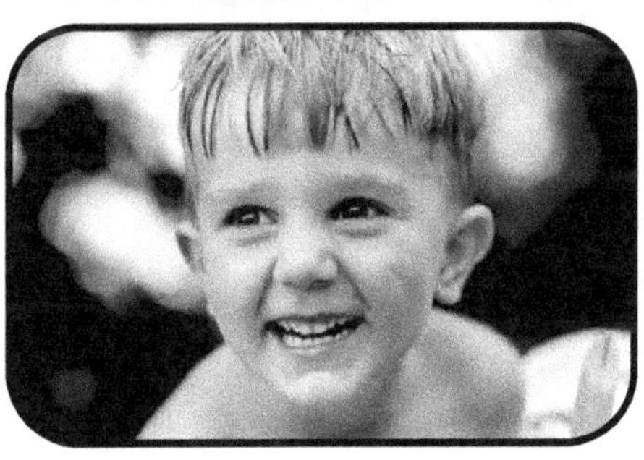

Solution: To redesign everything from the ground up with a new logo and a hard hitting campaign that would help launch a public awareness campaign and convince the industry and foundations to back it.

Strategy: To draw attention to the problems faced by these kids, a public awareness campaign was launched with Toronto Transit Commission and bus shelters posters, Ads, a DM piece and two television PSAs that focused on the importance of early intervention.

Result: The campaign acquainted people with the importance of the issues that children with mental health problems faced and the dire need for early intervention. **The strategy worked.**

- **The Silverman Foundation contributed $300,000 after reviewing the concepts and the campaign was launched in Ontario.**
- **The advertising community also rallied by donating over $780,000 worth of goods and services.**
- **Funds collected from industry and the public exceeded over $500,000.**
- **The entire campaign was picked up and also promoted by another charity called INVEST IN KIDS.**
- **The two hard-hitting TV spots generated over 40 calls a day each time they were aired.**

HANDY HINTS

If you think you have to wait for your direct mail response to come in before you start telemarketing, think again.

Research proves that it makes no difference. Besides, while you are waiting for the 1-2% to respond, the other 98-99% of your prospects are cooling off.

CHANNEL 5
TELEMARKETING

The telephone has always been a highly successful and convenient way of convincing current donors and recruiting new ones.

Since telemarketing is a very personal one-on-one interaction, it is a powerful tool for direct marketing. It provides immediate feedback on what works which means you can fine-tune your program as you go along.

Most charities either have the option of setting up their own telemarketing operations or they can hire a professional telemarketing company to conduct a variety of tasks or services on their behalf.

The most important services telemarketing provides are:

- Qualifying, prospecting and generating leads;
- Following up on prospects who have received a solicitation through direct marketing, promotions or another media;
- Receiving direct-response inquiries to TV, radio or print advertising;
- Selling or taking donations;
- Setting qualified appointments;
- Surveying, checking on customer needs and satisfaction;
- Providing, building and maintaining customer service and enhancing relationships with both inbound and outbound calling donors;
- Verifying, updating and enhancing the existing database and adding new customers;
- Tracking delinquent accounts and making collections;
- Gauging market and behavioural changes;
- Handling complaints and dissatisfied people;
- Making marginal accounts more profitable;
- Converting inquiries to donations;
- Helping political candidates or causes;
- Gauging a reaction or public opinion through surveys;
- Determining campaign or brand awareness;
- Covering distant donors economically;
- Reaching more prospects in less time.

HOW TELEMARKETING WORKS

There are two services that telemarketing firms provide and both require a high level of skill and training for the phone representatives and the managers who oversee them.

Outbound calls. This is when the telemarketer places a call. Here the telemarketer works with a database and a computer which automatically dials a prospect's or a donor's telephone number.

Up-to date information about the person being called appears on the screen. The telemarketer is provided with a prepared telephone script.

Inbound calls. These are calls that the telemarketer fields when a call is made to a toll-free number (1-800, 1-888). Here the callers must go through a variety of options that identify them or they must identify themselves with a series of codes. Here no script is provided but a guide on how to handle a variety of situations has been pre-established which the telemarketer must follow.

Inbound calls are automatically transferred to the first available representative who handles requests for information.

Many large organizations have their own telemarketing operations in-house.

For those that do not, the most important things for them to consider when outsourcing are professionalism and expertise of management and staff. This should be a crucial deciding factor because they will be handling your precious database, one of your biggest assets. It contains the names and addresses of your clients and their satisfaction is critically important to your success.

Here are some of the things to consider when out-sourcing telemarketing services:

- **Planning:** You need to consider the cost, your objectives for the volume/quality of data you desire;
- **Accurate data:** Providing accurate data is essential for success and that means continually updating;
- **A good script:** Although there are many books that advocate writing a script in advance for the service bureau staff, the most effective telemarketing script should actually not be a script at all. Telemarketers need a guide that steers them in a certain direction. Long pre-prepared scripts can be tiresome and unless the reader is one great actor, the script will sound canned. Also a good telemarketer should be able to handle the interruptions that so often come from a listener. The guide/script should be tailored to fit a variety of individuals but should be flexible enough to work with any individual response;

The introduction of the **National Do Not Call Registry** brought attention to the misuse of phone opportunities by certain unethical telemarketers. The media has often vilified telemarketing, sometimes for good reason. However it is a viable solicitation method and contact channel for renewing and informing your current donors and for cultivating prospective donors.

Telemarketing works best when members or volunteers of an organization touch base with their fellow members or donors.

If however you must use a professional telemarketing firm to acquire new donors, keep in mind that these companies operate on such a large commission basis that you can be left with 30% or less of the money raised in your name. The upside is that every donor goes into your database for your own future use.

People who participate in phone-a-thons give more when they are told about a big contribution made by a previous donor.

However, if the amount mentioned is too high, the gift amount is lower.

In addition, when callers were told that the gift was from a donor of the same sex as they are, they tended to contribute more than if they were told that the previous donor was of the opposite sex.

Source: nfpStrategy

- **Skilled telemarketers:** To achieve the desired outcomes telemarketers must have a good knowledge of the charity and its services, as they are acting as representatives of the charity. Telemarketers have to deal with all kinds of individuals and personalities, so they must be able to talk intelligently without getting side tracked or flustered by negative responses. They must talk persuasively to people at all levels.

Other advantages of out-sourcing are:

- **Low investment and overhead:** The set-up costs of establishing your own in-house telemarketing operation can be substantial and can include allocating space, phone equipment, telephone lines, cubicles, computer hardware and software and the employees' time.
- **Fixed cost estimates:** Most service bureaus provide a detailed estimate. The costs are usually based on a setup fee depending on whether the calls are inbound or outbound and the complexity of the calls. You are charged either on a per-call basis or per-hour basis. Per-call usually applies to inbound calls while per-hour calls apply to out-bound calls. The per-call charge is based on the amount of information and length of time to execute a call with a guaranteed minimum.
- **Immediate start:** Once a contract is signed, a script approved and database files delivered, the process can start at once.
- **24/7 service:** Most service bureaus provide a 24-hour, seven-day-a-week operation for inbound calls so that customers can place orders or leave messages at any time, day or night. Outbound calls are by law restricted to daytime and early evening slots.

GUIDELINES FOR A TELEMARKETING SCRIPT

The Start The telemarketer has to make sure the right person has been contacted and introduce themselves. Next they must:

- Grab the listener's attention with a hook in the first 10-seconds;
- Initiate a dialogue;
- Ask a relevant question, like, *"Mr. Smith, we've developed a way to save you up to $25,000 this year in taxes. Would you be interested in finding out more?"*

- Always address your prospect by name and keep the conversation going by making it a dialogue;
- Allow the caller to interact.

<u>The Middle</u> It should be a clear presentation of the benefits.

- Lead with a Question & Answer format. That helps clear up any misunderstanding and gets the respondent involved;
- Never interrupt when the prospect is talking;
- Have a prepared script or guide to follow;
- Anticipate as many questions as possible and be prepared with appropriate responses;
- Ensure that the script is broken up into sections;
- Stay within a length of up to five minutes.

<u>The Close</u> This is where the telemarketer asks for the donation and handles any objections.

FACTS ABOUT TELEMARKETING

Today telephone technology, software and linking by satellite have made it possible to place call centers far from your actual offices. This can save much money in venue rental, equipment costs and employee wages.

Telemarketing is a medium that one rarely uses on its own. It works best when it is integrated with your other sales and marketing activities. *You will learn more about this in Chapter 12.*

While telemarketing can play an important role for any organization from large to small, there is a downside to using telemarketing to agressively solicit donations. Though telemarketing success can be proven, invariably if asked people will tell you how annoying they find it. They don't like being disturbed at mealtime and badgered about a survey or asked for a donation. Telemarketing lacks prestige and occasionally a call ends with swear words and a slamming of the phone.

In the summer of 2003 a mandatory do-not-call registry was established in the United States and a year later more than 60 million people had signed up. Canada has followed suit and the **Canadian Radio-television and Telecommunication Commission** is looking after this. As a consumer you can register your number and file a complaint with them.

Finally, while telemarketing may not win any popularity contests, the telephone remains an important direct marketing channel to keep in contact with your donors.

Who can still call you even after you have registered for the 'Do-not-call' registry?

Consumers should understand that registering on the **National DNCL** would reduce but not eliminate all telemarketing calls. There are certain kinds of telemarketing calls that are exempted from the National DNCL Rules.

The exemptions include telemarketing calls made by, or on behalf of:

- **Canadian registered charities;**
- **Political parties, riding associations and candidates;**
- **Newspapers of general circulation for the purpose of soliciting subscriptions;.**
- **Organizations with which you have an existing business relationship.**

CHANNEL 6
INTERACTIVE COMMUNICATION (VIRAL MARKETING AND THE WEB)

DIRECT MARKETING WISDOM

The Internet did not create a new market, it only changed how existing markets work.

HOW BIG IS THE INTERNET?
This is a bit like asking how long is a piece of string?

The answer is we really don't know because it is unorganized, uncatalogued and continues to grow at a phenomenal rate.

However, the Internet World Stats, which is an International website featuring up-to-date world Internet Usage, Population Statistics and Internet Market Research Data, for over 233 individual countries and world regions, put the number of worldwide Internet users at 1.407 billion in 2008.

Another stat comes from a Google blog to which **Phil Bradley** alerted the author. According to this post *"… our systems that process new links on the web to find new content hit a milestone: 1 trillion unique URLs on the web at once!"* Wow, that's 1,000,000,000,000 URLs. This does not include duplicated content or auto-generated copies, so it's not as inflated as it may seem.

Any discussion of the web must be very fluid. By the time one records any facts or statistics about the subject, they may have already changed. But even with such challenges, the Internet is a dream come true for a direct marketer. It employs traditional DM principles with one major exception. While a direct marketing program must go out to seek prospects, the Internet brings them right to your door.

WIKIPEDIA DEFINES THE INTERNET AS :

"A global system of interconnected computer networks that use the standardized Internet Protocol Suite (TCP/IP). It is a network of networks that consists of millions of private and public, academic, business and government networks of local to global scope that are linked by copper wires, fiber-optic cables, wireless connections and other technologies."

THE MARKETING CYCLE IS REVERSED ON THE INTERNET

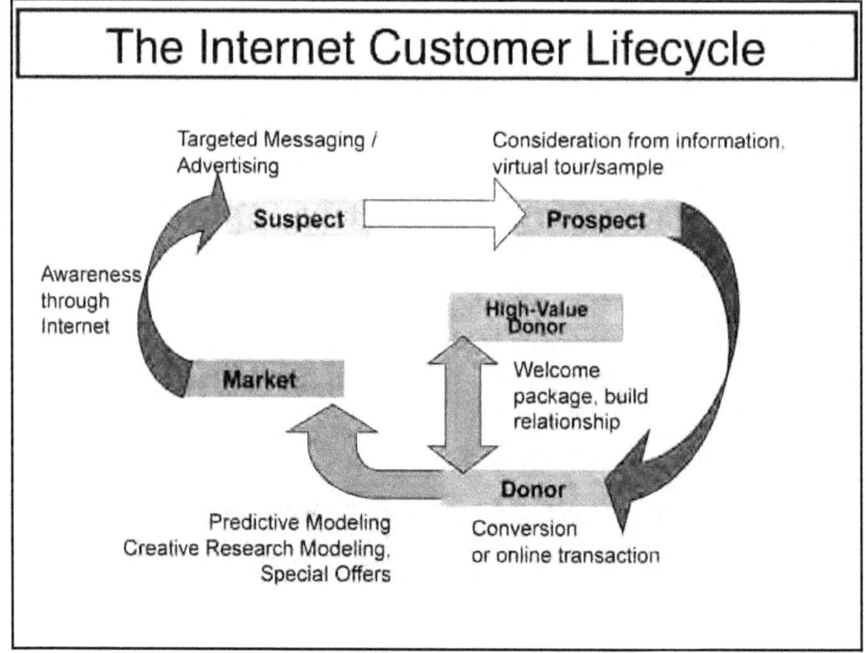

The Internet is the first mass medium that allows people to actively communicate with those who have a website. Here the interested parties or inquisitive browsers come to your website after surfing the web.

Once they land on your website they can browse or take a virtual tour to see if you have anything of interest for them. These people can then be considered as Prospects.

If during the visit they make an online transaction or donation, then they can be considered as Donors.

Donors who give more then once, or those that you build a relationship with, are then deemed to be Core Donors.

Finally, just like traditional direct marketing, once you know your donors and what they are looking for, you can adapt, amend and improve your website to cater to their needs and use the knowledge you've gained to attract more prospects to your web domain.

THE BENEFITS OF THE INTERNET

The Internet allows people to surf and browse various websites and to actively do one or more of the following:

- Respond to a marketing message instantly;
- Self-direct themselves to the required information to make a decision;
- Make the commitment/transaction instantly;
- Provide you with the necessary information to learn about their experience and help you communicate with them.

The costs to build the site are scalable: An information based site can cost as little as $1,000 to set up. E-merchant sites can cost less than $100/month to maintain.

Compared to traditional methods, a website can cost-effectively offer the following benefits:

- Provide instant updates or information;
- Disseminate information;
- Present marketing and communications plans;
- Lower your cost of acquisition;
- Build relationship opportunities.

It offers speed:

- Fastest to market;
- Immediate awareness, consideration and acquisition opportunities all within a matter of minutes;
- Real-time results analysis and comparison;
- Instant methods of initiating a two-way communication.

WHY PRINT IS EVEN MORE IMPORTANT NOW, IN THIS ELECTRONIC AGE.

There is no denying that a website today is essential for every business. The importance of a website and the amazing explosion in e-commerce over the last decade is phenomenal. It is a fantastic medium that people turn to for information on many subjects. And we all use it. A good website can act as a powerful lead generating tool. After all it is the most economical way of having a salesperson on duty, 24/7. But just having this sale sentry does not produce potential customers magically at your website's door. You actually need to drive the right people to your website first. Print and direct mail are far from dead; in fact they are more important than ever for the following reasons:

1. A website is not tactile. People can't touch it, turn it or store it away the way they can a piece of printed literature.
2. It is passive, relying upon a wandering surfer to find it. It cannot tap your most important prospect on the shoulder and say, 'Look at me.' It is buried in cyberspace.
3. A website coupled with a printed mailer or an ad can help drive customers to your website and inform them that you may have something for them. (A free newsletter, white paper, etc.)

IMPORTANT FACTORS IN WEB-DESIGN:

- **Stickiness** is a way of measuring the effectiveness of the content. Does the design hold the users' attention and entice them to complete their online tasks?
- **Slipperiness** is the opposite of stickiness. A slippery section of a site is one where visitor frequencies are low, users are few and visits are short.
- **Velocity** is the measure of user movement or how quickly a customer progresses from awareness, to deliberation, to decision.
- **Freshness factor** is the measure of how often content is refreshed, crucial for getting users to return to the site frequently.

It is easy to track: Online advertising provides instant and on-going results. By analyzing this data, you can determine:

- Brand effectiveness;
- Creative effectiveness;
- Which site segments are most attractive;
- What triggers a browser to come to you.

Everything that happens on your website is logged. By analyzing this data, you can determine:

- Usage patterns such as number of pages viewed on your site as well as monthly, weekly, daily or hourly patterns of use;
- Behavioral patterns such as frequency of visits, length of time per visit, purchasing patterns, common keywords used to find your website.

It can be used for personalization: By using tools to effectively build a profile of each of your customers you can:

- Provide a true one-to-one relationship with them – make them feel that you understand them and listen to them;
- Segment your users based on their profile and provide them with offers and benefits that will especially appeal to them;
- Build more complex profiles each time they return and interact with you online.

GROWTH AND IMPORTANCE OF THE INTERNET AND WORLD WIDE WEB

There are many reasons for the growth of the Internet, including these factors:

- Provides much higher computing power at much lower costs;
- Allows digitization of all types of information from text, graphics, audio to video;
- Permits access to mobile devices and wireless technology;
- Offers online donation opportunities. The Internet has created new markets and players because it offers marketers a rapid, flexible and versatile communication medium that is interactive and can supplement or enhance other media since it is cheaper, faster and more practical than fax, phone or mail;
- Allows a shift of power from charity to donor;
- Opens up much larger markets than just a local one;
- Produces new leads and opportunities;
- Eliminates intermediaries (e.g., many charities now sell products or tickets to events directly);
- Substantially trims the costs of doing business.

Ways the Internet is used:

- Getting information – publishing sites feature electronic brochures, catalogues, newspapers, encyclopedias and a wealth of other information sources;
- Retrieving up-to-date facts such as databases, forms and offers, letting users search for specific information;
- Creating personalization – you can create pages that cater to individuals' needs and tastes, anticipate user choices and suggest alternatives;
- Over 50% of new donors go to a charitable website for information about the organization before donating, so examine carefully how you present your organization to the world. Dedicate more time and resources to ensuring that your Web site shows off the great programs and personal stories that illustrate how your work makes an impact.

Conventional wisdom would suggest that if a person connected with an organization via a Web-based initiative the best way to reconnect with the same person would be through a Web-based communication. Extensive research shows that this is far from the truth. Most important successes resulted through direct mail follow-up. Simply put, people are people and how we reach out to them should never just be assumed.

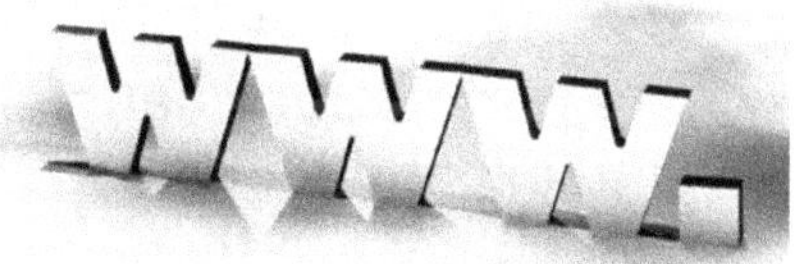

USING EMAILS TO CULTIVATE AND SOLICIT PROSPECTS VIA THE INTERNET (although it is not yet the star of the show)

Many companies have shifted their focus to online fundraising because it offers a promising glimmer of hope. That's because donors who make their first gift to a charity online generally give more than those who give their first gift by mail.

Also, many charities have been highly successful in raising millions of dollars with emails.

But, unfortunately most of them are US charities and most donations raised are a result of contributions made in response to a disaster or a special situation, like the Tsunami, earthquakes or food crises.

Using emails or viral marketing is still not a substitute for traditional campaigning for two reason: persuading donors to give online for the first time is not easy; it's harder to get online donors to become repeat or loyal donors.

If you are a charity and are having trouble raising money by direct marketing, don't expect electronic solicitations to be the miracle cure to help turn things around.

Although half the people who make a first-time donation may go to your website to decide, according to a recent survey in the US, 35% of overall donors still prefer direct mail as the method to

OTHER ELEMENTS YOU CAN ADD TO EMAILS:

1. **Quizzes, contests and games. People love a challenge and these are good involvement devices.**

2. **Surveys. Involving and inviting donors to voice their opinion can be very beneficial.**

3. **Videos and PSAs help solidify support**

4. **E-cards for holidays and special events allow donors to show their support for the charity and expand the reach when they use them to send to friends and family.**

5. **A leveraged gift. Getting a sponsor to match gifts by donors is a great way to increase funds.**

receive information from the organizations they will support. Of older donors (65 and older) 46% prefer direct mail; 36% of those age 40-49 prefer it; 25% of those age 30-39 want direct mail.

Unfortunately, just because E-marketing is cheaper it is still not the panacea that has replaced traditional ways of fundraising, although it is growing in popularity and should not be ignored.

With this in mind here are the important things to keep in mind when attempting to solicit via emails

LIKE DIRECT MARKETING, THE LIST IS STILL THE MOST IMPORTANT THING

Who you talk to is still the most important element in generating a response. Add to this the fact that if people have not opted-in or given you permission to email to them, your e-solication will either be stuck in a spam filter or deleted immediately.

It's a numbers game and you will need very large numbers of opted-in donors, just to generate a donation via e-marketing. Most email asks are filtered or deleted as spam. The open rate for emails falls between 20%-35%.

Fewer still are actually read and only a fraction of these who do read it are motivated to click on the link that goes to your website to make a donation.

NEXT THE MESSAGE ITSELF

The top area in an email, which is the prime real estate, must be effective in drawing the recipient into your email.

THE TWO MOST IMPORTANT THINGS WHEN COMPOSING AN EMAIL ARE:

1. THE SUBJECT LINE

The subject line dictates whether or not people will actually read what you have to say or simply delete it immediately.

Remember, with all the messages bombarding people today, they have probably developed some form of 'selective intake' mechanism.

- **Make it interesting (tease or arouse curiosity);**
- **Make it timely**
- **Make it pertinent.**

Make the subject line interesting: *For example:* For a children's charity dealing with learning disabilities: ***"How early can experts predict your child's future?"***

Make it timely: *For example.* For international relief charity: *"Help send drinking water to the flood victims of Brazil."*

Make it pertinent: *For example.* A membership organization: *"Last Call for Members to join the Orchestra at reduced prices."*

Make it short, no more then 50 characters.

Email formats vary in length as to how many characters your reader can see, so be on the safe side.

Avoid symbols.

Words such as Free, Sale, or symbols like $,!, CAPS, will land the email in the spam filter.

2. THE EMAIL ITSELF

- **Make it scannable**
- **Make it short**
- **Consider the 'preview pane'**
- **Consider the medium**
- **Use standard fonts**
- **Make hyperlinks easy to find**

Make it scannable

Most people only scan email messages. What catches their attention?

- Salutation
- First sentence
- Short paragraphs
- Underlines (use sparingly—only as hyperlinks)
- Graphic inserts
- Bolded or italic sentences (use sparingly)
- Bulleted lists
- Closing
- Identity of signer or sender
- P.S.
- Free offers
- Things to click on
- Interactive features (forward to a friend)

Make it short

Get to the point quickly. Present just one or two ideas maximum.

Consider the 'preview pane'

Preview panes reveal a small part of your message — the tip of the email on top. Consider the preview panel as precious real estate — your best chance to entice the reader further.

Banner Ads:

Imagine what it is like being stuck in a doorway.
This is the daily reality for millions of Americans with disabilities.

Click here to help them get through the doorway.

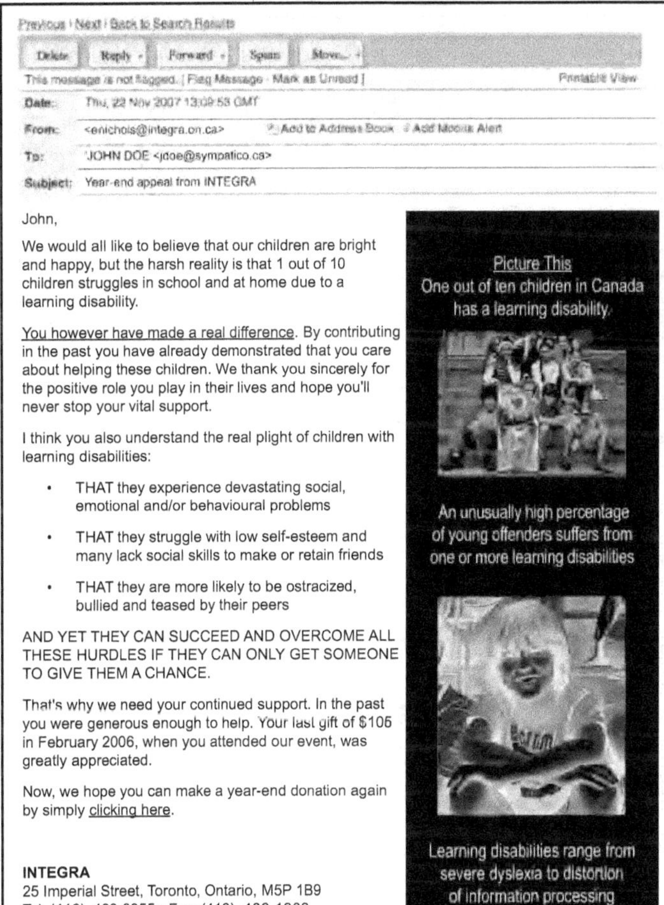

Previous | Next | Back to Search Results

Delete | Reply | Forward | Spam | Move...

This message is not flagged. [Flag Message - Mark as Unread] Printable View

Date: Thu, 22 Nov 2007 13:09:53 GMT

From: <enichols@integra.on.ca> Add to Address Book | Add Mobile Alert

To: JOHN DOE <jdoe@sympatico.ca>

Subject: Year-end appeal from INTEGRA

John,

We would all like to believe that our children are bright and happy, but the harsh reality is that 1 out of 10 children struggles in school and at home due to a learning disability.

You however have made a real difference. By contributing in the past you have already demonstrated that you care about helping these children. We thank you sincerely for the positive role you play in their lives and hope you'll never stop your vital support.

I think you also understand the real plight of children with learning disabilities:

- THAT they experience devastating social, emotional and/or behavioural problems
- THAT they struggle with low self-esteem and many lack social skills to make or retain friends
- THAT they are more likely to be ostracized, bullied and teased by their peers

AND YET THEY CAN SUCCEED AND OVERCOME ALL THESE HURDLES IF THEY CAN ONLY GET SOMEONE TO GIVE THEM A CHANCE.

That's why we need your continued support. In the past you were generous enough to help. Your last gift of $105 in February 2006, when you attended our event, was greatly appreciated.

Now, we hope you can make a year-end donation again by simply clicking here.

INTEGRA
25 Imperial Street, Toronto, Ontario, M5P 1B9
Tel: (416) 486-8055 • Fax: (416) 486-1282

Picture This
One out of ten children in Canada has a learning disability.

An unusually high percentage of young offenders suffers from one or more learning disabilities

Learning disabilities range from severe dyslexia to distortion of information processing

According to an AMA study, people who give both online and offline are the best performing donors. They have the highest frequency of giving, the highest annual giving, and are more likely to renew.

THE CCFC PACKAGE ONLINE

Here's an email solicitation that worked brilliantly to notify current donors about an emergency situation. It was for **Christian Children's Fund of Canada.** In the first week it generated $10,000 online.

THE E-MAIL

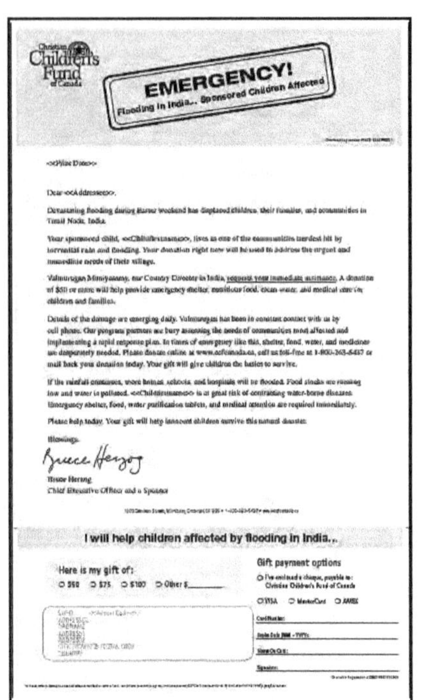

Christian Children's Fund of Canada

EMERGENCY!

Flooding in India... Sponsored Children Affected

Dear <<Addressee>>,

Devastating flooding during Easter weekend has displaced children, their families, and communities in Tamil Nadu, India.

Your sponsored child, <<Childfirstname>>, lives in one of the communities hardest hit by torrential rain and flooding. Your donation right now will be used to address the urgent and immediate needs of their village.

Valmurugan Muniyasamy, our Country Director in India, requests your immediate assistance. A donation of $50 or more will help provide emergency shelter, nutritious food, clean water, and medical care for children and families.

Details of the damage are emerging daily. Valmurugan has been in constant contact with us by cell phone. Our program partners are busy assessing the needs of communities most affected and implementing a rapid response plan. In times of emergency like this, shelter, food, water, and medicines are desperately needed. Please donate online at www.ccfcanada.ca, call us toll-free at 1-800-263-5437 or mail back your donation today. Your gift will give children the basics to survive.

If the rainfall continues, more homes, schools, and hospitals will be flooded. Food stocks are running low and water is polluted. <<Childfirstname>> is at great risk of contracting water-borne diseases. Emergency shelter, food, water purification tablets, and medical attention are required immediately.

Please help today. Your gift will help innocent children survive this natural disaster.

Blessings,

Bruce Herzog

Bruce Herzog
Chief Executive Officer and a Sponsor

I will help children affected by flooding in India...

Here is my gift of:
○ $50 ○ $75 ○ $100 ○ Other $______

Gift payment options
○ I've enclosed a cheque, payable to: Christian Children's Fund of Canada
○ VISA ○ MasterCard ○ AMEX

Consider the medium

Emails are less formal than direct mail pieces. While a DM letter starts with salutations like, "**Dear Mr. Doe,**" emails say "**Hi Joe,**" or "**Hello Joe.**"

The language is more colloquial, cryptic and casual.

Example: Just got home and wanted to fire off this message to you. Heard on the radio that parts of Brazil were flooded. Since you've sponsored a child in the region I wanted to make you aware of the situation and how you can help during this crisis.

Stay tuned.

Billy

Use standard fonts

The three common fonts are Times, Arial and Verdana. Anything else could be substituted but could alter the design unless it is sent as a PDF or in HTML format.

Make hyperlinks easy to find. Preferably in the top half of the preview pane.

While good copy writing applies to all media, writing for viral marketing has some distinct advantages and disadvantages.

THE ADVANTAGES

1. **Writing in real time.** A crisis occurs and you have the advantage of getting your message out at once.

2. **Your style of writing can also be more up-to-the-minute.** *An example:* In a DM piece the message may be: *"Thanks for attending our event. Your sponsorship matters."*

In email the message could be: *"It's midnight, just got home from the fun event. Whew! What a great night. Thanks for being a big part of it."*

In the US presidential race of 2008, **Barack Obama** used this to great advantage. The second his election was confirmed, each of his online supporters received a personalized thank you.

3. **Emails can be more conversational.** While a DM piece may say, *"We were honored by your generous presence"* an email can say, *"Glad you could come—that really made a huge difference."*

4. **You can use contractions and symbols in emails.** Many writers have to toe a fine line between selling and becoming chatty. Not so with emails. The Internet has its own jargon of cryptic writing in symbols and contractions, which appears more one-to-one.

5. Helps you reinforce your cause's campaign and acts as a reminder.

6. Prompts recipients to visit your website or learn more about the issue.

7. Email surveys are highly effective.

THE DISADVANTAGES

1. **You are competing with more noise in viral marketing.** People are barraged with emails daily so you have to learn to cut through the clutter to be heard. You have to be more persuasive.

2. **Low priority.** Studies indicate that most people read messages from business associates, family and friends, colleagues before they consider opening a fundraising solicitation.

3. **Sensitivity is a big issue.** Not everyone is willing to hand out information about friends or pass on your message to their friends, relatives or co-workers.

4. **Getting a second gift from the same donor still remains a challenge.** Donors responding to viral marketing are younger, with less disposable income. Also it is harder to relay an emotional message via a simple email—unless you lead them to a 'streaming video' that has all the desired impact. And that's often a two-step process.

5. **Emails have to be more precisely targeted.** They absolutely must be more relevant to the person receiving them in order to get the desired response.

A FEW MORE ESSENTIAL THINGS TO CONSIDER WHEN COMPOSING AN EMAIL APPEAL

Here are a few more things to consider when using the online medium to solicit donations.

1. **Follow-up email** – Re-sending the same email offer with slight creative changes or as a reminder can increase sales and profits by 20-40%. This has worked for direct mail so there is no reason why it will not work for e-appeals.

2. **Convert benefit-rich response links to call-to-action links** – This is the element that links your prospect to the next step in the sales cycle. Rather than "click here," convert benefit copy into links such as: "click here for a 5-day free offer".

Links early in the e-mail message get the highest response so try and include at least one link in the first screen shot 'above the fold' (visible on the screen when the message is first opened).

THE CCFC PACKAGE OFF-LINE

A few weeks later **CCFC** mailed a direct mail piece to those donors without an email address. This time they raised $20,100 the first week alone. An ROI of 4.7 to 1.

Outer envelope

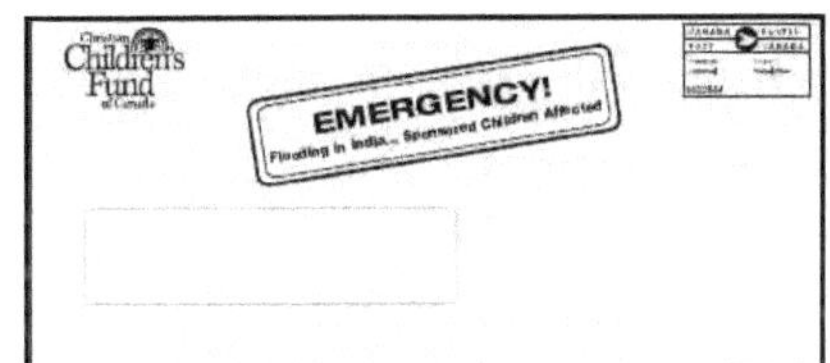

Letter (Front & Back)

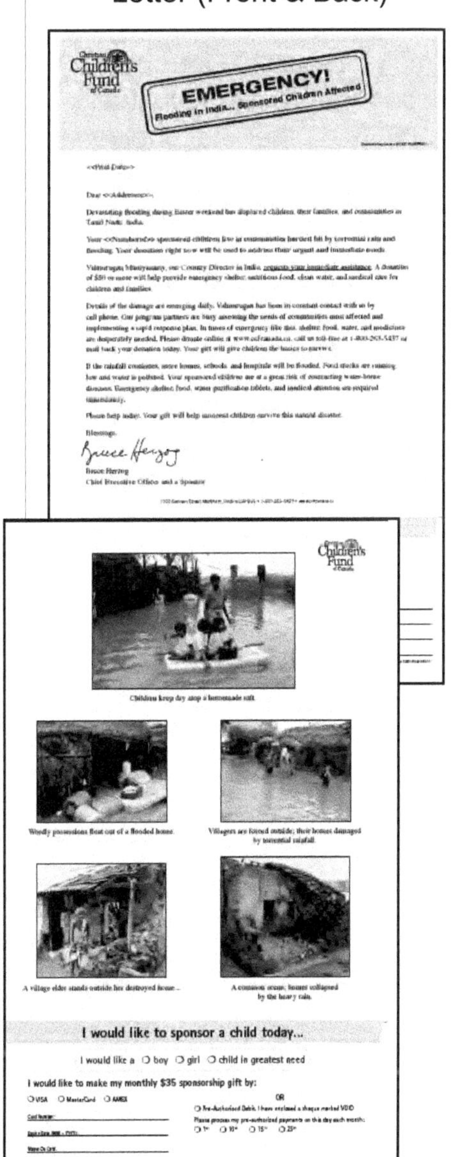
EMERGENCY!

I would like to sponsor a child today...

I would like a ○ boy ○ girl ○ child in greatest need

I would like to make my monthly $35 sponsorship gift by:

○ VISA ○ MasterCard ○ AMEX

OR

SOCIAL NETWORKING

Sometimes it seems like the whole world is busy ***facebooking, youtubing, myspacing*** *and* ***tweeting*** with little time to do anything else.

Many social network sites have millions of users. But, there is still debate about their real value to non-profit organizations.

On the one hand it is hard to be heard in the chaotic worlds of the web; on the other on-line social networking can make it possible for donors, board members, volunteers, staff and other stakeholders to interact with your organization and support an initiative.

Many claim that social networking has raised a ton of money, while others claim that, as of 2009, only 5% of charities have really benefited from social networking and most of them are still not in Canada.

3. **Cut copy way down.** Email recipients don't read, they scan for words and phrases of interest. Here's an effective copy-editing tip: Eliminate 50% of the words from the original copy, then go back and eliminate 50% more. It can be done and usually results in stronger copy with greater impact!

4. **Try using a video to capture your viewer's attention.** It engages, entertains and educates your constituents. Online video was the big trend in 2008. It helped attract millions of new and repeat subscribers to **YouTube, Facebook** and **MySpace** and it was part of a winning strategy used by **Obama** in his bid to win the election.

It can be a key technique for online engagement to help attract new viewers and a broader audience.

A FEW WORDS ABOUT SOCIAL MARKETING

There has been a tremendous buzz around social marketing. This 'friend help a friend' has worked for many charities sponsoring special events and getting people to rally around a cause to bring in new donations. However, many of these tend to be one-time gifts to support the activity highlighted in the email.

People who are engaged may lend their voices, but not necessarily their wealth. The only time they participate is when a friend urges them and generally their gift is a one-time donation and does not evolve into a loyal donor. Besides, this is a full-time job and your charity will need the necessary staff, the time, the hi-tech knowledge, a huge networking group and appropriate funds to pursue this properly.

The author's website below is quite simple.

CHANNEL 7
NEWSLETTERS
THE PERFECT WAY TO KEEP IN TOUCH WITH DONORS

LET US LOOK AT THREE IMPORTANT FACTS

First, what donors expect:

- Donors want to know how the money they gave was put to good use by a charity, What was the result of the project they gave the gift for?
- How effective is your organization in managing this money? How does it help promote and further the vision of the charity?
- How is the charity making a difference locally or globally?
- Did their help matter? Were they recognized for their contribution?

Second, what donors say:

A survey of donors found that the best ways to answer their questions is via newsletters.

Third, what donors really do:

Most donors seldom read the newsletters that charities send them.

Wait. We just said that donors like to have updates via newsletters but they don't read them? Most charities are under the illusion that the word newsletter by its very name should be a bearer of news so they fill it with:

- News about their office staff, or the inner workings of the organization;
- Photos of fundraising events with smiling people looking into the camera holding wine glasses;
- Articles about the cause.

All of which are the wrong things to put in a newsletter.

IT'S NOT ABOUT YOU.

The main purpose of creating a newsletter is showing your donor that he or she makes a difference. That should be the central message of your newsletter.

Your donor wants to hear one thing, that their giving matters.

This principle should guide all your decisions about your newsletter content.

So, ask yourself before you add any article in your next newsletter: "Does this demonstrate to my donor that his or her involvement matters?" If it doesn't, delete them.

Many charities can rely on Newsletter to generate funds from their donors.

One of the best ways to avoid these pitfalls is by not making these eight fatal mistakes:

MISTAKE 1

Forgetting the age-old 'WIIFM' (What's in it for me?) question. Your donors want to know how important a role their donation played.

This is the most important thing to keep in mind while writing your newsletter copy.

Use the word YOU often. It has strange magical powers. No other word, not We, Us or Ours, attracts the reader like the word, You.

Treat your newsletter as if it's a form of direct marketing letter. Direct your newsletter copy at your donors.

MISTAKE 2

Forgetting that a newsletter should have news that is relevant to the reader and worth reading.

Donors are not interested in what happened to your staff. They hardly know them.

When you write a newsletter, ask yourself: *"Why would this interest the donor?"* These are busy people. Is it any wonder that newsletters are the least read item you send to them?

MISTAKE 3

Forgetting that, like a commercial newspaper, the most read items are human-interest stories.

People give money to events like tsunamis or disasters because they have been moved by the plight of the people affected.

People give to help people; always keep that in mind. Make the stories interesting and involving.

MISTAKE 4

Forgetting donors want to know what you did with their money.

Make your newsletter 'donor centric'. Remember people don't give to your charity; they give through your charity. They want to help the cause you are working so hard for — be it improving the environment or people's lives.

Rephrase that popular saying from **Jerry McGuire**: "***Show me the money***" to ***"Show me what you did with my money."***

MISTAKE 5

Forgetting that your readers want to hear about your fiscal acumen.

They want reassurance that most of the money they donated went toward an important project and not toward administration, advertising or fundraising.

According to the *Chronicle of Philanthropy*, only 11% of donors think that the charities they support are doing a 'very good' job of spending money wisely.

The other 89% have their doubts as to how well the money is being spent.

To keep your donors on board, inform them as to how you spend their hard earned money. Merely including a pie chart with the breakdown of donations by percentage is really not enough.

MISTAKE 6

Forgetting your readers are already on overload.

Readers want to be able to skim through your newsletter quickly. We are all bombarded by over half-a-million dollars worth of commercial and media messages every day. As a result, today's audiences have developed a form of 'selective intake' mechanism.

Make it easy for the reader to skim through your material. Make your copy pleasing to the eye – capture their attention.

Cut down the number of words per sentence. Reduce the size of your articles.

MISTAKE 7

Forgetting to make your stories interesting.

Learn from newspapers as to what holds a reader's attention. Use headlines to first hook them. If your headlines aren't enticing enough to draw the reader's attention, your best article will never get read.

MISTAKE 8.

Forgetting to acknowledge your donors' support and hogging all the credit for your own accomplishments.

Your charity survives due to the generosity of your supporters, volunteers, sponsors and benefactors. They all need to be acknowledged.

Activities are what you do.

Accomplishments are why your charity matters to your supporters.

Donors are not attracted by your activities. They look for your accomplishments:
The reason they give to your charity is because you do something concrete, e.g., you give kids with physical disabilities a way of having fun and the opportunity to be self-reliant in the future and a chance to succeed in life.

This clearly demonstrates where their donations are going. Benefactors give you funds because they want to share in your accomplishments not because of the size of your organization or the number of counselors you employ at your camp.

CRAFTING THE NEWSLETTER

What kind of news you decide to feature will naturally depend on what you expect the newsletter to accomplish. Charities must consider two important aspects when planning newsletters:

1. **Think of the recipient; consider carefully what would make them want to read the newsletter.**
2. **What kind of internal news is meaningful to your readers?**

Writing for a newsletter is decidedly different from letter writing. Just like newspapers the format is different. Here is a structure to follow to make it newsworthy:

BOLD HEADLINE:

Be as intriguing as possible by playing with the theme in the article in a bold and captivating manner. It must summarize the key message in as few words as possible.

QUALIFYING LINE:

Explain the content of the article by giving meaning to your intriguing conceptual headline.

OPENING PARAGRAPH:

It must explain the main story as to what happened and its key features, accurately and clearly, and promise what's coming up in the article. It must connect the headline to the content you are about to present.

SUB-TITLES OR SUB-HEADS:

They help you break up your text into bite sized sections to lure skimmers into the story or make the story more palatable for the reader.

FOLLOWING PARAGRAPHS:

They present the full details in order of priority, explaining each new point in a new paragraph in a logical manner as to why it happened. Use a variety of sources if necessary; it must. however, read as a coherent train of thought.

CONCLUSION:

Highlight the point you are making. Draw a conclusion, include an editorial commentary or lead the reader to additional sources, if relevant.

PICTURES AND PICTURE CAPTIONS:

They help clarify and ensure the story makes sense.

You recall the story of Red Riding Hood, a bit of a yawner. Here's how it could have transpired if written in newspaper style.

Winter 2009

FUN RAISING TIMES

WOLF CAUGHT NAPPING IN DEAD WOMEN'S BED

Intended victim narrowly escapes

Headline

Qualifying Line

A cunning wolf was finally captured by the local police in an old lady's bed as he lay in it, after having eaten her. What seemed equally bizarre was that he was also wearing her clothes when the police nabbed him. A police spokesperson said, ***"I am not surprised because wolves are very sly and often try to disguise themselves."***

Opening Paragraph

Red riding hood was really the intended victim

Sub-Head

Earlier in the day the wolf had followed Red Riding Hood to the old lady's house. Miss Hood, granddaughter of the elderly woman, had made an apple pie and was going to deliver it to her beloved granny. The wolf confessed that the reason he was following her was because he really intended to eat the succulent Miss Hood and her pie.

Following Paragraph

Red riding hood pictured here safe after her harrowing ordeal with the big, bad wolf earlier today.

Picture & Caption

Artfully dodging behind trees and using stealth tactics, the wolf preceded Miss Hood into the house, gobbled up the sleeping granny, donned her nightie and was snuggled under the covers when Miss Hood arrived.

Investigators claim that the following conversation took place between the wolf and Miss Hood.

MH upon awakening her granny: ***"Grandmother, what big eyes you have."***

W: ***"The better to see you with, my dear."***

MH: ***"Grandmother, what sharp teeth you have."***

W: ***"The better to eat you with" as he lunged at the girl.***

However, Miss Hood had youth on her side, plus the fact she had not just eaten a huge meal, so she scampered away into the forest yelling for the police who were closing in accompanied by the animal control division.

Conclusion

Quick thinking by Little Red Riding Hood saved her as she ran from the wolf's jaws screaming. She will receive an Order of Merit for her bravery in helping bring this long sought predator to justice. She told reporters she will accept the medal in tribute to her departed grandmother. ■

HARD COPY vs. ELECTRONIC NEWSLETTERS

Make sure you provide your donors with a donation form and a (BRE) business reply envelope with your hard copy.

With electronic versions one should ask the recipients to go Online, fax, call a particular person or mail back a donation if they are so inclined. It is not necessary to push this, but do not neglect them either because even though this should be a soft sell, many donors are either touched or consider it a better method of giving

OTHER ELEMENTS TO ADD IN A NEWSLETTER

1. **Interviews with important people. This helps humanize your newsletter and makes it more appealing;**
2. **Hints. Short snippets of information can be very attractive;**
3. **Latest achievements;**
4. **Quizzes, contests and games. People love a challenge and these are good involvement devices;**
5. **Surveys. Involving and inviting donors to voice their opinions can be very beneficial;**
6. **A leveraged gift. Getting a sponsor to match gifts is a great way to increase funds.**

HOW TO RAISE FUNDS WITH NEWSLETTERS

Two simple ways to use a newsletter to raise funds from donors are:

1. Stories and visuals of one person in need creates more sympathy and funds than statistics. Donors give more to a charity when they read or hear about one individual as opposed to a group. People can make a stronger one-on-one connection with an individual rather than a vast faceless mass.
2. Donors are more likely to contribute to someone about whom they know one fact than to someone who they knew nothing about. This connecting through with the familiar can be helpful for charities using celebrity spokespersons or local known personalities that are viewed as charitable or warm people.

HOW TO GET YOUR MESSAGE ACROSS

When writing you have to give people the 'why' of a message before you can tell them the 'therefore.'

This is often referred to as framing, or context, because it opens the way to explain why a particular message is important.

Relevance is essential because, if you don't know what matters to your audience, how can you convince them to listen to what you have to say, never mind sell something to them? Try to see the world through your audience's eyes.

CASE STUDY

UNIVERSITY OF ST. MICHAEL'S COLLEGE

Background: On their 150th Anniversary **The University of St. Michael's College** launched a newsletter called ***Report to Donors**** that was part of their ***Faith, Hope & Charity*** Capital campaign.

Objective: To use the newsletter to raise funds by mailing it to two distinct groups—ex-graduates who had recently donated to the University and those who had not given.

Solution: The *Report to Donors* contained news about the different faculties that needed funding and listed the names and amounts given by the first group of donors.

An accompanying letter to the first group thanked them for their generosity.

The letter to non-donors pointed out the contributions made by their classmates.

Strategy: To thank the first group for their generosity and to show the second group the names and amounts of their generous classmates.

Result: The first newsletter collected over $55,000 from 305 people who had been in the non-donor part of the University's fundraising.

The next year it netted over $65,000 and now this newsletter has become a regular annual feature at the University.

* The *Report to Donors* is printed on newsprint

The first **Report to Donors** Newsletter

UNIVERSITY OF ST. MICHAEL'S COLLEGE

Celebrating our heritage, Building our future

Report to Donors

The President's Fund for Excellence in Research and Scholarship

Inside spread

Report to Donors 2003-2004

Successive Newsletters.

TYPES OF DONORS

OLD-TIMERS

People aged 75 and older are most comfortable with the old methods of fundraising such as direct mail and door-to-door.
THEY BELIEVE IN:

- Hard work
- Saving for a rainy day
- Respect for authority

WAR BABIES

Born between 1935–1945. Like old-timers, they too are comfortable with the traditional fundraising methods but are also tech savvy.

THEY BELIEVE IN:

- Saving for a rainy day
- Respect for authority

CHAPTER 8

TARGETING CONSUMERS

The two audiences that charities normally target when using direct marketing for fundraising are the general public and businesses.

Though different there are enormous similarities between these two groups. For starters both consist of people who are prospective customers.

Within these two categories, marketers select the desired audience (target group) most appropriate for their organization. This target group can be based on age, socio-economic status, sex, region, behaviour and lifestyle.

Reaching out and appealing to people is no different from selling. The same conditions, emotions and motivations that apply to good salesmanship also apply here. The biggest difference is that as a charity you are not selling something tangible, but something more elusive – a good feeling.

USING EMOTIONS

Fundraising is not just about asking for funds, it's also about inspiring others to embrace a good cause. In our clinical technology driven world, we lay too much emphasis on logic and reason.

We believe that what sets us apart from other species is our ability to work our way intellectually through problems.

Yet ironically, that's not what comes into play when we make many of our most important decisions.

Emotions, not reason, control many of our selection choices.

One of the most significant decisions we make has nothing to do with logic – the act of falling in love. It has little to do with reason. People don't coolly weigh the pros and cons of their attraction to one particular person.

Similarly people give to a charity from the heart and not from the head. Sure, logic is important but people generally give because they are moved, not because you have rationally presented a flawless argument.

Donors like to feel good. They like to feel warm or proud. They like to feel that their help has played an important part in what matters to them, be it the environment or saving lives. For the donor, writing that cheque is an act of love.

Emotions also lead us to buy certain brands for two reasons:

- One, we perceive them as better for us.
- Two, they make a statement about us.

Almost everything we choose makes a statement about us—our homes, our friends, our clothes, even the charity we support.

OUR DECISIONS ARE BASED ON TWO THINGS

We base our decisions on the external—being sold on a particular product or charity and the internal—justifying our choices.

So whoever is crafting the appeal—the head of the charity, a board member or a copywriter—their task is to sell to the donors while reassuring them that they are making a wise choice.

Even though the copy flow should be logical, the pitch has to be emotional.

CRAFTING THE MESSAGE

For starters, remember that we are all bombarded by over half a million dollars worth of commercial and media messages every day. As a result, today's audiences have become marketing resistant and have developed a form of selective intake mechanism.

More importantly, most recipients simply don't have enough time in their busy, complex lives to read anything other than material that interests them.

Howard Luck Gossage, a famous copywriter, once said: ***"Nobody reads an ad. People read what interests them ... and sometimes it's an ad or sometimes it's a direct mail piece."***

The decision to read or not to read comes down to one thing: Is the person interested in what you are saying and/or showing?

Although each generation is different they all have one thing in common—they are busy people. The reality is that they read very little of what we send them and this includes even the most loyal donors of a charity.

Too often they look at the package and go, *"Oh! Oh! They want money again,"* without reading the contents. Those who do look, either glance at the material or read less than 50%.

TYPES OF DONORS

BABY BOOMERS

Born between 1946 and 1964. This is the 'hippy' generation that marched to a different drummer. In this group women are the major givers.

THEY BELIEVE IN:
- Breaking rules
- Nostalgia

BUSTER OR GENERATION X

Born between 1965 and 1977. They are the true television generation who are comfortable donating by phone or online. They also participate in events.
THEY BELIEVE THAT:
- Irreverence is cool
- Communication means Electronic
- Life without computers is unimaginable

TYPES OF DONORS

BOOMLET OR GENERATION Y

Born from 1978 through 1992. The Internet age kids are into social media, networking and making small gifts and pledges online. They visit web sites that are youth-focused.

THEY BELIEVE THAT:

- Direct mail is un-cool
- They are event driven, web and e-mail literate and tend to scan not read.

Following old formulas of writing and design just don't seem to work like they once did. In his books: ***Purple Cow: Transform Your Business by Being Remarkable,*** and ***All Marketers Are Liars,*** **Seth Godin** stresses that the key to success is to find a way to stand out from the herd – to be the purple cow in a field of monochrome Holsteins.

How do we make our material interesting enough to get readers to pay attention?

FOUR WAYS TO GET PEOPLE TO PAY ATTENTION

1. SHOW OR TELL THEM SOMETHING NEW AND INTERESTING **(Tease them—arouse curiosity)**
2. TELL THEM SOMETHING THEY DON'T ALREADY KNOW **(Make it newsworthy)**
3. TELL THEM SOMETHING IN A UNIQUE WAY **(Give it a new slant)**
4. TELL THEM WHY THIS IS IMPORTANT RIGHT NOW **(Spur them to action)**

SHOW OR TELL THEM SOMETHING NEW AND INTERESTING

There are two ways to arouse curiosity. One way is to use words as in the example below. The outer envelope asks the question: **What's the biggest thing you can fit in an envelope?**

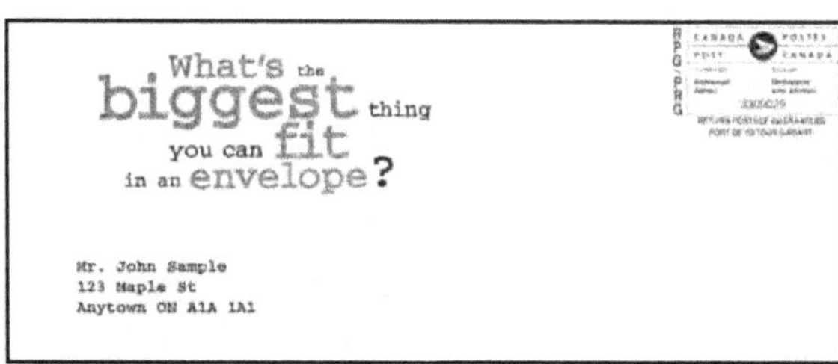

The folder alongside reveals the answer: **A child's dream**

Another way to catch someone's interest is with an item like a McGuffen. *(See page 67 or the Case Study on page 81 and 82).* A good reason for using a McGuffen to tell a story is because direct marketing is tactile — the recipients can touch and see what you send them.

TELL THEM SOMETHING
THEY DON'T ALREADY KNOW
(Make it newsworthy)

(See example of Hincks Ad alongside)

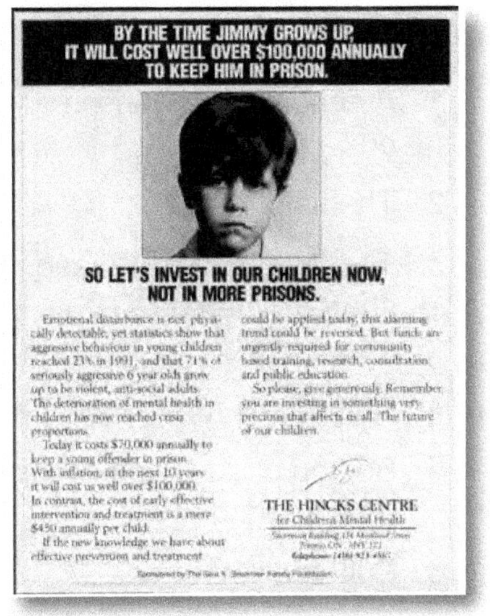

The Headline reads: BY THE TIME JIMMY GROWS UP, IT WILL COST WELL OVER $100,000 ANNUALLY TO KEEP HIM IN PRISON.

SO LET'S INVEST IN OUR CHILDREN NOW, NOT IN MORE PRISONS.

TELL THEM SOMETHING
IN A UNIQUE WAY
(Give it a new slant)

(See example of Oxfam Ad alongside)

The Headline: TEAMS OF WILLING WORKERS ARE NOW CLEANING UP THE BODIES IN EAST PAKISTAN.

Finding that the 'teams of willing workers' are vultures is the element of surprise.

TELL THEM WHY
THIS IS IMPORTANT RIGHT NOW
(Spur them to action)

(See FoodShare Case Study on pages 133 and 134)

The **FoodShare** mailing was aimed at loyal donors since the organization was being threatened with eviction. This direct appeal for help clearly gave donors a compelling reason to act immediately.

NEXT

After you have decided on your target audience go forward following this checklist of questions:

1. **Am I being donor-centric enough?"**

- Have I told my donors what amazing things the charity will do with their gifts?
- Have I mentioned worthwhile results? Real accomplishments?
- Did I celebrate the donor as a hero? Did I let them know, that this good work would not have been possible without their help?

WRITING & DESIGNING FOR BROWSERS

What catches a browser's attention?

1. A headline or Johnson box
2. The salutation
3. The first sentence (keep it short no more than 10 words)
4 Underlines (use sparingly)
5. Bolded or italic sentences (use sparingly)
6. Bulleted lists
7. The closing
8. Name of sender
9. The P.S.
10. Images (with captions)
11. Free offers (if any)

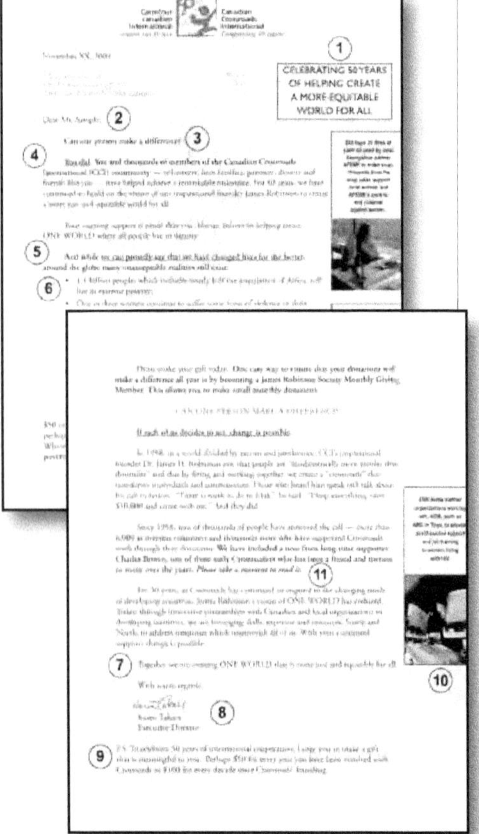

CELEBRATING 50 YEARS OF HELPING CREATE A MORE EQUITABLE WORLD FOR ALL

- Did I talk about the organization's cost efficiency? (*In survey after survey, donors often believe that charities are poorly run.*)

2. Make sure you are talking advantage of human psychology?
- Aim for the heart. Include all the emotional triggers that will spur people to donate;
- Make the tone conversational rather than formal.

3. Make sure the piece is graphically inviting and pleasing?
- Is it a quick easy read?
- Do the images help drive the narration? Are they compelling, not bland and predictable?
- Is the piece easily skimmed?
- Have the important elements that you want readers to retain been stressed? Have you used highlighting, underlining, sub-heads, etc. to help do this?

STORYTELLING. A GREAT WAY TO INCREASE RESPONSE

Storytelling has always been the most powerful way to got people absorbed. As children we could not get enough. As adults a book can enrapture us. A best-selling movie always has a good storyline.

And then there's the famous direct mail piece that generated over two billion dollars in subscriptions for the *Wall Street Journal.*
It started with the line:

"On a beautiful late spring afternoon, twenty-five years ago, two young men . . ."

Right away you can tell that it's a story and you are hooked and want to know more.

SOME HELPFUL COPY TIPS

TIP 1: Get them from the start.

The most important part of your message is the first line.

Imagine you are watching TV, flicking channels, and suddenly something catches your attention and you stop to watch. The first line acts just the same way. It's your best, and maybe your only, chance to capture your reader's interest.

It must have stopping power. Research shows you have only three seconds to grab your audience's attention and carry them forward into your message.

TIP 2. Get them involved.

Involvement devices always improve results. This can be anything from scratch cards to peel and attach 'Yes' or 'No' stickers.

(Example: Make-A-Wish 'Get Well Cards' alongside)

This Make-A-Wish mailing included a 'Get Well' card on which a donor could write a message to a child and send it back with a donation. It was instrumental as an involvement device and helped generate more funds.

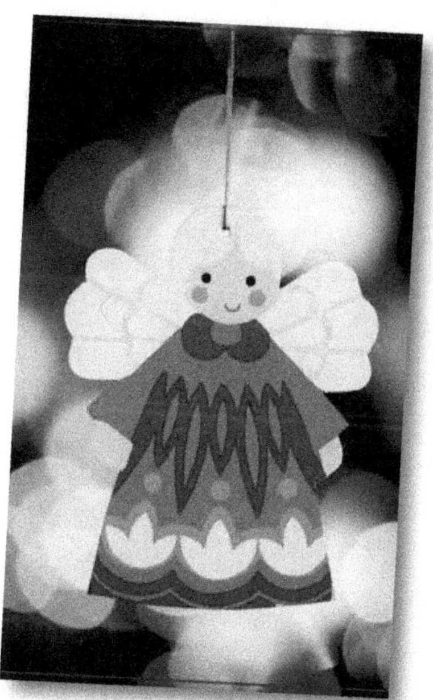

TIP 3: Show and Tell

There are two styles of writing: 'Showing' and 'Telling'.

If I said, "The girl was beautiful." I am merely telling the reader something about a particular person.

But if I said, "I was stunned by the lady in the yellow dress, by her beauty and elegant grace as she walked with her shoulders erect and her head held back. With each step her golden curls bounced ever so lightly. Her perfume drifted in the air and her blue eyes were wide and sparkling."

Now I am showing you something that you can imagine. The moment the reader can visualize the picture you're trying to paint, you're showing them, not telling them.

Most adjectives like, 'beautiful, attractive, fabulous or fascinating' are words that 'tell' us what to think. They don't reveal in specifics what is unique about the person or event you are describing.

As a writer you have the power to take charge and draw your readers, so show them rather than tell them.

TIP 4: Research on writing has revealed that the number of words in a sentence directly affect comprehension.

TIP 5: Large blocks of copy are best digested in bite-sized portions.

Long copy can be daunting to the reader. Smaller blocks look like less work.

(Example: FoodShare *letter alongside)*

Many people are doing everything they can, yet they are having trouble buying food to feed their families

Dear Friend,

I'm writing because they need your help.

Some have lost jobs

Some are single parents on social assistance who have had their benefits cut by 20 percent.

Some are what's referred to by policy makers as the 'working poor' – people who have a full-time job but still don't earn enough money to make ends meet.

TIP 6: Sections that are varied to look visually different are easier to absorb.

Having to plow through information that all looks the same can lead to boredom and a bored reader is a lost reader.

(See **International Eye Foundation** *example below)*

Enclosed is a book of famous lullabies especially for you. Let me tell you why . . .

Dear Friend,

In the enclosed book of lullabies you will find the most famous lullaby "Hush little baby don't you cry" right at the start of the book.

There's a good reason for that; lullabies have always provided a soothing way to help children fall asleep all over the world.

Mothers in many developing countries have their babies strapped to their backs and sing to them as they go about their day. They sing them to sleep and they sing to them when they cry.

But there are some things no song can soothe.

It is difficult enough to get a child to sleep when they are still hungry or malnourished. It is harder still when the child is sick and in danger of losing his or her sight.

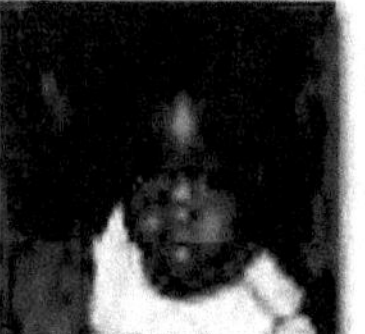

Just like the little girl Yama, who lives in a part of Africa that has the highest rate of river blindness.

This beautiful child was always full of life and energy. Just watching her smile and giggle filled one's heart with joy.

But when Yama developed a skin rash and little nodules on her head, the constant itching was so severe it made her often cry all night.

TIP 7: Follow the old KISS rule: Keep it Simple Stupid.

A 50-year old book by **Rudolf Flesch** called *The Art of Readable Writing* is chock full of great advice. You probably no longer can buy the book but there is a website based on his principles that let's you evaluate your copy.

Go to www.resources.aellalei.com/tools/writer/sample.php

You simply drop in your text and the website analyzes it for readability.

It will tell things like your average number of words per sentence or the average number of syllables per word. It will even tell you for what grade level you have written

For example: If you use 20 words per sentence with 1.5 syllables per word, you'll receive a 'Flesch Reading Score' of 60-70, which corresponds to the 8th/9th grade English level.

This is probably where you want your score to be because at this level people can quickly read your letter with easy comprehension.

TIP 8: Pay attention to your retention.

Why is this important?

Because when you fail to renew a donor, you lose any repeat gifts and the donor's potential for lifetime value.

Many charities find that renewal rates from first-time donors often drop by as much as 50%. Ninety percent of the remainder drop by the wayside within five renewal campaigns.

How do you stop this erosion?

You make subsequent mailings very specific about what the donor helps accomplish.

Any one who has run a campaign knows that being specific about the use of donations yields better results. Designated giving is a commitment by a charity to use donors' gifts for a specific purpose. This gives the donor a better understanding of why the funds are needed and makes for a more compelling solicitation.

(See **FoodShare** *Case study on page 133)*

TIP 9: Never miss a chance to send a reminder mailing.

Reminder mailings are key to lifting your response; most will bump up the response by as much as 2% to 4%.

Reminder mailings not only prompt those donors who set the mailing aside with good intentions for later but also gives you the opportunity to report on the progress of the fundraising and talk about what is still needed and why.

Giving your donors measurable results will spur more donors to give again.

(See **University of St. Michael's College** *example alongside)*

TIP 10: Finally, from time to time add a streak of outrage.

Vent your frustration. Get mad. If you aren't passionate about your cause then how can you convince others to be?

Besides it also makes the mailing memorable. Don't just preach social responsibility but evoke it too.

(See **Springtide Resourses** *Case Study on page 62 and* **CANFAR** *Case Study on page 87)*

THE ADVANTAGES OF SENDING YOUR DONORS A REMINDER MAILING CANNOT BE STRESSED ENOUGH.

Below is a reminder mailing from **The University of St. Michael's College**. It was sent to those who had not yet donated, reminding them with a no-nonsense bar chart that the university was still falling short of its target of $1.2 million.

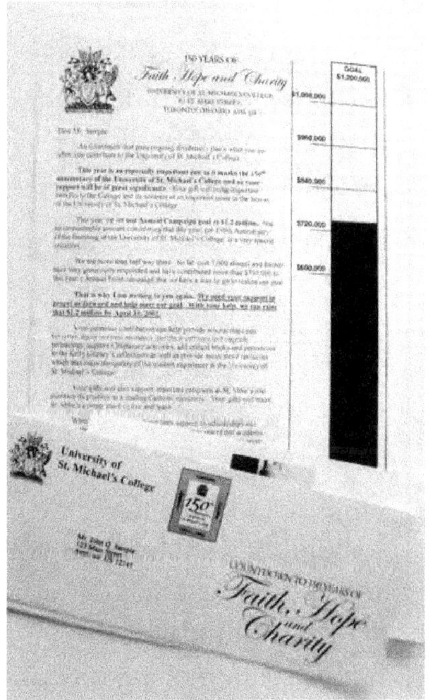

This reminder mailing quickly made up the shortfall.

CASE STUDY

FOODSHARE (Corporate Moving Campaign)

Background:: In the spring of 2006, FoodShare was informed that their main office and warehouse, currently at 200 Eastern Avenue, would have to to move to a new location.

They found a space at 90 Crotia Street, after having worked out a deal with city, provincial and federal officials to ensure that the relocation to their new home would be at no cost to them.

However moving could not interfere with:

- Children who were part of **FoodShare's Field to Table Program** and would still need fresh vegetables daily in over 90 schools;
- The **Good Food Box Program** that provided fresh affordable food to to thousands in the city could not stop;
- The **Good Food at Home program** for women during their cancer treatment relied on their 'Wellness Box' daily;

And deliveries had to be made without a hitch to the many shelters, seniors and other marginalized people.

Plus, a lot of work needed to be done to the new premises including constructing a new greenhouse and a new kitchen that needed to be completely gutted and refurbished.

Objective: To launch a **Rebuilding Capital Campaign** and request new and current donors for funds for the reconstruction of a greenhouse and new kitchen.

Joe Sample
123 Any Street
Any Where AA A1A 1A1

HELP US
REPLANT
OURSELVES

Outer envelope

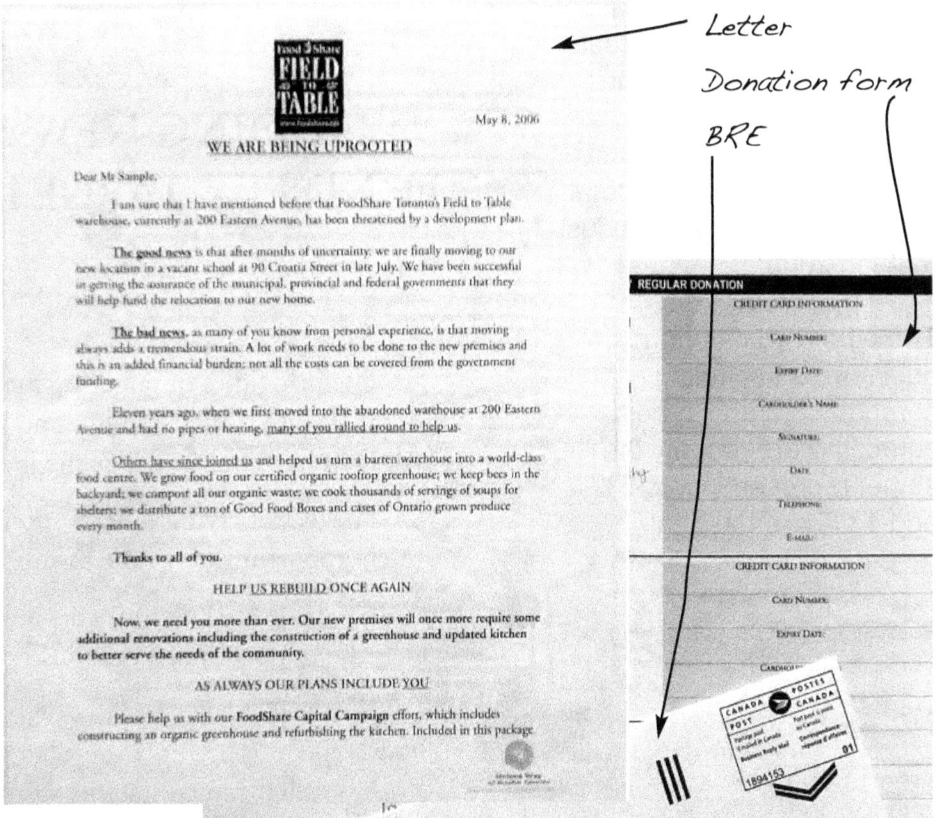

Letter

Donation form

BRE

Solution: Donors could gift either $500 towards both the greenhouse and the kitchen or $250 to either project in one lump sum or in installments. In return the contributing individual's name or their company's name would be inscribed on a branch of a 'Family Tree'. For just $250, either towards the greenhouse or the kitchen, a leaf would bear their name. This tree would be part of a beautiful at entranceway to the greenhouse.

Strategy: To demonstrate complete transparency, this package consisted of the following elements:

- A 9" x 12" outer envelope,
- 4 page letter
- 2 page donation form
- BRE
- Floor Plans, showing the two key projects – Greenhouse & Kitchen).

Result: Within a very short period of time they received pledges from 10.45% of the 7,000 people they had mailed to and collected close to $250,000 in pledges.

Floor Plans

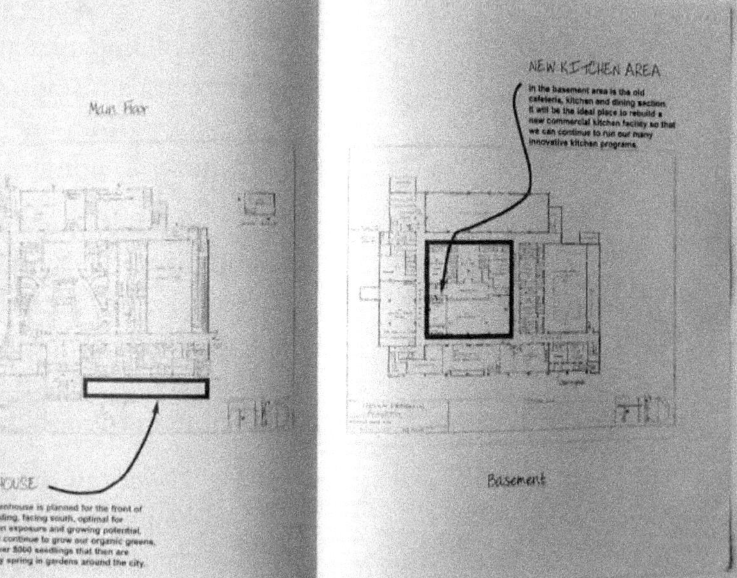

In 2006, 52% of healthcare giving came from individuals, compared to 61% in 2005.

Non-corporate foundations contributed 9.7% of the total in that year, compared to just 3.5% in 2006.

The other two categories, businesses (including corporations) and 'other sources' were roughly the same, representing 25.6% and 13.0% of the total, respectively.

Source: AFP Report on Giving

CHAPTER 9

FINDING NEW SOURCES FOR FUNDS BY TARGETING BUSINESSES

The principles of targeting businesses for direct marketing fundraising are similar to targeting individuals but are aimed at small firms and businesses at the local level.

This is not trying to gain sponsorship tie-ins but it could lead to such opportunities in the future.

The best prospects for corporate fundraising are those for which the nonprofit can demonstrate that there is a strategic payoff for both parties.

For example:

- A hospital can contact its vast network of suppliers and pharmaceutical firms to request contributions;
- Performing arts groups can point out the advantages to businesses of increasing traffic into the community
- Universities can approach firms who will benefit from hiring their well-trained graduates.

THE KEY DIFFERENCES OF TARGETING BUSINESS VERSUS CONSUMERS

Companies are in business to make money, not give it away. The company's priorities are its customers, shareholders, employees and the bottom line, so why would they give money, time, and resources to nonprofit organizations?

Corporate giving can advance a company's business objectives, its visibility and its standing in the community. They recognize the worth of the 'reflected glory' of associating their names with nonprofits. They also have a commitment to being good corporate citizens and will pay serious attention to a charity's obligation to social responsibility.

1. **Fewer but more expensive mailing packages will be needed.** You have to convince business owners that it makes sense for them to donate. Often these packages include cascading sheets of information, an annual report, testimonials or Lift Notes.

Your package must get past the so called 'Gatekeeper' (secretary, receptionist or who ever opens the mail). Often they are in charge of making the decision to pass on your fundraising piece to the right person. If it looks at all like junk mail, it may get tossed.

2. **Business donations are larger and more varied:**
   - **Donations.** Corporations can provide direct cash to a particular program, an event or both.
   - **In-kind support.** In-kind support could consist of donated products, equipment, services or space. Since in-kind support is easier and less expensive for a company to provide than a monetary gift, seeking it might be your first step in building a lasting relationship with a particular business.
   - **Employee involvement.** Some companies have employee volunteer programs. They might offer valuable services such as tutors for a school or executive staff for a charity in need of accounting expertise or help with public relations. Companies also make small matching gifts to organizations where their employees volunteer or donate.
   - **Non-philanthropic support.** Corporate help can also take the form of cause-related marketing (CRM). The funding comes not from money contributed for charitable contributions but from assistance such as marketing. *For example,* an advertising agency may produce all the advertising materials and public service ads (PSAs) for a charity in return for their own exposure.
3. **There is high likelihood that a corporation will commit to a steady stream of repeat business.**
4. **Partnership opportunities or event sponsorship are quite likely.**
5. **Corporate and employee support often provides a new source of volunteers.**

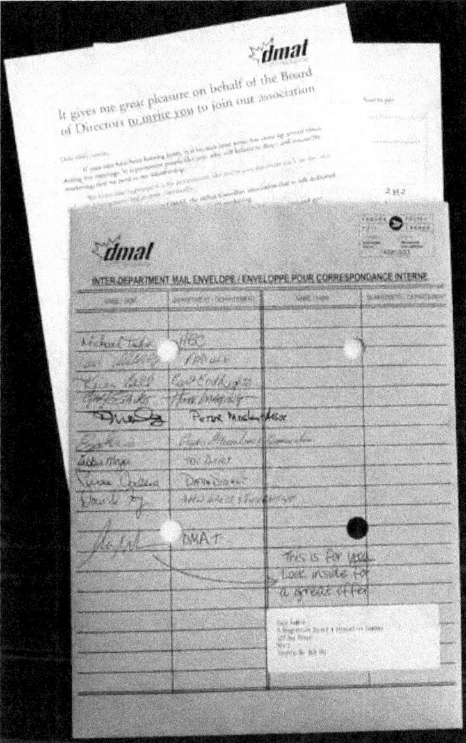

One way to break through the clutter and bypass the 'gatekeeper' is by the clever use of an Inter-department mail envelope.

This successful membership drive from the Direct Marketing Association of Toronto (DMAT) was sent to important people in the direct marketing community.

PEOPLE GIVE TO PEOPLE

This is especially true in soliciting funds from local businesses. Many valuable long-term relationships and sponsorship opportunities first begin as personal acquaintances. However, the biggest challenge is finding the right person in a business to contact.

Employees are constantly coming and going. It has been estimated that within a few years, 62% of a firm's people will either

This elaborate business package contained:

- Letter
- Donation form
- Lift-note
- Newsletter
- Booklet identifying the key players of the organization
- Annual Report
- BRE (Business Reply Envelope)

move within the company or leave for another one. This makes it hard for a charity to gain access to the right person.

Business lists are often too small and too expensive. The most successful lists are the ones painstakingly created by an organization using a variety of methods ranging from cold calls to referrals.

Companies differ in size, ownership and activity, so research is needed to determine the people who will best respond to your organization.

The initial direct marketing initiative may require targeting different people within the same firm. A multi-pronged approach is necessary to ensure that the right decision-makers receive the right information.

Lead generation may be initiated in various ways:

- As a cold call asking the receptionist who the best contact would be;
- As a website inquiry;
- Through someone who knows someone;
- Through networking.

Two important issues to be addressed – PERMISSION MARKETING and RELEVANCE.

PERMISSION MARKETING (opt-in or opt-out) is a whole new terminology that has surfaced because people are barraged with unwanted emails, traditional mail and phone calls.

Any list that does not have permission from its recipients to receive a solicitation risks not only irritating the receiver but also damaging the reputation of the organization sending the solicitation. Indeed new privacy laws make solicitation without permission illegal in many cases.

RELEVANCE. The list needs to be relevant to the product or the service being marketed, otherwise it wastes the receiver's time and the sender's money.

WHICH BENEFITS SHOULD A CHARITY PITCH?

Think in terms of mutual benefits for you and your corporate target group.

- Through a partnership with a non-profit, businesses can expand markets and access new sources and customers – WIIFM (What's In It For Me) factor;
- Increase employee morale and productivity;

- Increase customer loyalty;
- Enhance their image.

In addition to cash donations and volunteer support, there are other ways that non-profits can carry out their goals. More and more non-profits are turning to businesses to help lever support and to expand their limited reach and resources. In turn corporations see value in cause-related marketing, an arrangement by which a corporation seeks to increase its own sales by contributing to a charity. There are three methods of cause-related marketing:

- Corporations issue promotions;
- Businesses and charities jointly issue promotions;
- Portion of product sales go to a charity.

A business package for **Canadian Cancer Society**.

TYPE OF HELP	Description
Cause Promotions *Example*:	Supporting social causes by providing funds, in-kind contributions or other methods to increase awareness of the cause. **Bell Canada** has been a long-time sponsor of **Kids Help Phone.**
Cause Related Marketing *Example*:	Making a contribution or donating a percentage of revenue to a cause, based on sales. **Tim Hortons** donates coffee sales and collects public donations to send kids to camps.
Corporate Social Marketing *Example:*	Supporting behaviour change to improve health, safety, the environment or community welfare. **Nissan Canada** partners with **Meals on Wheels** to deliver hot lunches to the elderly.
Corporate Philanthropy *Example:*	Making a direct contribution to a charity as cash or in-kind services. **CIBC's Walk for the Cure,** contributes to the fight against breast cancer.
Community Volunteering *Example:*	Providing volunteers to the community. **Toronto Transit Commission** staff selling pizzas for **United Way.**
Socially Responsible Business Practices *Example:*	Adopting practices to support social causes. **Body Shop** promoting a ban on use of animals to test cosmetics.

CASE STUDY
SECOND HARVEST

Background: Second Harvest's mandate is built on a simple premise: there is surplus food in Toronto that goes to waste while people in the city go hungry.

Second Harvest drivers pick-up surplus perishable food from food stores, restaurants, etc. and distribute it the same day in their refrigerated trucks to over 120 agencies including churches, soup kitchens, drop-in shelters, social housing and inter-related agencies.

Objective: In the summer of 2001, Second Harvest was facing their most serious decline in food distribution in their 16-year history so something had to be done.

Solution: Appeal to people in Toronto to help feed the hungry.

Strategy: To raise awareness and recruit more companies to supply Second Harvest with food donations, a direct marketing program was developed to get information directly into the hands of decision makers within food companies around the GTA.

Creatively, the corporate direct mail package took an innovative approach by directly mailing senior executives a personalized proposal telling why their company should donate to a Food Recovery Program for Second Harvest.

Results: Second Harvest Food Donations reached 3.8 million pounds that year, exceeding the projection by 50%. This success was achieved with a total fundraising budget of only $30,000.

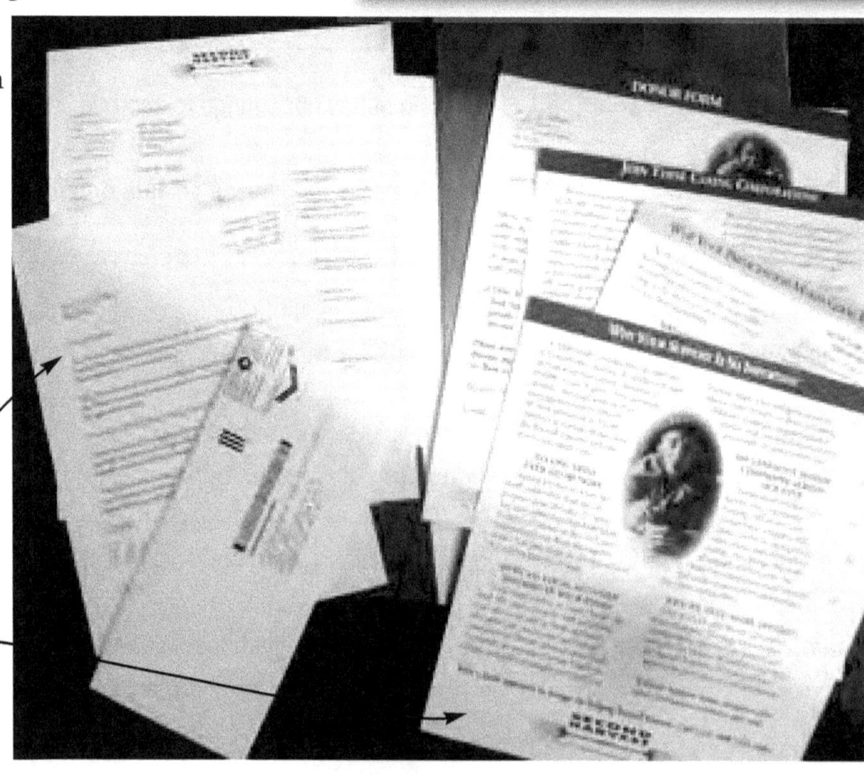

*A Lift Note by **Lucio Di Clemente**, President of **The Beer Store** accompanied the main letter*

Various sheets outlined the problem and solution

CHAPTER 10

DONOR STEWARDSHIP

Donors are a charity's most precious commodity and should be treated with respect and sensitivity

Acknowledge generosity promptly. Studies show a fast 'thank you' increases both individual and corporate donations. Also essential is making them feel confident that their gifts have begun to work as intended.

Welcome new donors into the family. Give a first-time donor additional information about your organization. Consider sending them a welcome package with small inexpensive tokens of your appreciation such as a calendar, bookmark or magnet. You could even get your volunteers to reach out to them with a 'thank you' phone call and better yet, ask new donors if they'd like to volunteer.

Start a two-way communication. Make it easy for donors to interact with the charity. Be sure to include a reply form and return envelope. Ask for corrections. Give them a chance to ask questions. Allow them to drive the relationship. Give them options as to how often they would like to be contacted. Would they like to receive newsletters, notices of events. Offer the option to receive communications by email and do all this before requesting another gift.

Most important of all, listen to your donors.

ACKNOWLEDGING GIFTS PROMPTLY

A study showed that 84% of individual donors and 83% of corporate donors voiced dissatisfaction about the quality of information and appropriate response they receive from the charity they have just supported.

The very least that most donors expect after they have made a contribution is:

1. Prompt personal acknowledgement of their gift;
2. Confirmation that the gift has been used for the purpose for which it was intended;

SURPRISE AND DELIGHT

The commercial world often uses a powerful tool called loyalty reward programs to secure and retain their best customers. It's called **'surprise and delight.'**

Often it is just an unanticipated **'thank you'** or unexpected **'recognition.'**

Both of these gestures are immensely valuable because of the old saying, **"it's the thought that counts."**

A rewards program can be an extremely valuable and powerful tool and yet charities very often fail to include this little gesture in their direct marketing plans.

Research shows that an extremely high number of Canadian charities send thank-yous, tax receipts, even simple acknowledgments of donations weeks, even months, after the gifts have been received—and sometimes, not at all.

How hard can it be to thank your donors warmly and promptly for their generosity?

This is especially astounding in an age of instant gratification and is a huge mistake that is guaranteed to to offend your donors and turn them into lapsed donors.

3. Measurable results achieved by the gift;
4. Updates about the status of the project or promotion for which the gift was requested.

Donors give to a charity because it is their way of sharing their good fortune with others, a way to help those less fortunate. A philanthropic deed is an emotional connection due to a personal experience, a family tradition or purely an altruistic wish to give back to society.

This emotional connection is delicate and should be nurtured. A donor's feelings can be easily hurt if they don't hear back quickly and especially if when they do hear it is in the form of a lacklustre standardized note that says:

On behalf of (Charity ABC) we wish to sincerely thank you for your recent donation of $XX

This is neither sincere nor personal and yet many charities continue to compose such dreadful thank-you notes. Worse still, many even have the gall to ask for an additional gift with their initial thank-you notes. Good manners play an important role in the lasting impression the donor has of your organization.

EXAMPLES OF HOW IT SHOULD BE DONE

Just like fundraising letters work best when they come from the heart, so do letters of appreciation.

Some tips for acknowledging gifts from High Value Donors:

1. **Your very first line is key to conveying your excitement and gratitude.** It should be a casual one-to-one communication and not business-like. Don't use 'corporate-speak' or 'committee-speak'. Avoid words like 'We' and 'Our', 'On behalf of', etc.

   Try something like this instead:

   Imagine my great surprise and utter delight when I walked into my office this morning and there on my desk was a donation from you.

2. **Have your closest link to the donor send the thank-you.** This could be a staff member, a board member or a client – whoever knows the donor best. Have them personally sign the thank you note in blue ink.
3. **If the donor's surname is printed in the greeting, have the person signing it scratch through the name and hand-write the first name.**

Also ask them to add a short personal note in the margin as shown below:

Hi John,
~~Dear Mr. Sample~~,

Your gift came in just at the right time. Thank-you

4. **Use a P.S. as you would in a normal letter.** It adds another touch of one-to-one communication between you and the donor.

   You can use the P.S to drive them to your website, tell them of upcoming events, give them a progress report or alert them to mailings and newsletters they can expect soon.

5. **Make the donors feel good about their generosity.** Tell them how their gift is being used, how it has helped the charity or how it will help ensure the vitality of your organization's mission.

6. **Add a way they can contact you in case they have any questions or wish to know more about a particular program.** Give them your phone number and/or your email address.

7. **Finally, if you or another staff member does not have a flair for writing,** I highly recommend that you hire a writer for this very important piece of communication, just like you do for your direct mail solicitations.

Thanking people quickly and warmly is crucial to ensure that your loyal donors stay and don't stray. Many donors also give to other charities. You want to build a warm relationship so they will think of you first when making donation decisions.

And remember this is a thank-you note. Make sure it is donor-focused with plenty of 'you, yours' in it.

Have a professional writer look at your current thank-you letter and make some suggestions or even draft a few new versions for you.

If you cannot respond quickly, then make a spontaneous phone call to your donors – regardless of the size of their donation. It will go a long way toward building a lasting bond. Just showing your appreciation does amazing things.

Remember, donor attrition occurs as a result of long silences or dull, standard responses. Your donors will come to the conclusion that:

1. The charity doesn't appreciate or need me.
2. The charity is not living up to its mandate.

How to craft an educational survey

1. Ask only questions about the charity that will illustrate its value.
2. Readers are more likely to finish a survey if it's not just 'yes' or 'no' options. Offer 'Undecided' or 'Not sure' in case their opinion differs from the norm.
3. More questions should lean towards a 'yes' option because many surveys end with asking the reader to take action such as signing a petition or making a memorial gift. It's hard to say no after having said yes to question after question.
4. Allow the readers space to express themselves with comments or suggestions. This way you learn more about what matters to them.
5. Always ask for a phone number or an email address in case you need clarification on some comments.
6. Keep the questions manageable; don't ask more than 11 questions. Odd numbers work best.
7. Don't forget a 'Thank You' at the end for the time and effort they have put into answering the survey.

Keep these facts in mind - on average many charities find that 50% of first time donors never give again and those who do gradually become lapsed donors after five renewal campaigns. Make sure your donors look forward to hearing from you

WELCOMING NEW DONORS INTO THE FAMILY

There are many ways to keep people interested. If you can afford it, send your first-time donors a welcome kit and include things such as:

1. A welcome letter saying how pleased and thankful you are to have them involved;
2. A statement about your overall mission with a synopsis of your core programs;
3. Contact info including your website address, a directory of key people, their job responsibilities, email addresses and phone numbers;
4. You could even include a donor preference survey. This is the first step to starting a two-way conversation with your donors asking questions like:
   - How often would you like to receive info or mailings?
   - What is the best way to contact you, phone number or email address?
   - How would they like to receive information – regular mail, email, fax?
   - Do you have a preferred method of donation – mail, phone, fax, online?
5. A low-key planned giving brochure;
6. Forms to make memorial or tribute gifts;
7. Brochure or leaflet outlining monthly giving benefits or a sustainer program;
8. A bookmark, calendar or magnet;
9. The charity's most recent newsletter;
10. High Value Donors should receive the charity's annual report.

DO NOT ASK FOR A GIFT AT THIS TIME!

STARTING A TWO-WAY COMMUNICATION

Activities like the ones just mentioned start a two-way communication with your donors and let you get to know each other better. Just be sure that you pay attention to their preferences and build their confidence by showing them you care about their wishes.

Alert your staff that if someone does contact them, they should keep careful notes to pass on to the person in charge of your database. Such notes are priceless when tailoring an approach. Knowledge is power and anything that you find out about your donors should be recorded and respected.

THE ART OF KEEPING A DONOR

The art lies in building and fostering a strong bond with your supporters. This is best achieved through compelling communications and quick responses to their generosity.

- Your appeal must give a persuasive reason for giving and should identify the financial goals essential to your charity;
- Work to understand your donors and offer them an appropriate plan of action;
- When a gift comes in, send a thank you promptly.

THE SCIENCE OF KEEPING A DONOR

The science is how you use the data, research and testing methods available to you.

- **Segment your donor files.** Remember the RFM (Recency, Frequency and Monetary Value) rules of direct marketing.
- **Spend more time, effort and money on people who have given more recently, more frequently and more generously.** They are the most likely to give again and could very well keep increasing their donation amounts.
- **They are also the ones who need to be constantly reminded about your organization and should receive more communication pieces annually.**
- **Research and test what works best for which group of donors.**
- **Use data mining to determine affinity for giving.** Some donors have a higher propensity to give than others. You could determine this by researching their lifestyle behaviour and or just by noting their postal or area codes.
- **Track your donors' giving history in terms of size and frequency of giving.**

MOTIVES FOR GIVING

Although there are many motives for giving, the following are the main reasons:

- Recognition
- Altruism
- Sympathy
- Empathy
- Self-esteem, self-interest
- Guilt
- Pity
- Social injustice
- Fear
- Reciprocation—paying back
- A gift in memoriam
- Prestige gained

KNOW YOUR DONORS

New donors are first time givers.

Transition donors are those who give sporadically. They have a history of giving once in a while in a 16-24 month period.

Core donors are those who have given a gift to the charity regularly either each year or within sixteen months.

High Value Donors are those who give big gifts.

Lapsed donors are those who have stopped giving. They fall into two categories:

- **Recently Lapsed donors** who have not given in the last 13-24 months;
- **Deeply Lapsed donors** who have not given in the past 25 months.

KNOW HOW TO DEAL WITH EACH GROUP INDIVIDUALLY

Most direct mail fundraising is designed on a volume-driven model with little regard for individual donors.

As a consequence, charities often find that renewal rates can fall by as much as 50% after a donor's first contribution. Worse still almost 80% of donors gradually fade off in less than five years and move to the lapsed category.

ADDITIONAL TIPS FOR KEEPING NEW DONORS

- **An early second gift appeal.** Ask them again within six to twelve weeks after their first gift. Invite them to become monthly donors or to give online. People who have just given are considered '**Hot Line**' givers so appealing to them again quickly makes sense.
- **Since on average only 50% of first time donors make a second gift, it is essential to approach new donors again quickly.** Many have the potential to become lifetime value (LTV) donors.
- **Present new donors with a strong incentive like a matching gift opportunity.**
- **Send your second request with a newsletter which shows good use of funds.**

- **Send them a first-year anniversary package in which you remind them of their gift amount and ask if they are able to up it a bit.**
- **Should you need to, send a reminder mailing after your approach.**

However, do not send more then two solicitations in the first year and always abide by any wishes they have expressed.

TRANSITION DONORS

Transition donors give sporadically to a charity. They are the occasional givers who sometimes give to a direct mail appeal or perhaps to a newsletter. They are the hardest to gauge as to when, how often or by what method you should approach them.

- **Some display a definite pattern of giving while others do not. Some give only to specific programs or events, others give only during certain times.**
- Odds are, if these donors do display a certain pattern of giving, then it is your job to figure what those patterns are and contact them appropriately;
- **Transition donors are also telling you something very important**—that they like your charity but obviously there is something that is holding them back from giving more often. It could be that they are retired or have large families with limited funds. They could also be upset by the lack of response from you or because they feel that you consistently keep mailing the same message all the time.

This very important group needs your attention. You should contact them either by phone or in person or through a survey to find out why they don't give more often. Perhaps they would like to give online on their own terms and time, or only give to certain appeal. You must find out before you mail to them again.

CORE DONORS

Core donors are your bread and butter. They regularly make a donation to your charity. They like and support your organization. By what methods and how often should you approach them?

- **Try and move them to monthly giving** because as monthly donors you are not hitting them up for money constantly. However always include a soft ask for an immediate contribution if they resist becoming monthly donors.
- **Keep a note of how often they give and when they give.** Try to figure out their giving behaviour pattern. After they have

In 2001 **Integra**, a children's mental health centre that specializes in helping children with learning disabilities, mailed a Christmas appeal that contained personalized bookmarks to a very select group of High Value Donors.

The result: Integra collected $10,600 and got a 45% response.

How valuable was that?

Would the donors discard a bookmark with their own name on it? Not in a million years. As **Dale Carnegie** said: *"There's no sweeter music than the sound of your own name."*

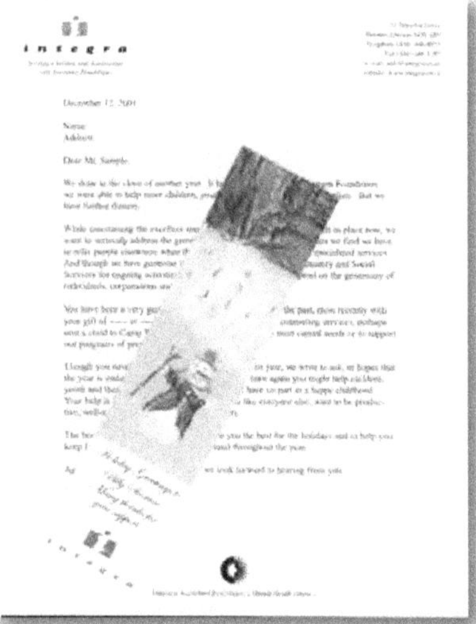

given in a year according to their normal pattern, you should stop soliciting them. You can send information within the same year but don't ask for money. They respect your charity so you must respect them too.

The last thing you want to do is alienate this group. **If there is a way to reward them, do so as often as you can.**

HIGH VALUE DONORS

High Value Donors are those who give big gifts – they are the 'saviors' of the charity.

You want to keep them involved and informed but should not overpower them. Do not include them in your mass marketing initiatives. They have to be treated differently.

- **Send them a closed-face large envelope** with their address hand-written and include a live stamp.
- **Ideally ask them only once a year in the form of an 'Annual Renewal' mailing. Include a detailed reply form which offers different ways they might respond. Print everything on high quality stock.**
- **Include a return envelope with a live stamp.**
- **Mention their last gift amount and date they made it and thank them for the gift.**
- **Tell them what their last gift accomplished, who it helped.**
- **Tell they what your needs are now.**
- **Have the sender personally sign the letter and add a P.S.**
- **Give them details about scheduling – when you need their gift. These are busy people and want making a decision to be as easy as possible.**
- **You could also indicate that you welcome gifts of stocks and securities, life insurance or a mention in their will.**

Understand a High Value Donor's true ability to give. The key to successful major gifts fundraising from these donors is having the right solicitor ask them for the right amount for the right campaign at the right time.

TRANSITION, CORE and HIGH VALUE DONORS are your most important givers. Treat them with the utmost respect and care because if they feel over-solicited and undervalued, they will take their money elsewhere.

LAPSED DONORS

- **Recently Lapsed Donors** should be included in the regular annual schedule of mailing. However, it is a hit and miss situation with them whether they will respond or not. They are not deeply committed to your organization and it may be best to include them as part of an acquisition mailing.
- **Deeply Lapsed donors** have very clearly indicated that they are not committed to your charity so to continue sending them a solicitation year after year is a waste of time and money. It may be more prudent to contact them by telephone to see if you can win them over. Failing that approach them by email.

In 2002 **Integra** once again selected 125 High Value Donors and sent them a personal letter and a small magnetic picture frame to thank them for their past generosity.

The result: The entire cost of the mailing was $218 and brought in $17,525.

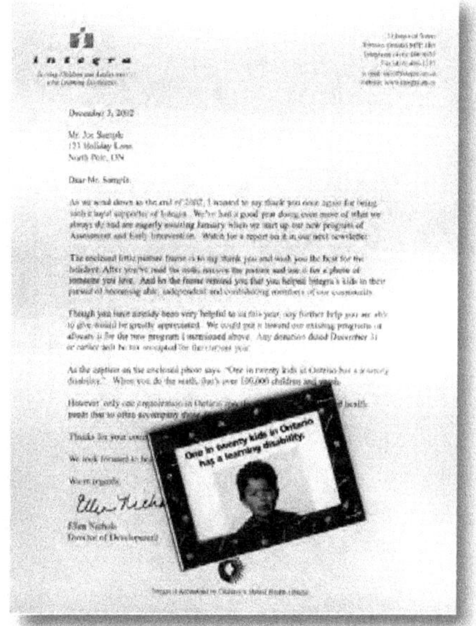

START WITH A CLEAR GAME PLAN

Research your donors' giving patterns, set up an annual schedule of mailings and stick to it. Whether you send two or twenty-two pieces of correspondence to your donors a year, you must stick to a game plan that works best for you.

Direct mail fundraising is most effective when you provide your donors with ample opportunities to support your cause without overdoing it. Not every correspondence you send them should be a solicitation for funds. You can include one or more of the following: a few direct mail appeals, newsletters, emails, annual reports, thank you letters and informational correspondence.

Chances are your donors also give to other charities and if you don't stay in touch with them constantly you risk losing them to charities that do. That old saying holds true - **Out of sight, out of mind.**

Stay in touch with them at least three or four times each year. That is the optimum number of mailings as per a survey that showed:

- Most people believe that up to three or perhaps four mailings a year is acceptable;
- Most people believe they receive six mailings every 3 months from different charities

However, test show that mailing seven or more times a year produces more revenue. What people say in a response to a suvey is often different from how they actually react in real life.

If you are afraid you are asking your donors too often and worry they may lapse, remember that not sending enough appeals each year is worse. Not hearing from you may cause them to lapse even faster.

Also, loyal donors appreciate the attention.

Individuals who have included a charity in their estate plans usually tend to be more philanthropic.

Engaging donors in this manner will benefit the organization now as well as in the future and donors get to experience the results of their generosity during their life time.

BEYOND THE 'WARM GLOW' OF DIRECT MAIL FUNDRAISING

Legacy fundraising. Legacies are an extremely important source of income for charities, yet fewer than half of adults have a Will and less then one in ten of those who do will leave a bequest to a charity.

Legacy giving is the final gift that a committed supporter can make to the cause they support.

Direct mail campaigns have so far been extremely important in putting the case to known donors. There has been a growth in telephone and face-to-face solicitation by trained representatives, which has the advantage of being able to deal with questions and concerns of prospects directly.

The trend of '**Giving while Living**' is another way that fundraisers should be talking with their donors about making a bequest. This could be the tax advantage of donating stocks or bonds or including a charity in their will as one of their beneficiaries.

What needs to change is the social and cultural stigma about planning for death, whether it be practical matters such as choice of funeral home or what you want to happen to the legacy you leave behind. Fundraisers must work at feeling comfortable in talking to loyal donors about wills, life insurance, trust funds and annuities.

It is a touchy subject, but keep in mind that if your charity isn't doing it you could lose the opportunity to another charity that is.

Gifts in memory. A gift in memory of a relative or friend is a positive way of dealing with grief. What better way to remember someone than by making a lasting difference in the life of a charity?

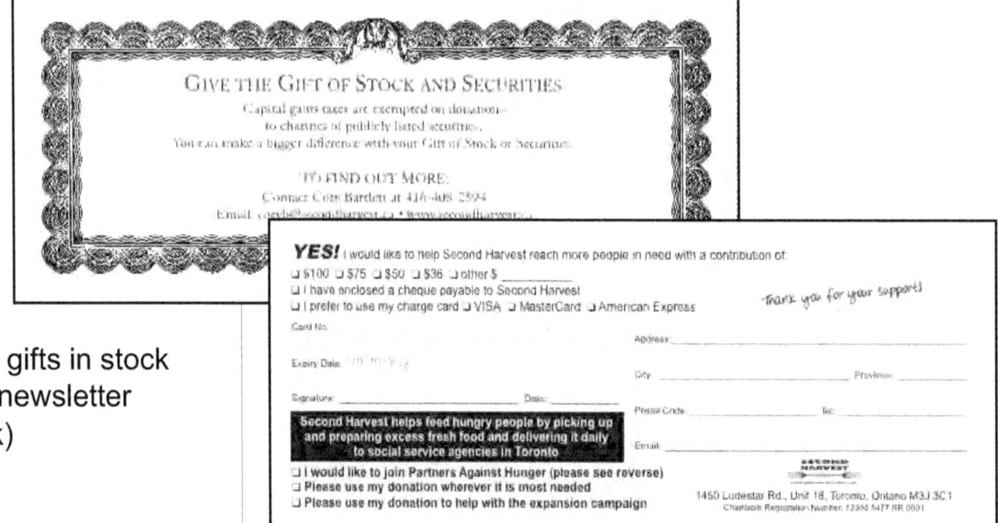

GIVE THE GIFT OF STOCK AND SECURITIES

Capital gains taxes are exempted on donations to charities of publicly listed securities.

You can make a bigger difference with your Gift of Stock or Securities.

TO FIND OUT MORE:

Contact Cory Barden at 416-408-2594

YES! I would like to help Second Harvest reach more people in need with a contribution of:

❑ $100 ❑ $75 ❑ $50 ❑ $36 ❑ other $ ________

❑ I have enclosed a cheque payable to Second Harvest

❑ I prefer to use my charge card ❑ VISA ❑ MasterCard ❑ American Express

Card No:

Expiry Date:

Signature: ________ Date: ________

Address: ________

City: ________ Province: ________

Postal Code: ________ Tel: ________

Email: ________

Second Harvest helps feed hungry people by picking up and preparing excess fresh food and delivering it daily to social service agencies in Toronto

❑ **I would like to join Partners Against Hunger (please see reverse)**

❑ **Please use my donation wherever it is most needed**

❑ **Please use my donation to help with the expansion campaign**

Thank you for your support!

SECOND HARVEST

1450 Lodestar Rd., Unit 18, Toronto, Ontario M3J 3C1

Charitable Registration Number: 13386 5477 RR 0001

An appeal for gifts in stock included in a newsletter (Front & Back)

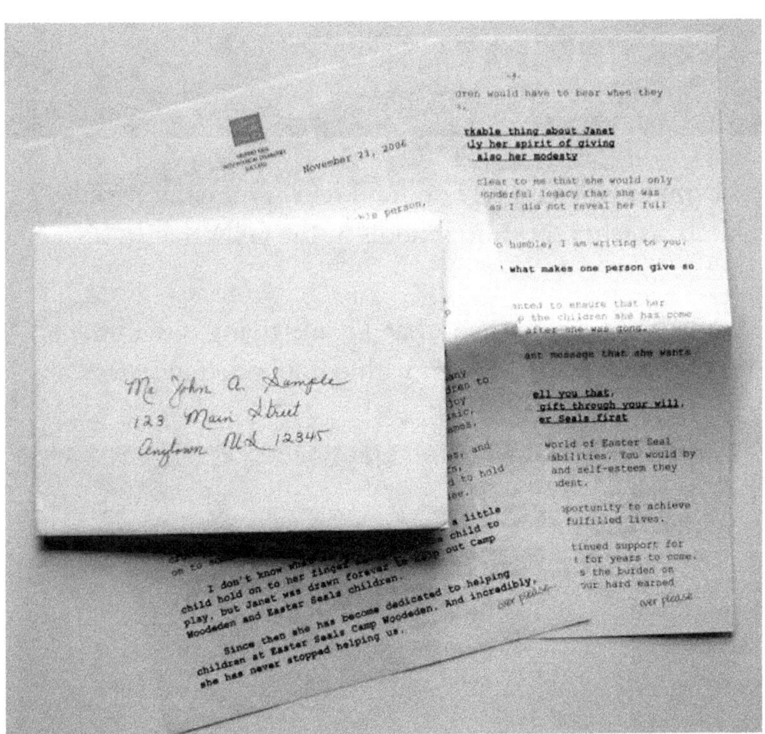

A range of Planned Giving material from solicitations to folders and kits.

A Planned Giving folder

A Planned Giving leave-behind kit.

CASE STUDY

SECOND HARVEST (THANKSGIVING)

Background: An estimated 93,000 families living in Toronto rely on food relief programs, social service agencies, emergency shelters, soup kitchens, churches and schools in the GTA that in turn depend largely on Second Harvest.

Objective: To appeal to new and current donors and remind them that Thanksgiving is the time to share the season's blessings not only with family and friends but also with complete strangers.

Solution: This appeal asked donors and new prospects to help their neighbours and not let them go hungry this Thanksgiving. It pointed out that just $5 could fill 10 plates with food. It asked them to open their hearts and wallets to the plight of their neighbours.

The message was simple and effective with the visuals on the side of the letter showing different people who would be helped by their generosity.

Strategy: To beat the traditional holiday Christmas giving rush, Thanksgiving – a highly respected holiday but not as faith based as Christmas – was selected. Another reason for choosing Thanksgiving was its close association with eating well.

Results: A 37% increase in donations from the year before. This piece was mailed to 6,957 donors and prospects and generated a 6.06% response, almost twice as much as the year before.

A reminder mailing produced a surprising 10.29% response.

Charity involvement: The charity telephoned over 200 select donors who had not responded by a certain date and got a 48.51% response to their calls.

Letter and donation form *Envelope*

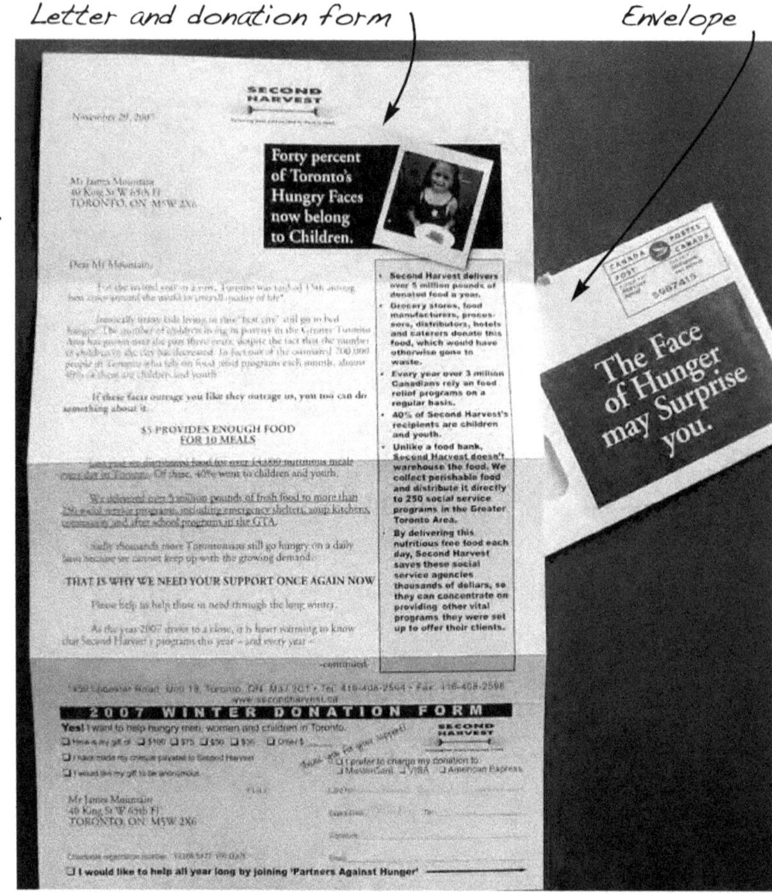

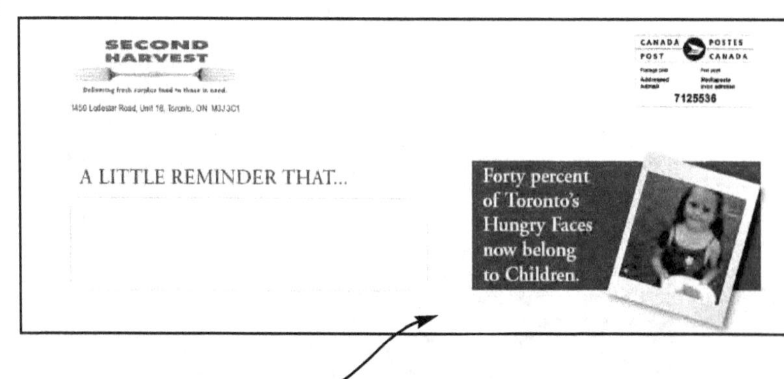

Reminder envelope with a one page simple letter

CHAPTER 11

BACK-END SERVICE: REVEWING HOW WELL YOU DID.

As defined in the beginning direct marketing is all about return on investment, relevance, responsibility and results. This section deals with the post-campaign endeavors such as fulfillment and marketing analytics. This helps us fine tune future initiatives to make them more effective.

CLIENT SERVICES

An Account Executive has to perform various functions up front as noted in Chapter 3. However, their work continues even after the package is produced and mailed. Everything from closing the docket to billing still needs to be taken care of.

Then there is the job of seeing how well the DM piece performed, beginning with analyzing the results right down to producing a final report for the client.

POST-PRODUCTION ANALYSIS

To analyze how well the direct marketing piece actually performed, one has to conduct thorough data analysis.

The list manager in charge of the data usually performs this function. They track the results along the various proposed clusters. The information is passed down to account managers who work with the list manager to decipher and analyze the results.

Many charities that do not have an advertising agency working for them must perform these important analyses themselves..

Analysis of the results includes:

- Tracking total responses and determining response rates
- Calculating cost per response or inquiry
- Determining cost per order
- Analyzing best-performing lists or media
- Calculating return on investment (ROI)
- Writing a final report

HYPOTHETICAL NUMBERS FOR ANALYSIS

Imagine a DM package that yields the following results:

- Total cost of package = $ 40,000
- Postage = $30,000
- Total number of packages produced and mailed = 100,000
- Number of donors who responded = 2,000
- Each donor's contribution = $100
- Fulfillment costs (cost to send a welcome kit) = $ 30,000

So the Total revenue was = $200,000

BASED ON THESE RESULTS WE CAN CALCULATE:

- **The Response Rate or Percent Response (%R):** [number of orders (2,000) ÷ total quantity mailed (100,000) x 100] = 2%
- **Cost Per Unit (CPU):** [total cost to produce packages ($40,000) + postage ($30,000) ÷ total number of packages produced (100,000)] = $0.70
- **Cost Per Response (CPR):** cost-per-package ($ 0.70) ÷ response rate (2%) = $35 cost-per-response
- **Fulfillment Costs Per Unit (FCPU):** total fulfillment cost ($30,000) ÷ total number of responses (2,000) = $15 per-response
- **Cost Per Order (CPO):** (cost-per-package ÷ response rate) ($0.70 ÷ 2% = $35) + fulfillment cost per unit ($15) = $50
- **Order Per Thousand (OPM):** response rate (2%) x 10 = 20
- **Cost Per Thousand (CPM):** [production cost ($40,000) + postage ($30,000) + fulfillment ($30,000)] ÷ [total quantity mailed (100,000)/1,000] = $1,000
- **Break-even response rate:** total cost ($100,000) x response rate (2%) ÷ total sales ($200,000) = 1%
- **Return On Investment (ROI):** gross profit ($200,000) – investment ($100,000) ÷ $100,000 = 1 or 100%

There are two ways of computing ROI:

1. ROI from a single transaction or program
2. ROI from the lifetime value of the donor or traditionally referred to as customer lifetime value (CLV)

DONOR LIFETIME VALUE (DLV)

Lifetime value calculations are easy when it comes to charities obtaining donations only. All you do is determine how long they continue to make donations per year to your charity.

They are harder to figure out when people buy something from a charity – like a product online or from a catalogue. In this case we will refer to the buyers as customers. However, when people pay for services that a charity provides – like going to a summer camp, then in that case we will refer to them as clients.

In the first case, the lifetime value of a customer is the sum of:

A) **Average profit generated per product sold**
B) **Number of orders per annum per customer**
C) **Number of years a customer buys a product**

A) **Average profit generated per order** is the most difficult to determine. It is important to calculate the profit rather than the sales. You need to deduct from your sales the cost of goods sold, the costs in processing the order and an allocation of your fixed costs.

B) **Number of orders per customer.** The best way to calculate this is to add the number of customer on your database at the beginning of the year and the number of customers left at the end of the year and divide this total by two.

To get the number of orders per annum per customer, simply take the number of orders you have received in a year and divide by the average number of customers on your database.

C) **Number of years a customer buys a product.** Again the number of years a customer buys a product is difficult to calculate, even if you have detailed computer records.

First, you need to determine when a customer has lapsed. This is different for different charities. A charity may sell a health care product to a customer every two months. In this case, if the customer does not place an order in six months then you may assume that that the customer has lapsed.

On the other hand, if every year for the last three years, a customer bought a goat to be given to a poor family in Africa but stops placing an order for two consecutive years, then you may assume that the customer has lapsed.

Every customer will have a different life span with your charity. What you need to do is calculate an average life span.

This is calculated by the formula: Number of customers at the beginning of the year ÷ by the number of customers lapsed during the year.

HYPOTHETICAL (DLV) CALCULATIONS

For calculation purposes let us imagine the following: Charity X has 10,000 customers at the beginning of the year. It obtains 3,000 new customers in the first year, but at end of the year it finds it has only 11,000 customers, instead of 13,000. So, the number of lapsed customers is 2,000.

Using this formula the average life span is five years (no. of customers at beginning of year (10,000) ÷ no. of customers lapsed during that year (2,000). That's 10,000 ÷ 2,000 = 5.

Now consider Charity Y that sells a service to a client:

a) **It makes a profit of $100 per child that goes to camp.**
b) **It gets two children from the same family going to camp each year**
c) **The average life span (i.e the number of years the children go to camp is 4 years.)**

Then the lifetime value of the client is $100 x 2 x 4 = $800

Lifetime Value is very important in determining future marketing plans. It means you can afford to spend up to $750 and still show a small profit to obtain a new client because on average you can expect that a client will generate $800 in sales during the CLV with your charity.

Consider other possibilities.

If your client generated a profit of $150 instead of $100, then the lifetime value of the client would increase to $1,200 ($150 x 2 x 4).

Similarly, if the client sent 3 children instead of 2 kids to camp, the profit would increase from $800 to $1,200 ($100 x 3 x 4).

And if the client stayed on for 5 years instead of 4, that $800 would increase to $1,000 ($100 x 2 x 5).

If you had 1,000 new clients then they would generate an extra $800,000 long-term profit.

However, the main purpose in obtaining new customers or a client is not just to replace your lapsed customers or clients. For a charity to continue to grow, you need to ensure that the number of new customers or clients they obtain each year is greater than the number of lapsed customers or clients.

The mathematics involved in the calculation of the lifetime value of a customer is important, but what's more important is your strategy to increase the lifetime value of each customer.

The hardest thing to do is to increase the average profit per order. Some of your options include increasing prices, improving efficiency by reducing your order processing costs, selling higher margin goods and services and reducing your fixed costs.

One of the best ways to increase the number of orders per annum is to market to your current customers. You can develop a loyalty program, have a sale, do one or more direct marketing campaigns to your own customers during the year or develop more products or services to supplement additional sales.

To increase the average life span of a customer or client, you need to increase the time it takes for a customer to lapse. Ideally you would like your customers or clients to continue to do business with you forever. But in reality, most stop doing business with you eventually.

TESTING

The adage, *"You cannot manage what you do not measure,"* is the main reason to test because it:

- Enables continual leaning;
- Proves conclusively whether or not a particular concept is working not based on opinion but facts;
- Pinpoints your greatest potential market and defines the best methods for reaching that market at minimum cost and maximum profit;
- Ensures that before you 'roll-out' a campaign and spend thousands of dollars, it will produce results.

Testing is all about gaining knowledge. Don't just look for what works, but also try to figure out <u>why</u> things work or do not work. Profits come from applying that knowledge intelligently.

Testing can be broken up into two categories:

Product testing, by which you test the viability of the one creative piece against another.

Comparative testing, when you change one part of a component of your DM piece, like adding a lift note or a buck slip in one sample and test the effectiveness of that change.

Product testing. Though product testing and comparative testing are interrelated, the success of product testing is determined by the concept, design and the offer.

Comparative testing. Comparative testing allows you to take a successful DM package and by changing just one of the elements, and test if a significant improvement takes place. *For example,* if half your targeted audience gets a brochure and the other half does not, you can determine if the incremental cost of producing a brochure is justified or not.

WHAT SHOULD YOU TEST?

You will have to decide what is worth testing, keeping in mind that testing little elements is not worthwhile. Test only larger important parts of your package and always test against your control package.

Some of the important things worth testing:

- Audiences to find your best targets
- Best donation amounts
- Best time of year to mail
- Creative themes, formats and techniques

Test everything you can think of that fits within these categories: creative, media selection and mix, copy, format, timing and positioning.

WHAT SHOULD THE SIZE OF A TEST BE?

The next thing to consider is the sample size of a test. Make sure your test cells are large enough to produce statistically valid results. Do not skimp on the size of test cells. A common rule of thumb is that your cells should contain a minimum of 5,000 names so you can apply statistical procedures and determine significant differences.

Rollouts. Start with a small but statistically measurable mailing. For instance, if you eventually want to mail to 1 million names, limit your liability by starting with only 25,000. Analyze the response. If it meets your objectives, then roll out another batch of 125,000. Gauge your results and then mail to another 250,000 and so on.

External factors. Many external factors between a test and the rollout can influence the outcome. There can be a sudden down turn in the economy or the entry of a new competitive player.

Seasonality, political and geographical issues or crises such as disasters can affect the timing of your mailing. Rollouts can behave differently from upfront tests when external factors are beyond your control.

Tracking your responses. This may sound elementary, but be sure to code accurately your mail/marketing pieces and record responses. Without the code, you will not be able to determine to which offer a donor is responding or from which list. When recording responses, be sure that accurate and complete data are entered into your marketing database.

Finally, know when to test and when not to test. If your mail quantity is so small that it will not be statistically accurate, then don't bother. Also, do not take someone else's test results as gospel even if there is a strong similarity in product or services. It may prove to be wrong for you because of unknown variables.

Additional helpful hints:

- Testing is vital in any acquisition program.
- Resist the temptation to throw out what may be boring but effective.
- Even if you love the new package, don't send too many. Only send enough to get a statistically valid response.

SOME VALUABLE HINTS ON TESTING

The outer envelope should be the first place to start when considering testing. It is the deciding factor whether recipients ever get to the rest of the mailing. It is also a relatively easy test.

Have a goal for every test. Decide what you want to learn. Test only one element at a time. Testing more than one element will confuse results.

This is not to say that you cannot test completely different packages against each other. Many tests are conducted against the control package to see if a completely redesigned package performs better. While major advances will come from testing, incremental gains result from single component testing.

A WORD ABOUT LOYALTY

There are five bonds that donors form with a charity:

Sympathy Bond. This bond is formed with a donor when the donor responds to a plea. It is the easiest form of bond to break as it is based on a single transaction.

Satisfaction Bond. A repeat donor is one who is satisfied and feels appreciated and whose donation has helped accomplish something important to them.

A loyalty program is like a good friendship.

How well a loyalty program works is often dependent on the way the charity communicates back and forth with its donors.

E-mails, newsletters, direct mail packages, 1-800 numbers and websites are all tools of the trade that one can use.

However, these communications devices are secondary to the messages.

Don't just rehash the mass marketing messages. You must establish relevant dialogue and foster a one-to-one relationship.

Don't forget that the foundation of many good relationships is 'listening.' Let customers tell you what they want and how they want it.

Too many relationships are reactive rather then proactive. Often when the competition offers something new, only then do many charities try quickly to respond.

Social Bond. This exists when a donor has a relationship with a staff member or a volunteer. As long as that person works with the charity, the chances are good that the donor will continue to support the charity.

Structural Bond. This is a bond of mutual benefit. *For example*, if a child was born in a certain hospital or treated there, the parents are more likely to support that hospital than another.

Emotional or Familial Bond. This is perhaps the strongest bond of all because it is built on a personal positive experience.

CHAPTER 12

INTEGRATED MARKETING: GETTING THE BEST FROM EVERY POSSIBLE SOURCE

Integrated marketing communications (IMC) involves the coordination of all forms of marketing communications into a unified program to maximize the impact or influence on customers.

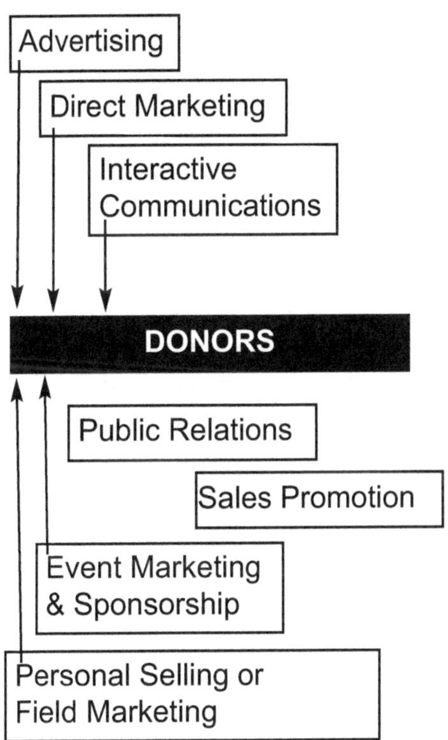

Integrated marketing communications (IMC) or multi-channel marketing means maintaining consistency in the use of all elements—slogans, images, font sizes, the key message, etc.

The answer to every marketer's prayers is a way to deliver a coordinated message to potential customers or donors anytime, anywhere and anyhow.

It is said that if the only tool you have in your arsenal is a hammer, then every problem becomes a nail. So, if you only understand direct marketing then the solution to every problem is direct mail. And if you only understand advertising then the solution to all problems is perhaps a television spot.

In our ever-expanding marketing universe where market choices are abundant, you need to know and understand other integrated methods available to provide the best counsel to your staff. Learn about other mediums like public relations, field marketing and telemarketing, to mention a few. You don't have to be an expert but you should know what they are capable of achieving.

EACH CHANNEL HAS A DISTINCT ADVANTAGE

Addressed Direct mail delivers your personal message to your intended audience right into their homes.

Unaddressed mail is a variety of literature delivered through the letterbox, but not bearing the recipient's name or address.

Telemarketing allows for one-to-one contact. It can increase response by an additional 50 to 200% as a secondary channel.

Newsletters allow you to provide crucial information and updates that your donors will appreciate.

Advertising involves mass communication to the public at large to create brand awareness and influence customer attitude. It is paid for by a sponsor or an advertiser.

Hundreds of people attend events like the annual Second Harvest 'Toronto Taste' event.

WHAT EVENTS CAN DO FOR A CHARITY

Events provide a great opportunity to introduce people to your organization and to bring in new capital.

Special events:

- Recruit in-kind contributions such as food, the venue or entertainment;
- Provide opportunities for sponsors to gain publicity when their names are displayed prominently at the site and in the promotional and program materials;
- Are good occasions for live or silent auctions that involve smaller sponsors who donate goods and services as items for bidding;
- Can generate publicity for the cause and all contributors;
- Build relationships by helping participants feel a connection with the cause;
- Provide 'face time' with supporters which can set the stage for large gifts.

However, not all participants who take part in an event can be automatically converted into future donors.

This is addressed on the next page under: **"HOW TO CONVERT PARTICIPANTS IN AN EVENT INTO DONORS"**

TV and radio advertising allows you to visually or verbally convey or showcase your message. Often TV or radio stations will run your ads free as public service announcements (PSAs).

Email and web marketing allow for high-level personalization. Emails are highly effective in imparting information or adding benefits on many levels. You can easily tailor elements to suit your target audience.

Event Marketing or Sponsorship can enhance participation of major players and drive ticket sales.

Sales Promotion consists of marketing activities designed to stimulate immediate action or sales of a product. Selling goods through mail or online catalogues is a good way of making additional money.

Personal Selling (street fundraising) or Field Marketing (door-to-door) involves face-to-face selling to inform, educate and persuade prospective donors to contribute. It is also a great way of gathering or imparting information and is excellent for doing research.

Public Relations includes activities that influence the attitudes, opinions and behaviour of the public toward a charity by issuing press releases. Also announcements generate free publicity through various media and add credibility in the eyes of the public.

HOW TO DEPLOY EACH CHANNEL

- A message that works well in one channel could fall flat in another.
- If each channel is not independently monitored and assigned a promotional code, then a spike in overall sales may be of little value if you have no idea which channel to credit.
- Start by restructuring your marketing initiatives by brand, not by channel, and encouraging and rewarding other participants in promoting other channels.
- Develop campaigns with the medium in mind.
- Keep offers consistent over channels so that you can determine whether the channel or the offer drove the sale.

BEFORE YOU BEGIN, ASK THESE KEY QUESTIONS

- Who is your target audience?
- What are their donation habits?
- What do they value?
- What motivates them to donate?
- Which channel or medium is the best way to reach them?
- What kind of message do they respond to?
- Which channel would be the most affective?
- Which medium or method do they prefer?
- Have you coordinated with other staff members involved an integrated plan (PR, events, direct mail, telemarketing, advocacy alerts, and fundraising appeals)?
- Are you ready to capitalize on the possibility of breaking news or events that affect your organization and get out timely, personalized messages?
- Can you drive recipients of direct mail and telemarketing appeals to your Web site for online donations, information and updates?
- Do you have online tools for immediate acknowledgment of donations and the capability to follow up quickly with a personalized thank-you to keep them informed and engaged?

HOW TO CONVERT PARTICIPANTS IN AN EVENT INTO DONORS

Many people attend an event because their friends persuade them; some have a strong link with the nature of the event itself; others attend because they have a strong affinity with the mission of the charity.

To segment this last important group and help identify potential future donors, a simple questionnaire can help.

On the registration form ask all participants to indicate if they or any family member or friend has been touched by what the charity does.

For example, in an event like **The Weekend to End Breast Cancer,** if a participant indicates that he or she is taking part because of a family member or friend, then you know that this person is more likely to become a future donor.

Someone who just tagged along because they like to walk or run doesn't have the same commitment.

CASE STUDY

INTEGRA FOUNDATION

Background: Integra Foundation is a small charity that helps children whose learning disabilities cause them to have mental health challenges as a result of ostracism, rejection and bullying. One of their biggest problems is that in a sea of big charities, they are generally lost and their voice hardly heard.

Objective: To break through the clutter it was important to tell the story of the isolation children with learning disabilities experience.

Solution: A small grant was obtained from the Ontario Trillium Foundation to design and launch an integrated public awareness campaign in different media with a common look and theme.

Strategy: To draw public attention to the problems faced by these kids, a public awareness campaign was launched with TTC posters, radio and television PSAs, online and with a DM mailing.

Result: This very simple approach reached out and touched every person by clearly demonstrating the serious side of loneliness for these kids.

The public awareness campaign acquainted people with the issues that children with learning disabilities face, how Integra has been helping these kids and how the reader can be part of the solution.

On a shoestring budget the campaign not only got a favorable response from the public but was also recognized by the Canadian Marketing Association when it received their 2006 Silver Award in the category Charity/pro-bono.

Integra received the following email: ***"These are excellent ads. You've obviously got a great firm working with you, not to mention a compelling message to deliver. Integra has already done Trillium proud. We appreciate the recognition in the ads and, more than anything, hope the ads bring results for Integra. You deserve the support!"***

Best,
Helen Burstyn
Chair, Ontario Trillium Foundation

Ad/ Direct Mail piece

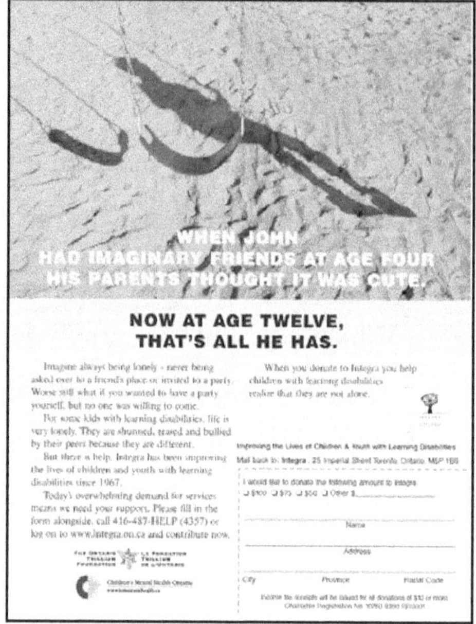

POSTER

TV Commercial

WEB DONATE BUTTON

IN CONCLUSION

Despite recurring predictions of the demise of Direct Mail fundraising, it continues to be the most practical way to raise funds.

Direct marketing can move new prospects along the ladder from First Time Donors to Advocates. Direct marketing has the ability to sell products, generate qualified leads, find new Suspects and then motivate them to become Donors and even Advocates.

However, direct mail works most effectively if you stick to the basic principles and follow them intelligently.

The Number 1 reason why people move from one charity to another is that the charity that they move to is more persuasive in convincing them that their charity was more deserving*.

As reported by the Indiana University Center on Philanthropy in a study called:* *"Why Donors Stop Giving to a Charity,"*** *that surveyed 1,000 lapsed donors from nine charities.*

THE SEVEN CENTRAL ELEMENTS IN DIRECT MAIL FUNDRAISING

1. **Follow a pre-planned program that goes out as scheduled.** This program should contain the complete series for the year, including all your direct mail pieces, newsletters, emails and reminder mailings.

   Giving your donors the right number of opportunities to support your organization is important and although this can vary from organizations to organization, depending on its size, one should never feel discouraged with low responses from one singular effort.

   Patience and persistence are key because what is important is the total income generated annually. However, always keep in mind that asking your donors too often may increase the rate at which they lapse while not sending enough appeals each year is worse.

2. **Never send a self-mailer.** It smacks of bulk mailing to your donors.

   If nothing else a fundraising appeal must include a letter in an envelope, because it is the single most important piece that talks one-on-one with your donors.

   Remember, a letter sells. In direct mail fundraising the letter is the workhorse of persuasion. A BRE (business return envelope) is optional. It is a nice gesture and facilitates response but it should be strategically employed to maximize response.

   For example: For your best donors, you can put a live stamp on the reply envelope. For smaller donors, sending a blank

People do not decide to give to a charity on the basis of facts and ratios.

They decide to give based on the causes they care about or the charity they have learned to trust. Some people give because they were asked by the right person at the right time.

Giving is not like selecting one product over the other. There are no concrete features to compare, no great offers to lure people.

Giving is all about asking.

People don't wake up in the morning and decide "I will give today."

They give because somebody asked them nicely to do so.

It's like the start of any relationship – somebody has to make the first move.

reply envelope and asking them to help defer the cost of the postage will not lower response.

You can use inserts, folders and lift-notes but keep in mind that they can distract and have been known to suppress response. Besides they will add to your costs per package.

However, once again there are exceptions. Just make sure that if your agency or freelance writer suggests using any one of these items, ask them to give you a very rational argument as to why.

3. **Avoid using premiums** like address labels, memo and note pads to acquire new donors. They only boost your cost and you will never get a decent ROI (return on investment).

   If you have been using premiums to get your donors to respond, you will find that the number of responses consistently dwindles each year.

   If you must send a premium to lure your donors, it may be better to convert the premiums from a front-end to a back-end offer. Use the premium as a carrot to get a gift.

   Surveys show:

- Premiums or gifts are considered a waste of money and act as a turn-off.
- 90% of donors think money spent on premiums might be better spent on the cause.
- 69% believe charities deliberately add premiums or gifts to make people feel guilty about getting something for nothing.
- An overwhelming number of people said they would stop sending donations if they repeatedly received premiums from the same charity.

4. **Segment your donor files.** Remember the RFM (Recency, Frequency and Monetary Value of your customers) rule of direct marketing.

   Spend more on people who have given more recently, more frequently and given the most. They are the most likely to give again and could very well even increase their donation amounts.

   They are also more likely to become monthly donors but you need to cultivate them. They also need to be constantly reminded about your organization and should receive more special appeals per year, as high as three to four mailings, which include direct mail fundraising solicitations until they donate, newsletters, informational mailings and Annual Reports.

A small percentage of your donors, 1% to 5%, is capable of giving more than the usual amount they donate. They are your High Value Donors. This group needs to be dealt with separately and not included in regular mailings. To get them to make larger donations they need to be handled more personally; everything they receive should give them the impression that they are special, from expensive stationary to a live stamp on the outer and inner return envelopes.

Another great way to make them feel special is by sending them a token of appreciation. (*See examples on pages 149 and 150 for Integra where the return on investment was 200% to 500%.*)

5. **An annual membership or donor renewal series of mailings is the most effective of all appeals.**

   Most donors only give once a year and in most cases the amount is less then $100. Reminding them that they gave and the amount they gave in the past is effective. The message need not be complicated. In fact it could be as simple as, ***'Please renew your membership or annual support."*** The reason why the word 'series' is used is because even the best donors often require reminders – we all tend to procrastinate and need to be jogged.

   Many often respond only after their membership has lapsed. Reminders are extremely important because they invariably bump up response rates by another 2% to 4%. Some have even out-pulled the original mailing. ***(See Case Study example on page 153.)***

6. **Sending a 'thank you' note as quickly as possible is absolutely crucial.**

   One of the key findings of many research organizations is that an extremely high number of Canadian charities send 'thank-you' receipts or acknowledge the donation weeks, even months after the gifts have been received and some times not at all. Just, imagine if you helped another person and waited and waited for a simple 'Thank you'. How would you feel?

   Donors expect, crave and need to be appreciated for their gifts. Not doing so promptly in an age of instant gratification is a huge mistake. Equally important is how you show your appreciation. It must match the size of the gift.

7. **You must continually acquire new donors.** Like the human body you constantly need fresh blood to survive. This is

perhaps the most expensive part of any direct mail initiative. Different things have worked for different charities. Some have had great luck with renting or trading lists from other charities; others have brought in new donors with radio or TV ads; some even use online petitions and social networking channels.

Different things matter to people at different stages of their life.

As **David Ogilvy** said, *"You are not marketing to a standing army. You are marketing to a passing parade."*

My advice is to see what works best for your organization, keeping in mind that the more mediums and marketing channels you can use to attract potential new donors, the better your chances of success.

Some charities use 'friend-get-a-friend' initiatives. Remember you are competing with commercial brands for hard earned dollars as well as other charities for your voice to be heard.

You may need to be more imaginative if you we want your mailing to stand out today. Unlike an ad which is two-dimensional, direct mail has the benefit of being three-dimensional and can appeal to all five senses: sight, hearing, touch, smell, taste. Yet most users of direct mail fail to take advantage of these.

You can make your acquisition piece more powerful by adding a foreign object to capture the essence of your message like a 'McGuffen' *(as illustrated on pages 61, 81 and 82)*, or even a fragrance or a sound (like the musical Hallmark Cards).

A lukewarm appeal is less effective than a burning passion. So get mad, express your outrage and feelings and tell people why your charity deserves their consideration and a donation *(as demonstrated on pages 27 and 28 and page 64.)*

People usually give to satisfy their own needs but you must touch them first.

CASE STUDY

INTERVAL HOUSE

The Lift Note from an abused woman's daughter acted as a motivator and also helped answer the reader's question as to why abused women continue to live with their abusers.

The main letter explained how women often have to abandon everything when they are fleeing for their lives

Background: Interval House is Canada's oldest shelter for abused women and their children. For the last twelve years they had a very successful control package that was unbeaten.

Objective: To beat the control package.

Strategy: Keeping the old elements that worked while introducing new creative.

Solution: One thing that made the control package so effective was a Lift Note from an abused woman's small child. The note was changed to come from a teenaged child to test the effect of having a more mature outlook.

However, the main idea in this test package was to emphasize the fact that a woman fleeing abuse has no time to pack when she's running for her life. To illustrate that, there was a toothbrush visible in a double windowed envelope.

The handwritten message on the envelope ***"There is no time to pack when you are running away..."*** *added a sense of urgency and despair.*

Result: In a head-to-head test, the new package beat the control by 33%.

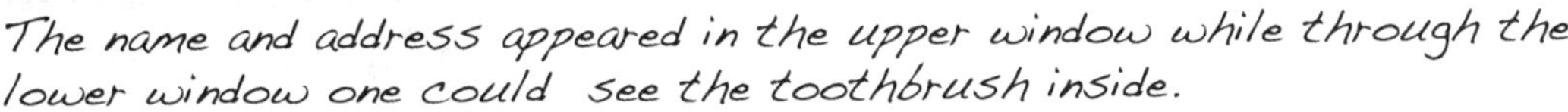

GLOSSARY OF TERMS

A

Action Devices
Items and techniques used to initiate a desired response. For instance, 'scratch-and-win' boxes or 'labels' that motivate people to get involved.

Active Donor
Previous donor who has made a donation or a commitment within the last twelve months.

Advertorial
Piece designed and written to appear like an editorial that is in reality a paid advertisement.

Address Accuracy
A program designed to encourage mailers to accurately address mail. An address is deemed accurate when all components are present, correct and match information on Canada Post Corporation's address database.

Address Correction Update
Option provided to regular donors or subscribers, to update their address or contact information. A detachable mail back form or email reply is sent back to the company of origin.

Admail
Refers to the family of Canada Post Corporation products that are primarily used for advertising by mail.

Audience
Individuals, groups or companies selected and targeted by a direct mail piece, a promotion or an advertisement.

Average Order
Mathematical formula that takes the total revenue generated from a program and divides it by the total number of orders.

Awareness
Knowledge of a charity,its mission, its products or its services.

Attrition rate
Percentage of donors who do not renew.

B

Back End
1. The activity necessary to complete a mail order transaction once a donation has been received, like sending a receipt and thank-you note;
2. A performance measurement once the donation comes in.

Bangtail
Pre-produced reply envelope with a flap for additional information; donation form or prepayment authorization that is perforated so that the donor can easily detach and return in the reply envelope.

Bill Enclosure/Bill Stuffer
Additional promotional literature piece enclosed with the initial direct mail piece to remind people to pledge

Bleed
A term used in printing to denote colour or an image that extends to the edge of a page. This is generally done by printing on an oversized paper and then trimming the paper to the right length.

Bounce Back
Complementary sales offer, traditionally used by catalogues, enclosed within the mailing to a supporter in fulfillment of an order.

BRC (Business Reply Card)
Response or reply card pre-addressed and often prepaid for lead generation mailings where no personal information is requested.

BRE (Business Reply Envelope)
Pre-addressed, prepaid envelope, included with the mailing to facilitate and thus increase response. It provides a safe way to send payment

Breakeven
When the funds or donations received equal the cost of the mailing

Brochure
Promotional pamphlet, folder or booklet included in a direct mail piece or as a take one piece placed in a counter rack.

Business List
List of business contacts that can be rented and used for direct mail and marketing purposes.

Business Reply Mail (BRM)
Consists of mail in the form of a card or envelope:

- Which bears the appropriate design elements approved by Canada Post Corporation for mailing.
- For which the applicable postage and fees are payable by the customer before delivery.

Bulk Mail
Large quantity of identical pieces with differing names and addresses, eligible for special postal rates.

Campaign
A series of ads, direct mail pieces or television commercials in a multi-media format.

Catalogue
A sales channel – a booklet mailed or placed on the charity's website that is either delivered to an individual or can be downloaded by the individual, showing multiple products and including descriptions and prices. Customers may order via mail, phone, fax or online.

Circular or flyer
Unaddressed piece of advertising or sales material.

Channel/Channels
Method a charity chooses to advertise its message such as mail, email, newspaper, TV, radio, etc.

Cold Call
Contacting a prospect unknown to you.

Cold Lists
Database of people with no prior relationship to the charity. Used to generate new leads.

Consumer List
List of names, addresses and telephone numbers of individuals.

Compiled List
List of names and addresses of people with common traits from different sources, including newspapers, directories, public records, government files and retail sales, etc.

Co-operative Mailing
Two or more items/advertisements from different sources, printed on a single sheet/card or coupon booklet, or mailed in a sealed bag, wrapper or envelope that prevents separation.

Consumer
Someone who buys a product or uses a service.

Cleaning/Cleansing
Process of removing names and addresses from a mailing list when the person no longer appears to be interested in your charity.

Co-op Mailing
Mailing with two or more participants with offers in the same envelope or carrier.

Control Pack
Direct mail pack that has been tested several times and proven to be a winner each time.

Copy
Charity's written sales message.

Cost Per Inquiry (C.P.I.)
Mathematical formula that divides the total cost of a mailing or an advertisement by the number of responses received.

Cost Per Order (C.P.O.)
Mathematical formula that divides the total cost of a Direct Marketing campaign by the number of responses received.

Coupon
Part of a promotion that a donor must fill out and return to the charity.

Cross-selling
Secondary relevant offers from a charity to a donor, e.g. T-shirts, caps, etc.

Collate
To collect individual elements of a mailing in a predetermined sequence to be inserted in a mailing envelope.

Commission
Percentage of sales charged by a company or individual as part of a contract.

Database
Collection of names and addresses merged into one master list.

Decoy or Seed
Name planted in a mailing list to verify list usage.

Direct Mail
Mail piece sent to generate a lead, get an order or to impart information to a prospect or customer.

Direct Mail – Addressed
Any mailed piece addressed to an individual.

Direct Marketing
One to one marketing approach designed to reach a specific audience using a specific database.

Direct Response Advertising
Advertising through any medium that generates a response that is measurable, e.g. by mail, telephone or email.

Demographics
Socio-economic characteristics that characterize a particular audience based on common traits such as country, city, postal code, group of households, education, ethnicity, income level, etc.

Donor
Someone who makes a contribution to a charity.

Drop date
The date when a direct mail campaign or piece is delivered to the post office for mailing

E

Enclosing
Insertion of printed materials into an envelope either by hand or by machine.

Expiry date
A preset date when an offer expires.

F

Format
Presentation of a mailing list.

Free-standing Insert
Leaflet or other printed material inserted in a magazine, newspaper or mailing package.

Frequency
Number of times an individual has donated over a certain period of time.

Fulfillment
Process of reacting to a customer's request from the time the order is placed to delivery of the order.

Fulfillment house
Place that follows up after a donation is received.

Geographics
Any method of subdividing a list using geographic divisions, e.g., postal codes.

Guarantee
Pledge by the charity to the donor to allocate funds received as promised.

Hot List
Segment of active participants who have made a donation in the last three months.

House List
List of current or former donors on a charity's database.

Inbound Calls
Incoming telephone calls from donors or prospective donors to a telemarketing service.

Insert
Promotional piece placed in an outgoing package, mailing or invoice.

Ink-Jet Printing
Process of printing by lettershop to print donor name, address, keycode and other variable data on each piece of mail.

J

Johnston box
A box or area at the top of a letter where a message appears highlighting the key message in the letter.

K

Key code
Letters or numbers (or combination of both), placed on the reply device (donation forms, reply cards), to identify a particular mailing so as to measure the effectiveness of that mailing.

L

Lapsed donor
A previous donor who has not made a donation for at least 12 months.

Lettershop/Mailhouse
Company that performs all the mailing details for a direct mail package including addressing, imprinting, collating, insertion and posting.

Lead Generation
Process of finding new donors for a charity.

Lifetime Value
Total profit realized over the active life span of a donor, customer or client.

List
Names and addresses (hard copy or electronic format) with detailed data re all donors.

List Broker
Specialist who acts as an intermediary between the list owner and the list buyer.

List building
Process of accumulating names and addresses and compiling them into a database.

Loyalty Programme
Programme designed to reward donors in line with their gift levels and behaviour.

M

Mailer
Person, supplier or company that sends out a direct mail piece. Also a generic description for a mail package.

Mail Merge
Merging mailing information from one or more lists.

Media Traffic Builder
Direct response ad intended primarily to attract donors to the charity.

Meter Impression
An approved impression placed on a mail item, reproduced by a printing die, which indicates that postage has been paid, the amount of the postage paid, the date and the meter number.

Occupant List
Un-personalized addresses, e.g. 'occupant' or 'residence.'

OCR (Optional Character Recognition)
Machine identification of printed characters through the use of light-sensitive devices in order to sort mail effectively.

Opt-In
Mail recipient requests to be included in a particular service or mailing.

Opt-Out
Mail recipient requests to be removed from future mailings.

P

Personalization
Using a database to put names and addresses on letters and other promotional materials relevant to the individuals.

Postage Indicia
A bilingual indicia obtained from Canada Post Corporation, which shows payment by deposit account and must include:

- Canada Post logo
- Product type
- Customer number
- Registration number
- Agreement number

Postage Meter
Machine that prints a postage impression on gummed meter tape or on an envelope inserted into the machine. The tape is placed on parcels, etc. as postage.

Premium
An item or gift offered to a donor, to encourage them to make a donation. A premium included in the mail package is called a front-end premium but a premium that the donor must request is called a back-end premiums.

Presort
Mail given a prior sort by the mailer in order to segment prospects or donors.

Prospect
Potential donors.

Prospecting
Using direct marketing techniques to generate future contacts.

Psychographics
Characteristics of lifestyles or attitudes of prospects and donors.

Purge
Removing duplicate names and addresses from a list.

Q

Qualified Leads
Individuals who indicate a genuine interest in the charity or its products or service as opposed to mere curiosity.

R

Recency
Last donation or other activity recorded for an individual or company on a specific customer list.

Relational Database
Database that shows the relationship between various pieces of stored customer information including donation habits, age, sex and communication history.

Rented List
Mailing list for which mailer pays for one-time usage. Usually managed through a list broker.

Reply Card
Response card included in a mailing on which the recipient indicates a preference (positive or negative) to the request. It can indicate a desire to donate and/or a request for more information.

Response Rate
Percentage of responses from a mailing or campaign. Direct Marketers usually measure leads, sales, opt-ins, opt-outs and even negative responses.

Rollout
Mailing out the remaining portion of a list after successfully testing a small portion of that list.

S

Seed
Placement of names and addresses in a rented mailing list to verify whether it is being used more than the agreed number of times.

Self-Mailer
All-in-one direct mail piece mailed without an envelope.

Solo Mailing
A single mailing, not part of a campaign.

Source Code
Unique alphabetical and/or numeric identification which distinguishes one list from another, used to track response.

Source Count
Number of names and addresses used from a given list.

Split Test/AB Split
Testing two or more samples from the same list by using a slight modification to see which performs better.

Standard Lettermail
A category of mail that includes letters, postcards, invoices, etc., weighing from 0 to 50g and meeting the requirements for Standard Lettermail described in the Canada Postal Guide and in the Canada Post Corporation Act and Regulations.

Statement Stuffer
Printed piece inserted in an envelope to a donor.

T

Teaser
1. Advertisement or promotion designed to induce curiosity about an upcoming event or promotion;
2. A headline on the outer surface of a direct mail package to entice the reader to open the package.

Tie-ins
Cooperative mailing involving two or more parties. This could be a tie in between a sponsor and a charity or between charities.

Tip-on
An item glued to a printed page. Tip-ons are generally used in magazines or newspapers.

U

Unique Selling Proposition (USP)
Distinguishing trait of a charity that provides a competitive advantage over another.

Universe
Total number of individuals that might be included in a mailing list, or all those who meet a set of specifications.

Upgrade
The process of trying to persuade donors to increase the size or frequency of their gifts.

V

Verification
Customer is asked to correct any mistakes in their contact details.

W

Window envelope
An envelope with a die cut hole covered with clear acetate, that reveals the mailing address, return address, premium or special messages.

Z

Zip-code
A code of letters and digits provided by Canada Post to be added at the bottom of each address to identify the recipient's address.

ABOUT THE AUTHOR

Billy Sharma has over 20 years of advertising and direct marketing experience working for many adverting agencies as a creative director or managing director in four major cities – Munich, Montreal, New York and Toronto.

Today he runs his own company, **Designers Inc.**, providing copywriting, design and consultancy services to many agencies and direct clients in Canada and the U.S. He has worked on a wide variety of accounts from the arts to not-for-profit.

He has a Bachelor of Science degree from Bombay University and Diplomas in Art, *cum laude*, from the J.J. School of Art (Bombay) and from the Hochschule für Gestaltung (Ulm, Germany), which was once considered to be the most influential design school in the world after the Bauhaus.

He has been a keynote speaker on direct marketing issues for **Canada Post**, the **Canadian Marketing Association** (CMA) and **Direct Marketing** newspaper.

He writes a monthly column called '**Direct & Personal**' for ***Direct Marketing***, a monthly on-line newsletter called '**Direct Forum**' and teaches direct marketing at both **Humber** and **Seneca Colleges.**

He has also judged many award shows including CMA's awards show for several years and has sat on the Board of Directors for non-profit organizations including **Change Canada Foundation** and **The Hinck's Centre for Children's Mental Health.** Currently he is a member of the Communications Committee at **Integra Foundation.**

Billy has won over 80 national and international awards including 11 CMA awards, a Gold Andy, the coveted Clio Award, Marketing Magazine's Gold, the Cannes Festival's prestigious Golden Lion and numerous Bessie awards.